D1236585

THE ILLINOIS

Books by James Gray

THE PENCILED FROWN
SHOULDER THE SKY
WAKE AND REMEMBER
WINGS OF GREAT DESIRE

Rivers of America books already published are:

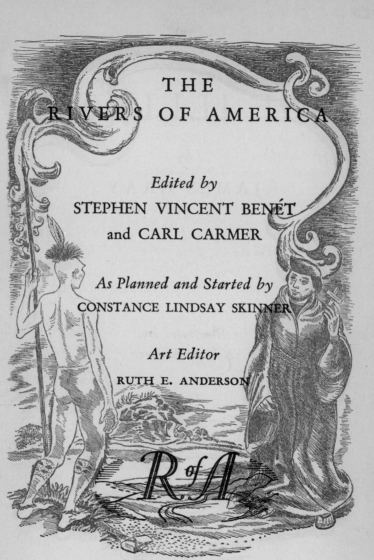

THE
RIVERS OF AMERICA

Edited by
STEPHEN VINCENT BENÉT
and CARL CARMER

As Planned and Started by
CONSTANCE LINDSAY SKINNER

Art Editor
RUTH E. ANDERSON

THE ILLINOIS

by

JAMES GRAY

Illustrated by
AARON BOHROD

FARRAR & RINEHART
INCORPORATED
New York   *Toronto*

001473183

IN MEMORY OF
TWO FELLOW WRITERS,
MY FATHER,
JAMES GRAY
AND MY MOTHER,
GRACE FARRINGTON GRAY

Contents

ix

BOOK I

Improvising A New World

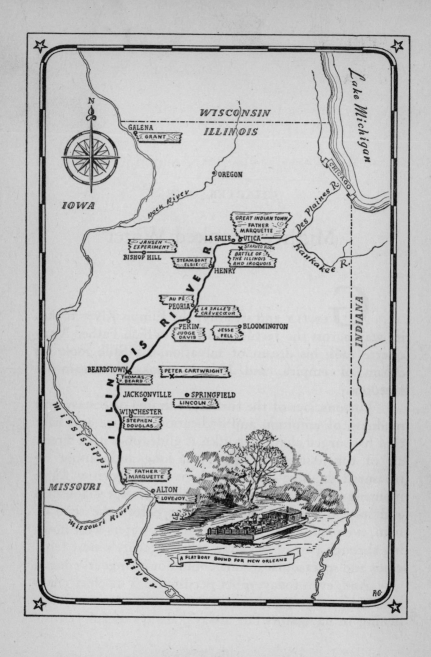

A FLATBOAT BOUND FOR NEW ORLEANS

CHAPTER ONE

Mighty Crooked Water

GENTLY and steadily, the Illinois River makes its way across the fertile prairie to which Father Marquette took his dream of salvation, La Salle took his dream of empire, and Lincoln took his dream of freedom.

Unconscious of the turbulent drama of ecstasy and madness, of ambition and dedication, of love and hate that has surged along its banks, it glides on with a serene air of timelessness. Its history is long and cannot be measured in mere centuries. If it could borrow for a moment our human faults of snobbery, superciliousness and spite it might remind us that before the time of man, even before the glaciers came, its waters were flowing through part of the same valley. Nature's most ferocious and spectacular drama could not change its course.

And, even today, quiet persistence is its chief characteristic, a characteristic that makes it sometimes maddening to navigators but always, always useful.

The Illinois has its source in the confluence of the Des Plaines and Kankakee rivers. This meeting occurs at a point approximately 45 miles southwest of Chicago and at a moment when the Des Plaines has achieved a condition which reminds an observer of Swinburne's sentimental descriptive phrase, "the weariest river."

It is the necessary, if not altogether happy, association with the Chicago Sanitary and Ship Canal that makes the Des Plaines lose something of its charm. At this critical moment, the Kankakee pours its sparkling fresh water into the stream. No eye could be so indifferent as not to respond with delight to its purity and no imagination fail to welcome the promise of refreshment.

Appropriately enough, at this point where the waters get a fresh start they also get a new name, and the Illinois begins. It began there, of course, long before the turn of the century when the Chicago Sanitary and Ship Canal came into existence. But the present day observer must be permitted to endorse, for his own reasons, the poetic impulse which made geographers decide that the Illinois begins with the union of the weary Des Plaines and the still sparkling Kankakee.

If the ancestry of the parent rivers were to be traced, the search for sources would carry an explorer up the Des Plaines into Wisconsin and along the Kankakee into Indiana. But the extent of the Illinois itself is contained neatly within the borders of the state.

It flows west at first and then, making a spectacular bend, turns south. After flowing 271 miles through country of greatly varied interest it loses its identity at last in the Mississippi at Grafton, 40 miles above St. Louis.

The names of towns and cities that dot the banks hint at the richness of the local tradition. Ottawa suggests the confused scene of an Indian battle, reminding one of treacheries and gallantries, catching the color of war bonnets resplendent in the sun. La Salle calls up the image of a stern-lipped man, intent on creating a new civilization in the wilderness. Hennepin makes one think, with amusement and annoyance, of a vain, pretentious priest who claimed the achievements of his betters and showered himself with praise. Peoria stirs a hundred memories of battles and sieges and also of the long period when, lost out of the world, its people managed to survive and even amuse themselves with wine and love and dances, danced by candlelight.

There is also the other curious tradition of the river names. The early settlers seem sometimes to have been ashamed of their newness. They sought to clothe it decently in the splendor of old names: Seneca, Marseilles, Utica, Pekin. They were reckless in their borrowings. Rome and Naples and Montezuma cherish their stolen glory secretly in little folds of the valley.

The appearance of the river varies greatly in its different stretches. Sometimes it flows through a valley the sides of which are gently terraced or sloping. Then, with a sudden show of resolution, it cuts its way through sandstone bluffs. These impressive jagged walls tower 120 feet directly over the water. In their forbidding aloofness they look like fortresses. And indeed the French explorers tried, with indifferent success, to make them precisely that.

A few miles beyond, the valley sides become low and inconspicuous. The trees and brush crowd down to the water's edge with vines climbing over them, turning the scene into a sort of stunted jungle. This wall of foliage shuts out the sight of whatever may be beyond, and a traveler has the impression of moving through an utterly uninhabited world. He tries to think that perhaps he is seeing the river as Father Marquette saw it when, sick but still eager for the salvation of souls, he entered these quiet waters and was grateful to escape from the turbulence of the Mississippi.

But it is not true, of course, that the present-day traveler can see the river as the explorers saw it. For the buffalo and the turkeys and the great congress of wildlife over which the French diarists were rhapsodic—all that is gone. In this jungle, greenness is the only tone. Tawniness of animal skin and red or blue of feather do not give their accents to the color scheme.

It is strange to travel from one great teeming city toward another and find oneself in the midst of such quietness. The smaller towns seem reticently to keep the evidence of their existence out of sight of the water. A bridge, a grain elevator, a tiny cluster of dwellings may declare that the throb of human life is near. But often its reality must be taken on faith as a traveler glides down the slow-moving stream.

But when silence has had its hypnotic effect and the traveler has surrendered to the impression of having withdrawn permanently from the world, a city suddenly begins to take form. At Peoria the river widens out into a charming lake. The valley indulges in a gracious and expansive moment. The sides pile up their height to 150 to 200 feet, looking almost mountainous in contrast to the scenes that have come before.

The waters of the lake are alive with craft: mercantile boats of every kind, sleek yachts looking like

well-groomed women in their slender grace, launches
shiny with red leather. The city climbs vigorously up
the terraces of the valley and looks down, handsome and
confident.

Then, on through a lock and into the wilderness
again.

There is a geological background for some of these
contrasts. The Illinois leads a sort of double life. That
part of it which lies below the great bend near Hennepin, flows south through the channel which it had in the
preglacial period. It made its bed ages ago, and continues, dutifully, to lie in it.

The part of the Illinois River that flows west from
the source is comparatively new, as time is measured by
geologists. It is excavating a course through the drift of
rock left by the glacier in its unimaginably majestic
progress.

But those same glacial movements, for all their
power, did not succeed in filling the lower valley with
deposits of earth. When the great natural melodrama
was over, the Illinois quietly re-established itself in its
old course.

The glacier had, however, effected important
changes. The Rock River in northern Illinois also follows
its preglacial channel. Geologists believe that it probably joined the Illinois at the great bend before glacial
action diverted its stream to the Mississippi.

Throughout its whole length, the Illinois receives
tribute of other streams. The Fox flows into it, and the
Vermilion and the Mackinaw. The Spoon River brings
to it all the tradition that the poet, Edgar Lee Masters,
has instructed us to associate with its name. The Sangamon brings in the Lincoln saga. Scores of other charm-

ingly named streams lose themselves in its waters: Peacock Slough, Spring Brook, Kickapoo Creek.

In the early years of its human history, the closest kind of association existed between the dwellers on the land and the river that passed through it. The Indians took their whole sustenance from the fertile soil along the river and from the abundance of wildlife that its waters attracted. The Illinois River brought the explorers who opened up the land to the white man. It brought the pioneers who settled on its banks. It carried necessary supplies to the founders of towns and carried away the produce of their farms.

Even the figurative language of early days reflected the closeness that man felt to his environment. In its own idiom, Illinois is the "sucker state." The reference is to the sucker fish which in the spring travels up the river to find a place for spawning just as, in pioneer times, the migratory worker used to travel up the river to find employment in such centers of activity as the mines of the northern section. "Sucker democracy," the phrase which the country was to learn when Lincoln appeared on the national scene, derived its bluff poetry from the fact that the man of Illinois identified himself with the life of the river.

It did not always serve him well. The man of Illinois learned that he could not depend on the river's faithfulness. Its caprices made navigation impossible above La Salle and difficult in other stretches.

But within the past few years, the Illinois has been brought under the complete discipline of engineers. It has been dredged out. Locks control its fall, which is comparatively precipitous in the first 50 miles of its westward flow. Linked to Lake Michigan by the Chicago

Sanitary and Ship Canal and the Des Plaines River, it completes a now unbroken waterway to the Mississippi. Its importance is greater than it has ever been before.

Though navigators may sometimes regret its sluggishness and, as they negotiate its frequent bends, complain of this "mighty crooked water," they love its steadfastness as much as any cursing captain ever loved the sea.

As it approaches the end of its course, the Illinois begins to flow parallel to the Mississippi. As though it were loath to lose its identity, it keeps a slender finger of land between itself and the great river whose chief tributary it is.

But when the final surrender can be postponed no longer, the Illinois goes quietly with the same circumspection shown throughout its length. To the end, it is the calmest and best disciplined of rivers.

CHAPTER TWO

Beautiful as Milk

OUT of northeastern Asia, across Bering Strait, came the first restless wanderers to settle down along the rivers of America. They had coarse black hair and copper-colored bodies suggestive of Asiatic origin. But in other respects—facial characteristics, for example, and bodily proportions—they much more nearly resembled Europeans.

For a long time science could not agree on any explanation of how the American Indians came to look as they do. Recent theorists find their development less mysterious. They believe that we have used the word "race" far too lazily as a crutch to help us limp toward an understanding of the peoples who share the globe. It may be, they suggest, that we are all much more closely allied than our vanity and snobbery have permitted us to believe. "Natural environment" alone may account for all those differences among racial types of which so much has been made in the past.

The American Indians, so the theory goes, became what they became because they lived under a particular set of conditions. It is even possible that Nature will patiently repeat herself, turning all of us who live on this continent into Indians once more. As we see Americans steadily growing taller and developing skins on which sun tan tends to become permanent, this is not difficult to believe.

Just before the arrival of the white man there lived in a region nearly identical with the present state of Illinois a confederacy of Indians the important tribes of which were the Peoria, the Kaskaskia, the Cahokia, the Michigamea, and the Tamoroa. Their name derived from the word "illini," meaning a full-grown man. There may have been a further self-congratulatory implication to the word. Father Hennepin, in his grandiose way, suggests that in its full significance the word meant something more nearly like "complete and perfect man." In other words, the Illini were trying to call themselves "he-men." It is not surprising. One of the most touching of human traits is the way in which all men seek to prop up faith in themselves by suggesting that their maleness is greatly superior to the maleness of neighbors.

The plural form of the name which the tribesmen gave themselves was Illiniwek. It proved to be much too difficult for the tongues of the French, who were their first white visitors. As visitors so often do, the French decided that the natives did not know how to pronounce their own language. A much prettier French ending was supplied, and the tribesmen became the "Illinois." It only remained for the English and Americans to come along and mispronounce the French form. And so was splendidly achieved the corruption of a corruption which has done so much to give our language its enchanting, if chaotic, variety.

It has ever been the way of the white man in his relation with the Indian, first, to sentimentalize him as a monster until he has been killed off or conquered and, second, to sentimentalize him in retrospect as the "noble savage." This routine somehow has served to soothe the consciences of men who had not yet learned the modern technique of dealing with the problem of overcrowding. The liquidation of the Indians was actually an early maneuver in the campaign to establish the point that on a crowded globe small groups of people cannot expect to keep large tracts of land to themselves. There was much cruelty and treachery on both sides before strength won its inevitable battle.

The French, who were the first Europeans to move into the Illinois valley, viewed the Indians much more realistically than did the English who came after. They lived comfortably among them and mated casually with them. They were not good colonists partly because they were so willing to surrender the privileges of domination to the ease of equality. But from the first these observers saw the Indians without any provincial desire to scold them for not being Europeans and without any sentimental desire to glorify them as heathen gods.

The Illinois Indians were handsome creatures. "They had legs," wrote the Sieur de Liette, author of the so-called *De Gannes Memoir,* "that seem drawn with an artist's pen." They moved under a load of wood as gracefully as a dancer. They had "the whitest teeth imaginable." They were good hunters, good runners. They were lively and intelligent, much given to the invention of games and the practice of social graces. In a pleasant, poetical confusion of mind, Sieur de Liette found also that they had faces "as beautiful as white milk, in so far as it is possible for Indians of that country."

But this catalogue of virtues did not dazzle the visiting Frenchman so much that he failed to observe their faults. They were, he said, "vain, licentious, hypocritical and perfidious." The men were possessed of an irresistible passion for gambling and often ruined themselves completely. Later these reckless ones took to begging as an inevitable sequel. Their morality as regards women was wildly confused. They invented ingenious humiliations for faithless wives, such as cutting off noses; yet they themselves did not hesitate to sell wives and sisters for trinkets.

From the standpoint of their own survival the worst of their characteristics was cowardice. The strength of their resolution was in direct proportion to their numbers. It was high if their forces were greatly superior to those of the enemy. But immediate was the wailing and the panic when they were faced by an army of warriors equal to their own.

Strangest circumstance of all, they had developed the vices usually associated with an effete civilization. The French were disgusted to find among them young men of shameless effeminacy. In a society which had somehow found a short cut from savagery to decadence, they played a curious, unpleasant role.

The testimony against them, in the French records, seems persuasive. Sieur de Liette's account is untainted by malice. Indeed, none of the French explorers could bring himself to dislike the Illinois Indians. All of them were amused by the whimsical ceremoniousness with which the great crises of human life were given poetic emphasis. A young man, wooing a girl, must carry to her parents' cabin presents of kettles, guns, skins, and possibly a slave, saying that it was only at her fire that he wished to warm himself. Etiquette required that these presents be returned by way of indicating that the matter was not so easily settled. This increased the young man's ardor so that he urged his father to give him more and better presents.

As many as three trips were made with this tempting array of merchandise before a maidenly surrender was permissible. On no account must the girl look at her young man while the negotiations were in progress because that would indicate a lack of modesty and the marriage could not be inaugurated with a proper display of decorum.

The ceremonies attending death were equally rich in drama. If the dead man had been a warrior with a pronounced taste for dancing, his career was celebrated by a great meeting of the villages in which the events of his career were represented in dance movements. If his passion had been for lacrosse, the game was played between teams from different villages by way of showing respect for his memory.

At funerals also there was a great exchange of gifts. Relatives of the dead man were showered with blankets and kettles. But it was all for the sake of ceremony. The next day the process was reversed. For a blue blanket, the relatives must offer the donor a red blanket; for a yellow kettle, a blue one must be returned.

When women were in difficult labor, the young men of the village would appear at the most unexpected

moment uttering loud and terrifying cries such as they
used in battle. They beat on the cabin with sticks. This
was to drive off the evil spirits that delayed the de-
livery of the child.

A favorite method of treating the sick was to permit the healer to fling himself upon the body of the
patient, howling as though he were mad and biting, with
great steadfastness of purpose, at the place where pain
had declared itself. Then the healer rose, having slipped
surreptitiously into his mouth the claw of a dog. This,
he declared, he had cleverly extracted from the sore
spot.

It is clear to see that there was not a dull moment
in the life of the Illinois Indians. A kind of spontaneous
showmanship made drama of all the commonplaces of
their daily life.

The same highly embellished formality marked the
beginning of every enterprise: the planting of the corn
in May, the setting forth for the buffalo hunt in June,
the launching of the year's military campaign in Feb-
ruary. All was orderly and according to the rules prescribed by tradition. The same feasts took place; the
routine speeches were made with whatever new adornments the imagination of the individual artist could
suggest.

When they embarked upon a military campaign it
was always to avenge the foul murder, in the last war,
of a brother, a father, or an uncle of a chief. At a mighty
gathering of the men, each would lay, upon a skin
stretched in the middle of the chief's cabin, the stuffed
bird which was his particular guiding spirit. To it he
made supplication, saying:

"Oh, falcon [or crow], I pray to you that when I

pursue the enemy I may go with the same speed in running as you do in flying, that I may be admired by my comrades, and feared by my enemies."

In battle they screamed the cries of their special birds. If three pursued a single enemy, the slave became, in captivity, the property of that warrior who had first touched him with a weapon.

It was not pleasant to be taken prisoner by the Illinois, though they were less adept in the refinements of torture than some other tribesmen. They killed only by fire. The prisoner was tied by his wrists to a little tree. Then torches of straw were applied to his body. At the end of six hours he was likely to faint, whereupon his thumbs were cut off; then he was revived, urged to run, pursued with stones.

In these exercises also the Indians were formalists. One who was suffering the attentions of the Illinois Indians once cried out in contempt at their lack of technical expertness.

"You know nothing of torture," he said scornfully.

Stung by this taunt, one of the women contrived a new device for inflicting exquisite pain. It had the proper effect, and the victim made a generous correction of his previous harsh judgment.

"Yes," he said, "that is the real torture."

The ceremonies of peace were just as definitely prescribed. When one nation came to visit another "to sing the calumet," the order of the day was fixed by diplomatic tradition. Good cheer was not lacking, but it was of the competently stage-managed sort. The calumet, made in the form of a hatchet with a highly decorated handle, was used as a symbol of friendship. It was shaken most vigorously at the chieftain whose pacific qualities were being extolled. But it need not seem surprising that a weapon was used for such a purpose. With the Indians, a peace conference led to war just as readily as it does in our civilized world.

The chief to whom the calumet was to be presented was led by his visitors onto a platform and around him the whole company grouped itself. Some beat drums, others sang, while two, who had the chief between them, pushed him gently to and fro "as a still more significant mark of the honor" they offered him. This went on day after day, presumably until complete exhaustion had set in for everyone, along with the temporary loss of singing voices and all interest in the loftier forms of histrionism.

The religion of these tribesmen was rudimentary in its philosophy as compared with that of other primitive peoples. The Illinois Indians thanked the Master of Life when they had had a good kill in the buffalo hunt. When one of their number died, they told each other that he had crossed the river where there was always plenty to eat, where one was never cold, and where women were always beautiful. Each man had his manitou which he worshiped, creating its image in the form of some wild creatures associated with the drama of his life: the buffalo, the buck, the bear, the lynx.

The Illinois Indian was not greatly gifted as a creative artist. The men exhausted the decorative impulse adorning their own bodies, which were tattooed on the back from shoulders to heels, and after they reached maturity, on the abdomen and arms. The women made dyes for feathers, mats, kettles, and blankets but there was less pride of workmanship among them than with many other tribes.

They lived in constant terror of their tribal enemies, the Iroquois. It is understandable that they should, for surely no group of men ever developed to a high peak of maddening consistency the technique of being annoying to other people.

No sooner had Indians or explorers built up something in which they could take pride than the Iroquois appeared out of nowhere with a splendid whoop of exuberance and tore it down. They were charmless early American playboys of the Western world, spiritual forebears of the gangsters.

Despite the richness of the Illinois valley, the timid, oppressed first inhabitants established a meager way of life in it. They succumbed perhaps largely through temperamental weakness, first to utter dependence on the traders, then to the malignity of their Indian rivals, and finally to pressure from the white man.

Gradually they were pushed farther and farther back across the fertile land, where they had grown their corn; over the marshes, where they had shot turkeys and ducks and cranes; away from the prairies, where they had ridden after buffalo; across the river, where they had dropped their lines for catfish.

The ceding of their lands finally removed them from their old home entirely. A little remnant of their number was placed on a reservation in Oklahoma, and today there is not one full-blooded Illinois Indian alive.

But in the late years of the seventeenth century, when other restless wanderers followed them along the Illinois River, there were some six thousand living in the region which they had made their own. For another hundred years and more they slip in and out of the drama, confusing its pattern with their own wild confusion of motives, inspired by their mixture of audacity and timidity, imaginativeness and meagerness of mind, splendor and simplicity.

If they are to be reborn out of the sun, in the bodies of the descendants of the Frenchmen, the English, the Swedes, the Germans who took their land, one can only hope that, in their regeneration, they will have all their old beauty and aptitude for drama, but a different sort of intellect and a more reliable kind of goodwill.

CHAPTER THREE

Father Marquette Lived Pleasantly

Destiny crept into the Illinois valley in a curiously gentle mood. No clash of defiant cymbals, no flaunting of a conqueror's banners accompanied the first scene in that quiet, pleasant place. To be sure, the innocence of such a beginning is deceptive. Conflict and confusion had been there before and conflict and confusion were to follow the white man. But for this little moment, when seven Frenchmen first entered the Illinois River in their birchbark canoes and found a ceremoniously hospitable welcome from the Indians living on its banks, the story has an idyllic quality.

The Frenchmen were Louis Joliet, Father Marquette, and their five assistants, who had been on a long adventure of which this was nearly the conclusion. They had been sent by Frontenac, governor general of New France at Quebec, to explore the mysterious Mississippi in the hope of advancing the kingdom of God and the fur trade. These two aspirations dwelt

together in the minds of many men of the period, allowing for each other's rights with a reasonable degree
of neighborliness.

It is true, of course, that emphasis was not quite
equally divided between the interests of religion and
the interests of trade. Even those spiritual leaders, the
admirable Jesuits, were not unconcerned with temporal
power. They distrusted the traders and hoped, through
their gift for organization, to create on the borders
of the Great Lakes another Paraguay where they could
control a nation of "converted and domesticated savages." Always the realist, even in his comfortably in-
direct approach to God, the Jesuit wished to have under
his authority all concerns of industry, education, ex-
ploitation, and defense. There were inevitable clashes
between the Jesuits and the lay leaders in New France.

But none of these difficulties existed in the mind
of Père Marquette. When he went with Joliet on the
mission of discovery, it was with a touching single-
mindedness of purpose. He wanted to take to the
Illinois Indians the radiant illumination of his own
love for the Immaculate Virgin.

Excitable writers on whom the examination of history exercises an intoxicating influence have sometimes
insisted feverishly that Father Marquette and Joliet were
not the first to travel on the waters of the Illinois.
There is in the life of La Salle a period that is not well
accounted for in the records, and the post-mortem defenders of his fame have decided that he was probably
busy discovering the Illinois during that lost time. But
the reasons for believing in such a journey are vague
and unpersuasive. Recent scholarship has disposed of

them as definitely as it is ever possible to dispose of volatile notions.

Similarly, writers have made much of an imaginary rivalry between Marquette and Joliet. Which was the leader of the expedition? Which was the real discoverer of the Illinois? Such spirited partisanship would greatly have surprised the two men concerned. They regarded themselves as partners in an enterprise. They got on well together. Apparently it never occurred to either to try to establish prestige over the other.

Joliet, a French Canadian born at Quebec, had been trained for the priesthood but had abandoned his studies to become a merchant. His early experience probably gave him a special kind of respect for Marquette, as a man who had become what he himself had once aspired to be. Joliet was always useful: a good organizer, an honest, conscientious man, a comfortable companion for the wilderness. But he did not have any imperishable brightness of individuality.

Father Marquette did have personal qualities of great charm and it was certainly his spirit that communicated itself to the whole adventure.

He was born in the city of Laon, where his father and other forebears before him had been men of substance and importance. Zeal for his vocation early inspired the young Marquette. He received an excellent education and showed a particular aptitude for languages. It may have been this gift which resulted in his being sent to the New World. He welcomed the assignment, as he welcomed each that came to him, with a shining hope that he might serve the Blessed Virgin.

A portrait of Father Marquette was discovered in Montreal in 1897 and it reveals with a curious unmis-

takability the gentleness of his nature. Though the oil
has checked so badly on the canvas as to obliterate
more than half of the study, still the spirit of the priest
shines out through the dimness. The large eyes have
the limpidity of a child's. There is a kind of confiding
wonder in them. They look out upon their world and
see nothing but the good. The mouth, even though one
must guess at its actual outline, shows the soft shadows,
the delicate curves, of sensibility and refinement. Those
lips surely could speak only what was gracious and
trusting.

His love was of the kind that loses none of its
vibrancy by becoming completely incorporeal. Its human warmth was not lost even in the spiritual form
that it took when Father Marquette turned his adoring
eyes toward the image of the Virgin.

Expecting good, he received it even from the Indians whose abstract gift for hospitality was not deeply
to be trusted. Many another Jesuit learned this when
living flesh was stripped from bones in that exquisite
refinement of torture which made of dissolution a spectacle on which its victim might look a long time before
he was permitted to die.

It was midsummer of the year 1673 when these
two young men entered the Illinois River from the
Mississippi. Father Marquette was thirty-five; Joliet was
twenty-seven. Weak from their hazardous journey and
undernourished by their meager, monotonous diet of
Indian corn and smoked meat, they had the satisfaction
of knowing that they had accomplished their purpose.
They had explored the Mississippi about which the
Indians had told them so many wildly conflicting
stories. They knew that it flowed into the Gulf of

Mexico. They had seen what were its opportunities for trade and wherein lay its real dangers.

They had defied all the horror stories with which the Indians had attempted to frighten them away from the pursuit of their mission. There is something highly humorous about the way in which the Frenchmen and the Indians played at that game of seeing which could tell the tallest story. They were like two groups of imaginative little boys, each of which hopes to gain a moral supremacy over the other by reducing its members to hysteria with tales that afflict the ear and set the nerves quivering.

The good, if not fastidiously accurate, Father Allouez, recommending submission to the Indians, remarked with superb disregard for truth:

". . . when our King attacks his enemies, he is more terrible than the thunder; the earth trembles; the air and the sea are all on fire with the blaze of his cannon; he is seen in the midst of his warriors covered with blood of his enemies whom he kills in such numbers that he does not reckon them by scalps but by the streams of blood that he causes to flow. . . ."

From the standpoint of either art or propaganda his was an excellent performance. But the Indians had the skill to match it. In his journal Father Marquette reports that the savages warned him to abandon his undertaking for fear of "horrible monsters which devoured Men and Canoes Together." He was told also that "the Heat was so excessive in those countries that it would Inevitably Cause Our Death."

He thanked them, as he says, "for the good advice that they gave me, but told them that I could not follow it because the salvation of souls was at stake, for which I would be delighted to give my life."

It must have been with a fullness of comfort in his own honest soul that Father Marquette proceeded up the Illinois. His mission of discovery was accomplished; his mission of salvation was about to begin. The scene delighted him and he set down the first impression that the eyes of a white man had ever received.

"We have seen nothing like the river that we enter as regards its fertility of soils, its prairies, and woods, its cattle, elk, deer, wildcats, bustards, swans, ducks, parroquets, and even beaver. There are many small lakes and rivers. That on which we sailed is wide, deep and still, for 65 leagues."

Seven miles below the place where the town of Ottawa now stands, Father Marquette and his companions came upon an Indian village which he calls "Kaskaskia." There he was received with the unctuous enthusiasm and the rhetorical exuberance to which the Indians so frequently treated their visitors shortly before the scalping began. One tribe of the Illinois Indians which Father Marquette visited assured him blandly through the eloquence of its chieftain that:

"Never has the earth been so beautiful as today: never has our river been so calm or so clear of rocks, which your canoes have removed in passing: never has our tobacco tasted so good, or our corn appeared so fine as we now see them."

All this sudden improvement in the face of nature and even in the private pleasures of the senses because of the arrival of seven Frenchmen! Hyperbole is the art of the uncomplicated. But it is pleasant to be able to report that in their application to Father Marquette these protestations had a certain degree of sincerity. At least he left the Indians with his skin whole.

It is not impossible to believe that the lack in him of any challenging arrogance and the presence of a spirit so gravely generous may have made an almost unique appeal to the savages. It may be that they found in him the embodiment of the masculine quality of fortitude which they admired and along with it an almost childlike confidence which it was not proper to betray. At least we find Father Marquette saying, again and again, that he "lived pleasantly" among these children of darkness whom he hoped to show the Virgin's brightness.

That he loved them there can be no doubt. Every description that he offers of their rituals, their dress, their domestic arts, and their efforts as entertainers reveals an extraordinary responsiveness. He likened part of the calumet dance to "a very fine opening of a Ballet in France," praise beyond which, surely, a Frenchman could not go. Of all the early travelers, he alone found their music to be something better than a nervous affliction. He was willing to see nothing but good in them.

This first visit to Kaskaskia, a name later applied to another place, was short. After living pleasantly with the Indians for three days, he hurried on to report the outcome of his mission to Frontenac. He promised, at the insistence of the Indians themselves, to return and instruct them. To do so became the object of his life and he fullfilled it at last, though at a terrible cost to himself.

It is not surprising to discover that Father Marquette's life in the wilderness had undermined his far from robust physique. But he never used ill-health as an excuse to escape his duty toward either the Virgin or her earthly children. Indeed, he seemed to glory in discomfort. He was very explicit, in his journal, about his digestive problems, for example. But each mention of them is made in the tone of elation.

H. L. Mencken has somewhere referred to the gnawings of indigestion as "cryptic reminders that God is love." Mencken's irony was Father Marquette's faith. For, like the true martyr, the more he was permitted to suffer for his belief, even through the slightly grotesque medium of the stomach, the more sure he was that his services found favor. One entry in his journal rhymes on all his favorite themes:

"The blessed Virgin Immaculate has taken such care of us during our wintering that we have not lacked provisions, and have still remaining a large sack of corn with some meat and fat. We also lived very pleasantly, for my illness did not prevent me from saying holy mass every day."

A terrible ordeal of the flesh had to give Father Marquette its satisfying spiritual reward before he was able to get back to his Indians at Kaskaskia. The scene of his return was a deeply touching one. He was received, according to Father Claude Dablon's report, "as an angel from Heaven." (The Illinois braves would have had another way of putting it since their happy hunting ground was not peopled with angels; but it is clear that there was great enthusiasm.)

Like a good organizer, Father Marquette immediately set about preparing these people, whom he had adopted, for the adventure of the spirit which he had to offer. Those rugged but rudimentary gestures toward salvation which satisfied the Spanish explorers in their relations with the Indians did not seem sufficient to the French priest. He could not be content with a hastily organized troop movement toward heaven. Instead, he went patiently from wigwam to wigwam, talking with grave intensity, first to the chiefs and elders and then, when "the first seeds of the gospel" had been sown, to all the people.

He chose a great unsheltered prairie under the sky as the setting for his first mass. The time was the Easter season and the generous air of spring must have conspired with Father Marquette to lend a simple, direct-appealing drama to his interpretation of the Resurrection. Above him as he stood addressing the two thousand men, women, and children, four images of the Virgin, attached to pieces of Chinese taffeta, moved gently on their standards and seemed, perhaps, to beckon to those being received into the mysteries of the church.

The Indians listened, not as they sometimes had listened to other teachers, with a noisy and exuberant appreciation of a new kind of magic, but quietly. Father Marquette made them as grave as himself and perhaps he did actually manage to give them an oblique glimpse of his own touching faith. He celebrated the mass a second time and, as Father Dablon says:

". . . by these two, the only sacrifices ever offered there to God, he took possession of that land in the name of Jesus Christ and gave to that mission the name of the Immaculate Conception of the blessed Virgin."

He was not to possess it for long. The knowledge that he was already dying prompted him to hurry back to Quebec to report on his success. He promised the Indians to return. So he disappears out of the story of the Illinois. For like an actor in classic drama he had the reticence to let the end come off-stage. In the wilderness he died, calling softly upon Jesus and Mary.

Perhaps it may appear that he left the scene unchanged and the drama not yet begun. The Indians may not have remembered him for long, but the world finds a curious fascination in his history and in his temperament.

And there was significance to his experience on the Illinois River because it foreshadowed that of other men who were to come. He saw the beauty of the place, touched its abundance, knew its hospitality. He also felt the heavy hand that it could lay upon the frailty of men's bodies. On the banks of the Illinois Father Marquette had his greatest success and it killed him. That was to happen to others.

CHAPTER FOUR

Struggle for Empire

THE scene along the Illinois River ceased to supply the background for a charming idyll the moment La Salle appeared. His was a striking, martial figure, wearing the costume of gallantry and the mien of resolution. Even in the wilderness, when his clothes were frozen so stiff that they had to be thawed out at a blazing fire before they could be put on, he managed to retain in his flaring coat and bright-colored sash a fastidious and commanding presence.

One draws upon imagination, of course, in supplying to his image such details as well-brushed long hair and scrupulously tended mustache. But the evident awe in which he was held by his followers indicates that he possessed those qualities of personal dignity which help a man to command. One sees him as an anticipation of the modern ideal of gentleman-exploiter who bathes with zeal precisely because the conditions are hard and who dresses for dinner in order to dazzle the natives.

Sculptors who have cast their notions of La Salle, appropriately enough in bronze, give him a chin that protrudes aggressively and eyes that lower with defiance. They follow, of course, the long-accepted interpretation of La Salle's character, that he was a man of the greatest determination who failed of his purposes because so many people betrayed him.

But there is more than one way of analyzing so conspicuous a display of strength. It may be simply a mask worn to conceal a sense of inadequacy. Certain latter-day observers of his exploits are inclined to believe that this was so of La Salle.

His letters and reports were filled with complaints that he was being betrayed by those who were supposed to be his backers; that his men were robbing him, shooting at him out of ambush, putting poison in his food: that, in fact, everyone was against him. Such obsessions do belong to a paranoid pattern. It is possible that La Salle was persecuted more in his mind than in actuality. Even the fact that his followers did revolt, to rob and finally murder him, does not necessarily prove that he had been right about their treachery from the first. A man who does not know how to use power fairly forces his subordinates to rebel. La Salle's fear may have produced out of itself the crisis it had so long anticipated.

Certainly he suffered from the neurotic's love of analyzing and justifying himself. In one of his letters, he admitted, pathetically, that timidity was the undermining flaw of his character. But he was really convinced that even this represented in him a superior moral refinement. His men, he thought, did not like him because he lacked "popular manners." This rigidity of his code was deeply offended by the debaucheries in which his followers indulged to distract themselves from the hardships of the wilderness life. Incapable of any adaptation, La Salle sacrificed the possibility of being an effective leader by never trying to understand his men.

But allowing for all his flaws of temperament, one still respects him for the fact that he was a man of great creative imagination. Into the Illinois country he introduced, not Father Marquette's gentle religious philosophy, but the modern man's doctrine of opportunity. His fundamental purpose was to establish on the banks of this conveniently situated river a colony of French and Indians where, as partners, they could defend themselves against those artists in destruction, the Iroquois. La Salle's plan was to establish on the Illinois River a fortress to be used as a storage place for the furs of all the western tribes. By adding other strongholds on the Mississippi, he hoped to provide an outlet for the trade of the whole region.

In many ways René Robert Cavelier was well trained for just such an undertaking. He was born of a rich burgher family at Rouen in 1643. His designation, Sieur de La Salle, was borrowed from the landed estate which had long been possessed by members of his line. He had had his early training under the Jesuits, in whose school he displayed unusual intellectual gifts and especial aptitudes for geography, mathematics, and history. It is evident that he must have taken certain preliminary vows which, by French law, barred him from claiming any share in the family inheritance.

But his imagination was too restless and his view of himself as an individual too demanding for the cloistered way of life. He left the Jesuits, took in a lump sum the allowance which his family was willing to make to him at the age of twenty-one, and sailed for the New World where a brother had proceeded him in the black gown of the priesthood. He made good use of his resources of imagination, energy, and capital. Renouncing temporarily his youthful dream of exploration, which had as its goal the discovery of the Northwest Passage, he took advantage of the opportunity offered. He accepted the grant of a large tract of land near Montreal and became a feudal lord of the wilderness.

But a larger ambition kept knocking persistently at his mind. Its demands were stimulated by the descriptions which he heard from wandering Indians of a beautiful river flowing to the sea. He was the sort of man who must follow the leaps of his imagination even when they led him away from security into danger. Accordingly, he disposed of his lands and set on his first journey of discovery. It is this period of his life which remains obscure in the records. His stanchest admirers make claims for him which cannot be supported by evidence.

When he returned to Canada from this prelude to adventure, he found a new governor in charge of the colony. Count de Frontenac was temperamentally sympathetic to La Salle. His aristocratic pride declared itself in imperiousness and high temper. La Salle's self-esteem was masked in decorous reserve. But the two candidates for greatness understood each other well and straightway became allies. The design for immortality which they wished to give their activities was the same. Both hoped to transform the wilderness into an ordered world, teeming with trade.

Frontenac's purpose was frankly colored with the

hope of immediate and personal gain. He had left the cultivated world behind not because he loved the wilderness solitude as neurotic La Salle did, but because his fortune needed repairing. He was zestfully, and not always judiciously, on the make. He did not intend that the Jesuits should have the fur trade all to themselves or that the English should invade his territory. When regulations interfered with his private plan, he disregarded or got around them with less scrupulousness, perhaps, than an official should show. But he was an effective person and, with the strenuous agility of the doer, he vaulted over obstacles. He saw in La Salle a man whose ambition also soared.

Besides sharing the same view of opportunity, Frontenac and La Salle shared a gift for dealing with the Indians. Pooling their talents they hoped to bring order to the New World, and to the Old a great stream of profit.

It was natural that Frontenac should further La Salle's personal ambition. He sent his lieutenant back to France with eloquent letters of recommendation to the king. The young man, just past thirty, applied for and received two things: a title of nobility as payment for past services; a feudal grant of lands which were among the most valuable in the New World.

Life appeared to mean well by him at the moment of his return to Canada. A rich estate awaited him as lord of the domain; he had a powerful partner in the governor; friends and family were eager to share in his good fortune by investing in his enterprises. Not being permitted by law to seek out the Indians for purposes of trade, he was able to persuade the Indians to settle about his fort where trade could be conducted with

complete legality. "If," wrote a contemporary friend of
La Salle's, "he had preferred gain to glory, he had only
to stay at his fort where he was making twenty-five
thousand livres a year." The equivalent of $5,000 must
have made him a rich man in 1675.

But the urgings of ambition won every argument
in the secret councils of La Salle's mind. He could not
be content for long even as the virtual king of a busy
small domain. Again he felt "immortal longings" in
him and again he sailed for France to seek support for
his plan of creating a midland empire.

Before the minister, Colbert, he placed a persuasive
report, phrased in his usual direct and plausible style,
of what he had seen on his first journey of exploration.
He said of the land:

"It is nearly all so beautiful and so fertile; so free
from forests and so full of meadows, brooks, and rivers
so abounding in fish, game and venison that one can
find there in plenty and with little trouble, all that is
needful for the support of flourishing colonies. . . .
They would be increased by a great number of western
Indians who are in the main of a tractable and social
disposition; and as they have the use neither of our
goods, and are not in intercourse with other Europeans,
they will readily adapt themselves to us and imitate our
way of life as soon as they taste the advantage of our
friendship and of the commodities we bring them, inso-
much that these countries will infallibly furnish within
a few years, a great many new subjects to the Church
and the King."

The exuberant optimism of this survey (which
might have been taken as the model for all Chamber of
Commerce reports which were later to enlarge if not

enrich American letters) becomes touching in its sincerity as one reads the later story of La Salle's hardships.
For he found that even in the midst of this paradise
it was possible to be hungry. The Indians were not so
willing, after all, to renounce their lice, their lands,
and their tribal rituals of slaughter at the first sweet
urgings of reason. The history of the land along the
Illinois River was to be for a long time one of violence,
of poverty in the midst of plenty, of chaos for want of
planning.

But the important thing at the moment in 1678
was that La Salle's desire won its end. The king's "dear
and well-beloved Sieur de la Salle" received a patent,
good for five years, permitting him to explore, to build
forts at such places as he thought necessary; and to
"enjoy possession thereof under the same clauses and
conditions as at Fort Frontenac." But Louis the Putrid,
as Mark Twain bluntly called him, knew how to mix
generosity with caution. For all this was to be done at
La Salle's own expense. He was further ordered not to
interfere with the trade in peltries which should properly flow through Montreal, though he was permitted to
trade in buffalo hides. Once more a monarch proved
that kings are the most hard-bargaining of traders. A bit
of scarlet-ribboned prestige in return for a man's unending toil, his financial resources, his health, his hope,
and finally his life! Quite tidily inexpensive at the price!

But La Salle was grateful. He probably would not
have assumed to judge the king for his penuriousness.
And certainly he would have been shocked by Mark
Twain's expression of disesteem. The boy whom the
Jesuits had trained had grown now into a man who

hated loose language and punished it severely in his followers.

La Salle's success with the king brought him followers and backers. One of the most important was Henri de Tonty, an Italian whose father had migrated to France as the result of political upheavals in Naples. Tonty was physically frail and in the Sicilian wars he had lost a hand. Yet he was to become the stoutest in spirit of La Salle's lieutenants.

With Tonty and other new lieutenants, La Salle returned to Canada. There he was joined by another associate whose name is written large across American history in the Middle West. He was Louis Hennepin, the Recollet father who became the chronicler of the expedition.

Hennepin comes into the story on his sandaled feet, a curious figure, destined to give it some moments of unconscious humor. For under his coarse gray capote, bound about his middle with the cord of St. Francis, Father Hennepin carried the temperament of a braggart. Lacking in neither courage nor ability, he could never resist the literary artist's temptation to wanton with facts. His worst fault was that of denying to other men their due. Successive editions of his journals grew progressively unfair to his leader, especially after La Salle was dead and could no longer defend himself.

No doubt Father Hennepin persuaded himself that his sly misrepresentations somehow served God and his order. For, as a Recollet priest, he was bound to advance the claims to greatness and power of his own brotherhood as against those of the more conspicuous Jesuits. It is certain, in any case, that he developed a pretty talent for arranging the wilderness about himself

s a central, dominating figure. His snapshots were anything but candid.

Still, there must have been something appealing
about him, as he went about the wilderness carrying his
altar strapped to his sturdy back. If he made love to
himself on paper, it is no more than many another ex-
perimenter in autobiography has done. His infatuation
with his own intrepidity and resourcefulness falls short
only of his passion for his own eloquence. His journal
mentions several occasions on which he encouraged his
fellow adventurers in the "most touching" language.

Hennepin had an adventurous spirit along with a
weak stomach, and that is a sad combination. Even in
his youth at Calais, when he hid behind tavern doors
to listen with insatiable appetite to the stories of the
sailors, the smoke of their pipes was sickening to him.
Yet the mind triumphed over the frailty of the flesh
and he wrote: "I could have passed whole days and
nights in this way without eating."

To his observation about being unable, in the presence of his sailors, to swallow food, Father Hennepin
might have added the rueful comment, "Au contraire!"
for he is very explicit about the effect their pipes had on
his digestive system. But there was no frivolity in the
man. Indeed, even the stern La Salle, who also boiled
with principles, found him too much on the pedantic
side.

There were many problems and disasters before La
Salle's party reached the headwaters of the Illinois River.
Most serious of all was the loss of his ship, the *Griffin*,
in Lake Michigan. But at last in December, 1679, they
arrived. For days they had lived on little besides acorns.
La Salle, lost in the woods while looking for the portage

to the Illinois, found his way back to his followers in the morning, carrying two opossums at his belt. He had killed them with a stick as they hung from a branch of a tree. For the moment the starvation diet was over.

They set their canoes at last on the waters of the Kankakee. The surrounding scene cannot greatly have cheered the half-starved travelers. The only signs of abundance, which La Salle had described so rhapsodically in his memoir to the French king, was the rank growth of reeds in the marshes. Their rustling alone disturbed the immense solitude of the oak barrens. The only souvenirs of that teeming wildlife which he had said would provide food for prosperous colonies were the bleached bones and skulls of many buffalo. They found just one alive, a bull mired in a slough. The men killed him and dragged him out with a cable. Thus, they had had their first taste of the country's capricious hospitality.

The second came when they reached the spot where four years previously Father Marquette had instructed an audience of some two thousand on the mysteries of the Blessed Virgin's love. La Salle and his followers came, on their trip down the river, to the inviting meadows bordered by gracefully rolling hills on which stood the great Indian town of Kaskaskia. They saw the lodges, made of rush mats thrown over a framework of poles. There were, by Father Hennepin's count, 460 of these cabins. But there was no greeting, either cordial or forbidding. No dogs barked at them from the shores. No men held out the calumet of peace. The village was deserted. The Indians were still away for the winter hunting.

Desperate for food, La Salle permitted his men to

find the Indians' caches and help themselves to a supply of corn. He was scrupulously honest about this appropriation, almost fussily so. The means of repaying the Indians, whenever they might be encountered, were resolutely set aside.

On New Year's Day, 1680, the explorers landed once more to hear mass. It was on this occasion that Father Hennepin spoke those touching words which made such an appeal to his own fancy.

The struggle for empire had really begun.

CHAPTER FIVE

"We All Are Savages"

THE Indians in their winter quarters on the banks of the Illinois River were startled and frightened enough when one day in January, 1680, they suddenly saw a party of armed white men gliding toward them on the water.

But they were not so frightened as they should have been. For when La Salle came round the bend of the river, it was the beginning of the end for the way of life that these people had established. Not much longer would they retain their traditional right to the fertile land which supported them in a comparative degree of comfort and gave them more of leisure than their neighbors had. Not much longer would they marry their dozen wives apiece; love their children; torture their captives; peddle their slaves. What was good and what was charmless in their social life, all of it presided over by their philosophy and their religion of terror, was bound to be discarded. Lost out of time for ages, the

Indians had enjoyed the privileges of unhampered movement in a huge realm. But the ancient yesterday was
over; the modern world's today had overtaken them.

And there was La Salle to enforce the authority of
change. He came not knowing to what an overwhelming
degree he was a conqueror. Because he made a permanent
settlement on the Illinois River and gave civilization
a foothold in the wilderness, the world would never be
again what it had been. Yet he arrived with little more
than the modest resolution of a man of affairs leading a
little band of badly disaffected followers.

His party approached the camping ground of the
Illinois and threw it instantly into panic. La Salle had
ordered the eight canoes to be put in a row across the
stream, each of the men holding his gun in a brave
display of military strength. Woefully inadequate as it
actually was, this was sufficient to impress the Indians,
who relieved their feeling of anguished surprise in bass,
treble, and falsetto howlings. La Salle leaped to shore.
Hennepin, that wily diplomat, began winning the children round with attentions which he states were irresistibly beguiling. The Indians, for their part, hastily
decided that it was a moment for discretion and offered
the calumet of peace.

In the savage, as in the civilized world, a peace conference calls for a banquet, and La Salle's men soon
found themselves treated to some extraordinary gestures
of hospitality which included rubbing the feet with
bear's grease and feeding the guests as though they were
helpless infants. In his postprandial address of the evening, La Salle confessed about the appropriated corn;
promised gifts as compensation; slipped in a threat between a compliment and an offer of partnership as he

explained that he had come to build a fortress among them; and altogether acquitted himself of an admirable piece of oratory.

The moment of mutual goodwill did not, however, last for long. Some neighboring Miamis came in the night to warn the Illinois against the French visitors. In the morning La Salle had his job of conciliation to do all over again. He did it patiently and bravely in the midst of evident antagonism.

In his best vein of horror fiction, the chieftain, Nicanopé, warned La Salle away from an attempt to conquer the wilderness, picturing the usual frightfulness in the jaws of unnatural monsters. Though La Salle was able to outdo the chieftain in veiled threats and to win his indulgence once more, he was not able to control his own men; before morning, six of them decamped, overcome by fear of the freak show of the Mississippi for which Nicanopé had acted as barker.

No matter how much he may have been tormented in his private thoughts by actual desertions and by imaginary betrayals, La Salle acted in public with consistent resolution. His imagination produced so elaborate a system of persecution that he came to believe intensely in the danger to his plans. His character, at the same time, was able to produce the grim determination to combat that danger. He had the unstable individual's touching hardihood which makes him turn to face, with equal gallantry, either an actual crisis or one conjured up out of his wayward fancy.

If La Salle's brilliance had in it the flaw of irrationality, it nonetheless served him admirably in the moment of critical decision. Despite the discouraging circumstances of his welcome among the Illinois Indians, he set immediately about the building of his fortress on the banks of the river. It was the third link in the chain of defenses he had planned. The other strongholds had been built already on Lake Ontario just below Niagara Falls and at the mouth of the Miami River.

He called the new fort Crèvecœur. Its literal meaning, "broken heart," has been interpreted by one earnestly sentimental historian after another as being a reflection of La Salle's woefully depressed state of mind. It is difficult, however, to believe that so arrogant a man would have advertised his worries to the world. The more he thought himself to be the victim of persecution the less he would be inclined to make a self-consciously tearful confession to his enemies.

La Salle's Fort Crèvecœur was probably named for a Fort Crèvecœur which, in his time, stood at the junction of the Dieze and the Meuse near Hertogenbosch in the Netherlands. His lieutenant, Tonty, is known to have fought in a battle there and it was he, no doubt, who suggested the name. La Salle's heart never needed nursing even if his overworked imagination did.

The work was begun in the middle of January when, in Father Hennepin's words, "there came a great thaw." The site was a low hill "two hundred paces from the bank of the river," just below the present site of Peoria.

"Two deep, wide ravines protected the two sides and part of the fourth side where the entrenchment was completed by a ditch connecting the two ravines. . . . The top of the knoll was left in its natural shape, an irregular square and merely edged with a good parapet of earth capable of covering all our force. The men's quarters were placed in two of the angles of the fort so that the men would be ready in case of attack."

As the fortress neared completion La Salle became the strenuous man of affairs once more. He must replace lost supplies if the rest of his plan for creating a new empire for France was not to be delayed two years or more. He split up his party, leaving Tonty to hold the fort, sending Father Hennepin on a trip of further exploration, and returning himself to Fort Frontenac for needed equipment.

With characteristic passion for his own nobility, Father Hennepin explained the arrangement:

"In this extremity, Sieur de la Salle and I made a decision as extraordinary as it was difficult to execute. I was to go with two men into unknown territory where one would be at all times in great danger of death. Sieur de la Salle was to go on foot to Fort Frontenac more than five hundred leagues away."

Hennepin mentioned also that he tried, at the last moment, to funk his assignment. His brother friars urged him on, assuring him of the glory that would come to him along with death in the wilderness. La Salle's argument had probably more weight. He said very succinctly that, if Father Hennepin refused to go, "he would write my superiors that I was the cause of the scant success of our mission."

The story of La Salle's journey is one so filled with evidence of hardship that the character of the rugged individualist, seventeenth century style, commands respect for its physical and psychic resolution. Between the lines, a present-day reader fully acquainted with the dangers from infection and disease reads a second narrative of escape from germs which seems no less miracu-

LA SALLE WALKED AMONG THE DEAD. ON T

NFINISHED BOAT HE FOUND A CRYPTIC MESSAGE.

lous than the recorded story of escape from Indians. Somewhere in the course of developing scientific method, we must have lost a technique of holding off death by sheer moral authority.

Tonty, left at Crèvecœur, was to carry forward La Salle's dream of prosperous colonies by building a ship for further explorations down the Mississippi and by fortifying the eminence on what is now called Starved Rock. He did not, like Father Marquette, live very pleasantly in his wintering; for no sooner had he set out on the second of these assignments than the members of his party gave themselves up to an orgy of protest. They wrecked Crèvecœur, stole guns, ammunition, provisions and furs, and deserted. One of them, who possessed a brutally whimsical turn of mind, wrote on the side of the unfinished vessel: "Nous sommes tous sauvages." With that effective exit line, he and his confederates disappear out of history, to meet no doubt with an appropriately unattractive end.

Two who were faithful to La Salle hurried off to Starved Rock to tell Tonty what had happened. In his turn, Tonty sent messengers to La Salle and then, making the best of utter confusion, settled down among the Illinois.

There he and the remnant of his band, including two Recollet fathers, employed their enforced leisure by trying to improve the minds and the spiritual outlook of the Indians. In the midst of the reek of many fires and the effluvium of many bodies in close congregation, they made what contribution they could to the empire of Louis XIV and to the empire of God. All around them squaws worked in the fields; naked warriors mended their weapons or gambled with cherry

stones; children tumbled over each other in play. The
Frenchmen were not well content, as Father Membre's
journal reveals. They did not like the Indians' lack of
reticence in physiological and amatory matters, their
coarseness of language, their habits of letting their shirts
rot to pieces on their backs, of eating from unwashed
receptacles, of chewing lice.

But the monotony of their days was better than
the interruption which was to come. Suddenly the
Iroquois appeared on one of their exuberant missions of
annihilation. Two of the advance guards had had the
humorous notion of dressing up to look like a Jesuit and
an explorer. The latter, they hoped, would be mistaken
for La Salle himself. The fear-stricken Illinois believed
for a moment that the French had turned against them.
They paused in their preparations for flight to attack
Tonty and his men. A suggestion of a fighting alliance
appeased them. But the tempo and pitch of panic
mounted.

There followed a series of those indescribable military maneuvers which so baffled the dramatic genius of
Shakespeare that he set them down as "excursions and
alarums" and let the matter go at that.

The Iroquois advanced, whooping. The Illinois retreated, screaming. Everyone shot at everyone without
much thought of aim or objective. There were armi-
stices, designed to lend suspense to the horror of the
tale. Tonty went as emissary for the Illinois and persuaded the Iroquois to believe that a great company
of French soldiers would presently come to the rescue
of the besieged. A jittery Illinois hostage gave the truth
away. The Iroquois turned on Tonty and prepared to
scalp him. Remembering afterward the delicacy of his

position and writing like the gentleman that he was, Tonty achieved a masterpiece of understatement. "I was never," he wrote, "in such perplexity."

Presently a treaty was concluded in which Tonty gained a measure of security for his Indian allies. The Iroquois almost immediately repudiated it. They pursued the Illinois, stopping long enough en route to wreck the town, disinter the dead, and put skulls on stakes to celebrate their triumph. They then rushed on to the dearer delight of tormenting live flesh.

The wave of frenzy, a regularly recurring feature of Iroquois psychology, had washed over the Frenchmen and tossed them aside. Only one, the benign Father Ribourde, had been killed. The rest made moccasins of the dead priest's frock and prepared to travel north. They lost their way, fell ill, nearly starved, and finally reached the camp of some friendly Ottawas near Green Bay.

Meanwhile La Salle had reached Fort Frontenac and was returning with a fresh band of followers and also with supplies needed to outfit a vessel for the trip down the Mississippi. The moment seemed auspicious. The prairies, which had shown themselves so bleak and forbidding on his earlier trip down the Illinois, were now alive with the movement of buffalo. The strange, shaggy beasts glared out through tangled hair at the invaders. La Salle's men, coming fresh to the wilderness, delighted in the sport that such game afforded. They had great feasts of buffalo meat and topped off with helpings of venison, of goose and swan. This was the paradise that La Salle had promised himself in that exuberant memoir to the King of France.

It was just such a moment of sun-drenched hopefulness as those relentless fatalists, the creative writers, always choose for the striking of a heavy blow at man's hope. For when La Salle came within sight of what should have been the great Indian town, he saw nothing but heaps of dead. Crows and buzzards, soaring above, completed a macabre design in black and white and gray. Bleached skeletons that had been torn from graves hung upon scaffolds.

La Salle walked among the dead, touching the skulls, fearing that one might be that of Tonty. But he found only those of Indians.

He returned to his boat and paddled on down the river. Each of its turns added further proof that here was another interruption to the adventure that he had begun so many times.

There was no sign of a fortification on Starved Rock. Crèvecœur was in ruins. On a plank of the uncompleted ship he found the cryptic message:

"Nous sommes tous sauvages."

Nothing gave him hope that Tonty might still be alive. Yet he went on and on, searching until he came to the Mississippi. To reach the great river had long been his objective. But he stood at last upon its banks, robbed by his anxiety of the satisfaction that he should have had in this success.

He turned back toward the site of Crèvecœur, leaving for Tonty a pathetic note attached to a tree. There was nothing for him to do but return to the nearest of his fortresses—the one on the Miami River—and prepare to begin all over still another time.

On the return trip he saw a comet and made orderly notes on the phenomenon in his journal. Europe, seeing the same apparition, was terrified into hysterics. But La Salle, feeling that thunderbolts especially addressed to him from on high showered upon him daily, could afford to remain calm about something so impersonal as a comet.

CHAPTER SIX

Great Medicine

LIKE the career of La Salle, the early history
of the Illinois valley was one of many false starts and
many interruptions. There were moments when its
scene was crowded with drama and there were also long
stretches when, almost literally, nothing happened at
all.

The violent incident of the Iroquois assault on the
Illinois Indians was a spectacular climax of the kind
for which a storyteller yearns. Its three phases—death
in the afternoon, abomination in the evening, and horrible, haunting silence on the morning after—present
the perfect pattern of drama. The inevitable anti-
climax followed with the episode of La Salle's lonely
search for his friend.

Having achieved these fine effects, however, history failed to build upon them as the cunning, calcu-
lating storyteller would have done. Drama simply disappeared from the scene. In the stillness of the years,

the gently flowing river continued to cut its graceful line through the pleasant prairies. Nature began to heal the wounds of earth made by the passion of man. She covered violated graves with the discreet exuberance of wilderness growth. Back to the fertile valley came the stubborn buffalo. But no event of human significance interrupted the long silence that followed the tumult and the shouting.

It was, in fact, more than two years later, in 1682, that La Salle took up his unfinished business with the Illinois. When he appeared again it was in one of his moments of triumph. In the missing time he had recovered Tonty as a lieutenant and Frontenac as an ally. He had made a thorough exploration of the Mississippi, claimed the new domain for his king and given it the name Louisiana. One important modification to his design of empire had been made, however. Instead of using the approach to the rich valley from Canada with its hazards of cold, enmity, and hardship, he planned to go back and forth in the interests of trade through the Gulf of Mexico and the Mississippi.

On Starved Rock he and Tony built the fortress which had for so long been with La Salle an idée fixe. A naturalist, a poet, and a military man would all have agreed that the place was beautiful. Its view of the valley was (and is) one of those heart-lifting sights that spoils the American eye for much more famous European rivers, which have less of natural beauty and nothing of a sweet, spacious wildness.

But La Salle and Tony were perhaps more impressed by the fact that "Le Rocher," as they called it, rose straight and sheer above the river and had from the rear a narrow, easily defended access. To their new fort they gave the name St. Louis.

Here the two men developed their plans for bringing the Indians of many tribes together in a close confederation. La Salle offered himself to the Indians as their defender against the Iroquois. He offered the further inducement of French goods to be exchanged for furs.

He was enormously successful, as always, with the Indians. They flocked back in great numbers to land once made horrible in memory by the violence of the massacre. La Salle had about him some four thousand warriors and sixteen additional thousands of men, women, and children of various tribes. He held seignorial rights over this domain by patent from the king. But what was more important, he held psychological authority over the Indians by virtue of temperamental characteristics which appealed to them. The savages knew how to value his silence and his love of solitude.

In this pleasant moment of triumph when he had accomplished at least a small part of the great thing he meant to do, La Salle's importance to the story of the valley begins to diminish. There was still much for him to do. He must wrestle again with problems of his own and his rivals' making. He must venture on still another trip to Paris to win once more the affirmative support of the king's ministers. He must sail to America for the last time and, after he has built in Texas another in his projected chain of fortresses, he must meet a tragic death—but one that had been inevitable from the beginning—at the hands of his own disaffected followers.

La Salle was modern man living in advance of his

time. His time repudiated him. Obsessed by an idea which seemed to him sacred, he sacrificed his own comfort and exploited his followers. They avenged themselves on an unloved leader by killing him and submitting his dead body to a final indignity. It was stripped naked and left to rot in the bushes.

Toward a demanding, and perhaps not altogether normal, imagination La Salle had fulfilled his duty by opening up a new way of life in the New World. He had earned his fame. But the rough justice of human history demands the judgment that he had probably earned his death as well.

As inheritor of La Salle's spirit, his plans and his holdings, the Sieur de Tonty sat in Fort St. Louis, high above the river, on his craggy eminence. Tonty would be a romantic figure even if it were not for the fact that he had an iron hand. That is one of those sheer luxuries of imagination in which fate sometimes indulges. The hand which Tonty had lost in the service of the French Army during the Sicilian wars, had been replaced by a metal one which he wore gloved. The loss must have seemed disastrous to Tonty, himself; but to an onlooker at his story, all these centuries later, it is more than made up for in dramatic value. Tonty completely defined himself in that moment when, with his own remaining hand, he cut away the ragged bits of flesh that the grenade had left.

Indeed, the iron hand had many advantages. In the wilderness, despite his frail physique, Tonty was more than once able to drop an Indian with his firm administrator of justice. The savage enemies of the Frenchman came to have a deep respect for that hand, describing its admirable potency, in the poetic idiom of their language, as "great medicine."

But it was the iron of his mind that really mattered. There was no soft place in it for self-pity. A masculine austerity of outlook is impressively evident in the records that he left. The blunt directness of his writing style suggests that it, too, was the product of his iron hand.

Much has been written about La Salle's ship, the *Griffin,* which was mysteriously lost in one of the first misfortunes of the expedition. But a reader listens in vain for the moan of despair in the accent of Tonty's account. His history of the *Griffin,* in only slightly abbreviated form, runs like this:

"We found there [near the Falls of Niagara] some cabins of the Iroquois, who received us well. We slept there, and the next day we went three leagues further up to look for a good place to build a boat, and there encamped. The boat we came in was lost through the obstinacy of the pilot. . . . The boat was finished in the spring. . . . We got into it and continued our journey as far as Michilimakinac. . . . M. de la Salle sent his boat back to Niagara to fetch the things he wanted. [Later in Illinois] He determined to go himself by land because he had heard nothing of the boat he had sent to Niagara. . . . As for his boat, it was never heard of."

That is as deep a glimpse as this brave man cares to give into his heart. Yet he was brave to the point of recklessness and far beyond. In that tense moment when he was trying to act as mediary between the suspicious Iroquois and the almost equally suspicious Illinois, he had very nearly arranged a truce when some of the more belligerent Iroquois suddenly developed a capricious appetite for Illinois flesh. They would, Tonty was told, eat only a few. But even in his embarrassing position, Tonty refused to find their ideas of moderation attractive. He upset the peace conference by repudiating the proffered tokens of goodwill. "I kicked away their presents," he wrote, "saying that I would have none of them since they desired to eat the children of the governor." Tonty surpassed even La Salle as a representative of the type of man who can be strong and silent without forever pointing out how strong and how silent he is being. "As it was necessary to fortify ourselves," writes Tonty with a beguiling mixture of directness and naïveté, "we built a fort."

Tonty and his partner, La Forest, had been left in charge of Fort St. Louis while La Salle continued his explorations in the South. There they received the remnant of followers who had fled up the Mississippi and the Illinois after the murder. Among them was La Salle's own brother—"Monsieur Cavelier, the Priest," as Joutal calls him in his journal. It seemed best to say nothing of so unpleasant a matter as murder. The priest still had the letter of credit given him by his brother. He presented this to Tonty who, "believing M. de la Salle was still alive, made no difficulty of giving him the value of about 4,000 livres in Furs, Castors, and Otter Skins, a Canoe, and other effects . . ." So with a pious sense of duty done, M. Cavelier proceeded on his way, leaving to the stubborn, loyal Tonty the obligation of making a totally unnecessary and very dangerous trip to find La Salle, of whose earthly remains the vultures had so long since greedily disposed.

When at last they were convinced that La Salle was dead, Tonty applied for and received from the French king the concession of Fort St. Louis.

"On this lofty rock," one observer has written of Tonty, "he reigned like a monarch over the surrounding tribes and his inspiration and diplomacy banded them to united action in repulsing the Iroquois. The advance of the Five Nations was thus checked and the conquest of the English on western soil delayed for many years."

There are some pretty grim records showing how effectively Tonty repulsed the Iroquois. He asked the Illinois to estimate the number of the enemy they had killed and to the French authorities went the report that 334 Iroquois men and boys, women and girls had fallen under their guns and tomahawks.

These statistics, intended to prove the value of Tonty's activities, had exactly the opposite effect. Louis XIV had now lived long enough to repent of his youthful licentiousness. At forty-seven he had married the sentimental bluestocking and royal school-mistress, Mme. de Maintenon. Knowing nothing of the Iroquois but being full of a variable and untrustworthy kind of sweetness and light, Mme. de Maintenon decided that the fur trade was the cause of all the difficulty. Under her influence the king decided to forbid all dealings with the Indians. Their souls alone were to receive attention from the French. Having done her good deed for the day, Mme. de Maintenon could then persuade the king to revoke the Edict of Nantes, thereby setting back the cause of religious tolerance for another long, grim period.

It was this sort of fatuous interference from ignorant rulers, half the world away from the Illinois country, that made the early life of its white inhabitants hard. First the French, then the British, and finally the United States governments had a fling at languidly mismanaging a country and a people about which they knew nothing and arrogantly refused to learn anything.

At first, through the influence of their powerful friends in France, the company on the Illinois River was exempted from the prohibition against trade. Tonty and his nephew, Sieur de Liette, persuaded the Indians to move from the vicinity of Starved Rock to a more favorable neighborhood near the widening of the river which the Indians called Pimitoui and which is now called Peoria Lake. The inaccessibility to wood and water, in case of attack, made the fort on Starved Rock impracticable though picturesque.

The Indians were glad to go. Father Gravier, their spiritual leader, followed and built a new chapel near the larger fort which was first called St. Louis, after the old one, and later Fort Pimitoui.

From that time on it seems probable that there was always a settlement on or near the lake. There are gaps in the history, preventing the present natives of Peoria from proving that theirs is the oldest permanent white settlement in the West. But further investigations are tending more and more to close the gaps, and eventually their pride of venerability may be satisfied.

The prohibition against trade had its most grievous effect on the Indians, who had become totally dependent on the fur industry for many of their necessities. Their bodies suffered, but Mme. de Maintenon was not concerned with such matters. She continued to brood over their souls.

The anti-imperialist influence brooded so successfully over the Illinois country that finally Tonty and La Forest were obliged to give up. The latter returned to Canada. Tonty went to join the growing colony in the South where d'Iberville was developing imperialistic plans very like those which La Salle had had for the Illinois country. In 1704 he departed forever, leaving his nephew as his lieutenant in the Illinois country.

Legends, which grow as luxuriantly in the Illinois country as in any fertile place, have the man with the iron hand returning to sit on his high rock either in the flesh or in some incorporeal essence to revisit the glimpses of the moon.

But the harsh and unromantic truth is that he died of a fever, poorly requited for all the energy, courage, endurance, and loyalty he had displayed. He has been badly served even in history for his name is overshadowed by that of La Salle, who was perhaps his inferior in significance as he was surely his inferior in nervous stability.

CHAPTER SEVEN

Little Ways of Being Gay

FRANCE, having saved the souls of the Indians, proceeded to forget the explorers, the voyageurs, and the coureurs de bois who had gone into the Illinois country believing they should be free to make the most of its opportunities for trade.

But they were cheerful, adaptable creatures who made the best even of this dreary business of pious betrayal. Life must go on and it did proceed for them with a shrug, a "Qu'est-ce que vous voulez?" and a "C'est la vie!"

Because they were adaptable they mated with Indian squaws, lived the life of the country, learned its language, allowed their own to be corrupted, and even forgot to measure time in the old way. They dated events from "the time of the great waters" or the "time of the strawberries."

Because they were realistic they knew that their weak communities could not stand alone and presently they began to huddle together in a group of towns on the banks of the Mississippi just south of the confluence of the Mississippi and Illinois rivers. The reasons why the people drifted south were several. It was an advantage from the standpoint of safety to be near to one another. It was an advantage from the standpoint of profit to be closer to the French colony on the lower Mississippi. It was an advantage from the standpoint of ease of life to live on the soil which the periodic floodings of the Mississippi made fertile as the land of Egypt which the Nile enriched with its whimsical risings. Egypt, the land came to be called, or the American Bottom, in a different idiom.

Even the name of the old Indian town on the Illinois River was carried away. Kaskaskia is henceforth to be identified with the Mississippi. Near it Cahokia, Fort Chartres, and Prairie du Rocher came into being.

Within these towns life became a sort of meager idyll. If its range of interests was not wide, neither were its harassments, its disappointments, or its failures many. The French found what Gertrude Stein calls "little ways of being gay." To continue an appropriate borrowing: "They were gay there; not gayer and gayer; just gay there."

The society was organized as simply as possible. Each man had his bit of land. It lay in a long narrow strip running from the river back to the bluff. His neighbor's land was just alongside, two furrows away. The whole of this "common field" was enclosed by a fence and each man was responsible for the upkeep of that part which passed over his land. In addition to the common field, a community tract, called the common, served as pasture ground for the cattle of all the villagers. So they worked side by side with companionable closeness which had the added virtue of safety. When a young man married and needed to establish his own domestic economy, a strip was taken from the common and given to him as his field.

There was, however, no self-conscious notion of a classless society. Those who profited most had more of life's comforts and adornments. The gallants of Kaskaskia had diamond buttons to their coats. Their elegant wives copied the fashion of Paris and did as much as they could to re-create in the wilderness the great world they had once known.

The simpler folk clothed their anonymity in garments which looked alike but gave everyone a kind of jaunty picturesqueness. The capote made of white blanket material covered the body and had a hood for the head in cold weather. Pantaloons were of coarse blue stuff. A kerchief tied about the head gave each man an opportunity to express his individuality. Each man tried to wear his headgear "with a difference."

And there were slaves, too, to complete the category of classes. They were introduced into Illinois in 1719 by Philippe François Renault for the purpose of working mines which were believed to offer fabulous wealth. Stopping off in the West Indies en route to the New World, Renault bought five hundred Negroes and added them to his company of two hundred mechanics and miners.

The presence of these slaves is ironic and dramatic, for it made Illinois early acquainted with a problem which she was early to solve, for herself at least, by outlawing slavery.

All classes lived together in harmony and the love

of God. On Sunday morning they went to mass to express their respect for His might; on Sunday evening they danced to express their trust in His indulgence and understanding.

They danced a great deal. On the last day of the year, the young men disguised themselves as beggars, in picturesque tatters. They danced through the village, in and out of every house, inviting its occupants to a ball to celebrate the end of one year and the coming of another. It was never long between parties. On the sixth of each January, there was another traditional fete. Four beans were baked into a cake and the four gallants who found them in the pieces with which they were served, became the four kings whose regal obligation it was to plan the next party. Publicly they chose their queens, amid a pleasant flurry of kissing.

The houses of all classes looked much alike. Most of them were of wood. Heavy posts made the framework of the one-story structure, the intervals between them filled up with mortar made of clay and cut straw. The floors were of heavy split logs called puncheons. Crude tools smoothed away some of their roughness and the dancing did the rest. The outside of the houses was whitewashed to give them a neat, well-kept look.

Within the houses class differences were evident. The aristocrats, whose persons flashed with diamonds and billowed in satins, also had other means of "conspicuous consumption." Their silver plate was heavy, their linen fine, their candelabra many-branched and gleaming.

Visitors to these little islands of civilization, lost in the wilderness, reported variously about the character of the French. As people who know little of hardship are likely to do, some of these early tourists chided the men for backwardness in their agricultural methods and their wives for untidiness. They were inclined to be severe about drunkenness among these pioneers in the wilderness. But perhaps their concern was not entirely impersonal. The French in Illinois soon learned to make very potable wine of the native grapes. Indeed, it was so good and so plentiful that in 1744 the French in France had to forbid its import into their country for fear of having their own industry ruined.

One questions whether any of the charges against the French meant more than that the travelers were far from home, uncomfortable, captious, and capricious. For the picture is a pleasant one as one reads between the lines of many a casual record. The small, wiry French—joking, inventing games, drinking, dancing— make a restful page in the history of pioneering life. It presents a lively contrast to the ponderous page of sermons, of punishments, of inhibitions and dark sub-terranean escapes from inhibitions, that one follows in other corners of early America. The French laughed in the sunlight of utter normality.

They worked too. Despite their crude agricultural implements and the endless labor that the oxen made of plowing, the French often were able to help their neigh-bors. When, in 1745, a storm destroyed the crops of lower Louisiana, the Illinois French sent four thousand sacks of flour, each weighing a hundred pounds in its stout deerskin container.

Not even those stern observers who appear to have felt that it was slightly immoral of the French to be so happy seem ever to have doubted that they had a good life. Day after day, for fifty years, these villagers led the same pleasant, if meager, existence. They were still on excellent terms with the Indians. No effort was ever made by the laymen to change the habits of the tribes-folk. The citizens of the town probably felt a gentle pity for the Jesuits who, as Father Marest wistfully said, spent their lives "in rambling through thick woods, in climbing over hills, in paddling canoes across lakes and rivers to catch a poor savage who flies from us and whom we can tame neither by teachings nor caresses."

An epitome of the history of this time shows only a scattering of events: the annexation of Illinois to Louisiana in 1711, for example, and a French military expedition from Kaskaskia to Peoria on the Illinois River in 1730. There was little more until the beginning of the French and Indian War in 1754. The villagers were a happy people whose annals made scanty, though not dull, reading. They did not even need law courts to settle their differences.

That there were differences no one need doubt. The manner of settling them is described in a sketch printed in the *Illinois Magazine,* the issue of May, 1831. The anonymous author was, in fact, the editor, James Hall. He achieved a French comedy of justice which Molière would have rolled under his tongue.

The story begins much as all stories, in the time of man's literary innocency, were supposed to begin: "On a pleasant day in September 1750, two horsemen were seen slowly wending their way along the road leading by the margin of the Mississippi River from the French village of Notre Dame de Kaskaskia to Fort Chartres." One of these figures proves to be the commandant of Fort Chartres, governor of the French settlement in Illinois. He is, of course, "gay, martial and elegant."

The other is the superior of the Convent of Jesuits at Kaskaskia, a "tall, lank, homely" man with an air (purely for purposes of atmosphere) of being "cunning, mysterious, and austere."

As they approach Fort Chartres, they see "under the spreading catalpa," a woeful figure. It is the central character of the narrative, Michel de Coucy, who has never been known before to be anything but merry. The able exposition reveals that he had been a boatman, born in Canada where, as he came to manhood, he was the darling of his crew. "None sang with truer cadence" and none "could skin a deer, cook a fish, or scrape a fiddle with equal adroitness." To this list of talents and amiabilities, he added another: "On Sunday he shaved the whole company."

But when the story opens Michel has not been a boatman for many years. Married to an amiable tyrant, father of a beautiful daughter, he lives on his land outside Fort Chartres. But his French thrift has not permitted him to keep the savings of his lifetime, a hoard of Spanish dollars, under the floor of his house. He has invested them in trading: bought furs and merchandise; taken for the merchandise "notes of hand and fair promises." When his customers have failed to pay what was owing to him, Michel has been obliged to go for ready cash to a rich man on the opposite side of the river.

This Pedro Garcia, living in the Spanish settlement across the Mississippi, is an "ill-looking fellow," the sort of disagreeable person who, in all comedies of justice, earns general dislike by wishing to be paid. He comes roaring across the river and goes to the minister of law for a hearing. The minister of law considers the matter

deeply and tells Pedro Garcia, at last, that he is amazed
to find a Spaniard attempting to sue a subject of the
Grand Monarque within the territory of France. The
French official's legal sense is properly outraged at such
an indelicacy.

But Pedro is a persistent fellow. He goes next to
the military. The Chevalier Jean Philippe de la Val ex-
amines the document and calls Father Felix to his aid.
In what language is this document written? the Chevalier de la Val wishes to know.

"It is Spanish," says Pedro Garcia, "a language
which your excellency no doubt speaks with the elegance and propriety of a native Castilian."

This contemptible effort at slyness gets Pedro nowhere. "You do my excellency unmerited honour," the
Chevalier de la Val replies, "I am not presumed to know
any other language than my own"; and he adds: "A
paper written in Spanish can be of no validity in a
French court for there would be an obvious absurdity
in requiring the minister of justice to decide on that
which he can not read."

And now Father Felix takes a hand in the comedy
of justice. He reads Pedro a brief, improving moral lecture on the iniquity of legal documents. They betray
a lack of trust and take the place of conscience in a
debtor. The Spaniard has been guilty of a great wrong
in making such a godless arrangement.

Tormented beyond his strength, Pedro makes
threats of calling Spanish law to his aid. The priest
exclaims:

"Worse and worse! if his excellency, the commanding officer, should undertake to decide upon the validity
of a Spanish functionary it would doubtless be con-

sidered by his most Catholic Majesty a very indelicate interference . . . and the consequence might be a war between two Christian princes."

As though the villainous Garcia had not been already sufficiently rebuked for the guilt of wanting his money, the Chevalier de la Val, studying the mark which the illiterate Michel had made by way of signature, says that the whole thing is undoubtedly a forgery. Pedro, "fearing that he might be in the end handed over to the inquisition," is obliged to beg for mercy.

But his sense of being badly treated returns to him once he is back on his own side of the river. He visits a Spanish notary, getting no comfort at all. The notary quietly extols the courtesy and sense of the French.

Maddened by a sense of injustice, Pedro turns recklessly toward just such a solution as a movie scenario writer would devise. He kidnaps Michel's lovely child, Genevieve, leaving a placard reading: "Meshell Coosy, French rascal! pay me my money and you shall have your daughter back."

Michel is inconsolable! The male population rises to the rescue! Excursions! Alarums!

And now we return to the first scene with Michel wailing under the catalpa and the commandant arriving in the nick of time. The commandant orders all those interested to appear before him at Fort Chartres.

The leisurely narrator now interrupts his climax to give a glimpse of the fort itself. It is an irregular quadrangle, with walls two and a half inches thick and twelve feet high. There are loopholes for musketry and portholes for cannon.

"If," he goes on, "any of my fair readers should be desirous to ascertain what is meant by an irregular quad-

rangle with bastions at the angles, I am happy to inform
them that they may obtain an exact idea of the figure
intended by laying on the table before them, an old-
fashioned square pin-cushion of which one side is a little
longer than either of the other three, with large tassels
at the corners. Such was precisely the shape of Fort
Chartres."

Within the fort the case proceeds to its conclusion.
Pedro is there looking very sad, for it appears that Genevieve, in all the fury of her twelve years, has given him
a bad time. She is there with him and Michel's heart
lifts. Some aged chiefs of the Kaskaskia line the walls.

The commandant reads the document and pro-
nounces justice. The conduct of the French has been
wholly decorous and proper, he declares. Pedro must be
paid back but without interest. The interest due him
will take the form of a fine against him for having committed violence in French territory. This pleases Michel,
whose friends, learning of his difficulties, have come forward with their debts to him.

It pleases the Indians, who through their spokesman
declare:

"Father [referring to the commandant], we came
to see you do justice; we opened our ears and our hearts
are satisfied. The cunning black spider crawled into the
nest of the turtle and stole away the young dove; but
our father is an eagle, very strong and brave; he is wiser
than the serpent; he has brought back the young dove
and the old turtles sing with joy. Father, we are satisfied;
it is very good. We bid you farewell."

Everyone is pleased but Pedro who, like his literary
forebear Shylock, deserves no sympathy.

Michel has learned three great truths: ". . . first,

that French laws surpass all others in wisdom and justice; second, that Spaniards with black whiskers are not to be trusted; third, that it is safer to bury money under the floor than to embark it in traffic."

So the French, like Father Marquette, lived very pleasantly in Illinois.

CHAPTER EIGHT

News from Au Pé

"Sir," said Dr. Johnson, ". . . large tracts of America have been added by the last war to the British dominions . . . the barren parts of the continent, the refuse of the earlier adventurers, which the French, who came last, had taken as better than nothing."

He referred to the territorial gains of the peace treaty signed between England and France in 1763. Included among them was the rich and beautiful Illinois country. Dr. Johnson's airy dismissal of them as worthless lands was due partly to prejudice, partly to misinformation, an arresting combination of which had always made him such a voluble and effective speaker. The further addition of ill-temper made Dr. Johnson irresistible to a certain audience and attracted to his feet one of English literature's greatest if most slavish, biographers.

Despite the fact that imperialistic hypocrisy preferred to have it appear that the new acquisitions were nothing but a burden, the English had long been nervously elbowing the French in their determination to control this region and, through it, the fur trade. But having reached the objective to which so many years of busy, boyish plotting and trouble had been devoted, no one seemed to have definite ideas of what to do with the Illinois country.

At first the English were not to blame. The Indians stood stubbornly in their way. The diplomatic genius of the Indian leader Pontiac had united the tribes against "these dogs in red clothing" as he emphatically called them. He had stood, a tall imperious figure, before British authority and said: ". . . you can go no farther without my permission."

It took two years to crush Pontiac's "conspiracy" and in that time one force after another had been flung back with grim resolution. In the meanwhile, the three thousand French living in their cluster of little towns just below the Illinois River, and on it, continued calmly with the business of hunting and growing grain. They lived as best they could in the midst of their little civilization, while chaos howled all about.

Eventually, of course, British persistence won. Captain Stirling penetrated the Indian encirclement and took possession of Fort Chartres. And still no one could make up his mind about the political future of those three thousand Frenchmen who were decidedly and definitely wrong no matter what they did. Policy wavered between resentment at their being on what was now British soil and a desire to leave them there so that they might be exploited. The latter, more sensible attitude prevailed among the officers. They were able to extract pleasant little fees for this and that service,

which the French did not in the least want, without fear
of being called to account for irregularities. For England steadfastly refused to give the towns any organized
government at all.

That was not, of course, sheer perversity. Away off
on her island Britannia was having an attack of the
vapors. It was a moment of great confusion in her political history. With ever-hopeful capriciousness, she looked
with favor on one ministry one day and on another the
next. Each, arising in its turn, reversed the policies of
the one before. Those towns in the barren country to
which Dr. Johnson had referred were the last to get
anyone's thought.

It is not difficult to understand why the British rule
was unpopular with the French. It is true that they had
experienced the same kind of neglect from the French
government. But when one is treated badly by a father,
that is discipline; when one is treated badly by a neighbor, that is oppression. Being realists, the French escaped
from the unpleasantness of tyranny by living, working,
and rearing their families with as little protest as possible. Those who had the greatest amount of pride (and
the greatest amount of money to support them in their
pride) sold their possessions and moved away to join
the French settlements to the south. The others stayed
on and made the best of it.

History, being obliged to follow the main current
of events, has a way of dismissing from any kind of
personal consideration the figures of drama who lose
out. The Indians are permitted their moment in the
center of the stage until the white men come bustling
on. Then they become merely the off-stage menace, to
be shot as soon as possible. Actuality, in its less orderly

way, has to juggle many human stories simultaneously. In the Illinois valley, for example, a small but lively three-ring circus was in progress during the middle years of the eighteenth century. One of these rings was occupied by the English, another by the French, and a third by the Indians. The members of each of these groups thought of themselves as important. That flesh was sweetest which "clung to their own bones." It is interesting to let one's glance flash between one ring and another to see what very human things were going on.

When Pontiac had to sign his ignominious peace with the British he was still not reconciled to their rule. With his followers he left his old home because he would not live with "the red-coated dogs" and established a new village on the Kankakee River, just above the point where it joins the Des Plaines to form the Illinois. He was still "tall, manly and unimpaired by the years," still a leader.

But no people in the world has ever been eager to receive refugees. Among the Illinois tribes, Pontiac and his Ottawas were regarded as aliens. Even as they were raising their lodges in the new land, trouble began. Kineboo, an Illinois chieftain whose territory this had always been, resented the intrusion. There were "border incidents," acrimonious disputes, and finally a peace conference which turned out to be neither a conference nor anything resembling peace. In the midst of it, Kineboo, overcome with a need to express eloquence, announced that rather than accept such terms as were offered "we will sacrifice the last drop of blood in our veins and leave our squaws and papooses to be tomahawked."

That, as it turned out, was precisely what hap-

pened. For Kineboo's next act was to stab and kill
Pontiac. A devastating war was the result. The Shaw-
nees, the Chippewas, the Miamis, and the Kickapoos—
all the tribes that had once fought the British as Pontiac's allies—joined together to avenge his murder. They
cut off his head and legs, boiled them (reverently) to
remove the flesh, and then, with skull and crossbones
nailed to their standard, set out to do battle.

This is not the orthodox story of the death of
Pontiac. What is usually said (perhaps to save time) is
that he was killed returning from a debauch at Cahokia.
One of the liveliest of the early writers has a different
story to tell. The Indian killed at Cahokia, Nehemiah
Matson believed, was a handsome, prepossessing Ottawa
who, having a taste for masquerade, appeared at St.
Louis wearing a French uniform and saying he was
Pontiac. He ranged about the country attracting an audience, indulging his taste for liquor, and spreading the
holiday spirit among the unruly. The party ended as
such parties are likely to end, with a paid killing. The
masquerader had become a nuisance and this seemed the
best way out. A young trader, Pierre Chouteau, erected
a monument over his body, but when he discovered that
he had been imposed upon and that this was not Pontiac
at all, he destroyed all identification on the mound.

It may seem a small matter how Pontiac died. To
quarrel over it may be like saying that the poems of
Homer were not written by Homer but by someone of
the same name. But the resolution of Pontiac's character
does not seem to fit in with the story of the drunken
debauch. It is also consoling to that part of the mind
which tries to heal shock with reason to know that
there was an explanation for the bitter Indian warfare

which broke out in the Illinois valley and led to the incident which gives Starved Rock its name.

A relentless fight, of the kind that the Indians knew well how to conduct, swept through their country. The Illinois were driven before its power until they took refuge at last in the great town where Marquette and, later, La Salle had found the tribesfolk. Here they thought themselves safe. Some semblance of normal life was returning when the attack began again and a battle lasting twelve hours devastated the land.

At last the remnant of the Illinois took refuge on the rocky eminence where La Salle and Tonty had had their fort. Here they were besieged, day after day, by their very thorough enemies, who now saw an opportunity of completing with a minimum of effort their plan of annihilation. The Indians on the rock had neither food nor water. Still they tried gallantly to hold off death. Cutting up their buckskin clothing and twisting the strips into long cords, they lowered vessels to the river and tried to draw up water. But each time the Ottawas on the river level broke the vessels and destroyed the cords.

There were romantic stories of devotion told of the siege. A half-breed boy named Belix had joined the Illinois in their village to marry the daughter of Chief Kineboo. Tradition, having proper respect for drama, says that the Indian girl was beautiful. Their marriage rites were interrupted by the attack and Belix fled with his bride to the rock. There he fought as resolutely as any of the braves to hold off the besiegers. But at last his head was split open by a tomahawk and, when she saw young Belix die, the Indian girl flung herself from the rock into the river.

Of all who were besieged on the rock only one, according to the legend, escaped. He was a half-breed boy who, under cover of night, slid down one of the buckskin cords, dropped into the river, and swam to safety. The story follows him to Peoria where he embraced Christianity and became known, in all honor and respect, as Antonia La Bell. It seems an odd name for a former savage, but no doubt it satisfied some compensatory yearning after softness. Perhaps he had had enough of harshness in his life.

Captain Jean Baptiste Maillet and Felix La Pance, returning from a trip to Canada, passed Starved Rock a few days later en route to their home at what is now Peoria. The Indian village was a wasteland where wolves scurried among the bones of the dead. And over Starved Rock buzzards swooped. The final triumph and the final reward of patience was theirs.

This glimpse of Captain Maillet prompts a closer examination of his way of life. He was a prominent member of the white settlement living on the Illinois River at the point where it widens out into the beautiful lake. It was convenient for him and other traders like him to live near the gathering place of the Indians. From them Captain Maillet purchased furs to take to Canada and in payment brought them the supplies they needed.

The name of the village in which these white men lived is variously given in different records. Sometimes it is Au Pé, sometimes De Pé, and again Le Pé. After that the variations begin to show a higher order of ingenious variation. "Lee Pee" is one of them and "Opa" another. This lack of agreement is hardly surprising, since everyone who used the name was illiterate and those who made the first brave attempts to spell it knew nothing about French. The British were no better at mastering the difficulties of the French language than the French had been at mastering the intricacies of the Indian languages. Each nation in turn gave to place names its own rough-and-ready twist.

Au Pé was once thought to be a corruption of the phrase "au pied du lac," referring to the townsite at the foot of the lake. Maturer judgment has come to believe that Au Pé was an abbreviation for "Au Péorias," among the Peorias. That explanation has the great recommendation of making sense.

It had been the home of traders for many years when, in 1761, Jean Baptiste Maillet decided to move a mile and a half down the river where the land was drier and the water better. Others followed him, and there grew up a new settlement which many years later came to be called "La Ville de Maillet." This fanciful notion irritates historians of the sterner type, who say that La Ville de Maillet was just some more of Au Pé. The two settlements together formed Greater Au Pé, as it would have been called in our day of population wars. There never was any Ville de Maillet except in the imagination of Governor Edward Coles who liked the fine flavor of the phrase and used it in a legal document.

In Au Pé the French lived together, in sickness and in health, apparently being little affected by theoretical changes in overlordship. Through many years of neglect they had got into the habit of thinking that they belonged principally to themselves.

They did not always live together quite wisely. For example, there was that bad moment in the village life when Captain Maillet, who was later to prove himself a character of great firmness and resolution, allowed his sentimental nature to be played upon by a lady who was the wife of someone else. Her husband, Louis La Vossière, was a "high-toned gentleman from Europe" and her preference for Captain Maillet must be attributed to one of those vagaries of the flesh that do so much to make drama.

M. La Vossière had his own gifts in the dramatic line. Having discovered that he was being deceived by his wife, he plotted a revenge of such ingenuity that it would have delighted the velvet-draped imagination of Edgar Allan Poe. The truth of this story has been doubted; but the best proof of its authenticity seems to lie in the fact that only a genius could have invented it. And since the man who first told it was no literary genius, he must simply have been telling the truth.

What M. La Vossière did was to invite to dinner all of his friends including the reckless Captain Maillet. The party was gay; it was, perhaps, even a little tipsy. Not so much so, however, but that someone noticed a peculiar quality to the merriment of the host. A kind of rumbling prophecy of doom ran through his laughter. He kept disappearing on mysterious errands, and everyone became extremely nervous.

At last Captain Maillet persuaded all the guests to leave the house. Conscience had made a coward of Maillet not a minute too soon. For, as the company stood outside, wondering shamefacedly why they had run away, M. La Vossière's house blew up. That had been the design of his little Gothic romance; to blow his wife, her lover, and himself all to blazes at the height of a frivolous party.

The proper moral ending to the tale would be that

Captain Maillet and his mistress parted in chagrin, each to devote his life to good works. But the French are realistic and in the wilderness there were plenty of opportunities for mortifying the flesh without inventing ridiculous sacrifices. Very sensibly, Mme. La Voissière and Captain Maillet married. They lived happily ever after, or at least until Captain Maillet got himself killed in a brawl.

The history of Au Pé was infrequently interrupted by melodramas of this sort. For the most part it jogged along quietly with one event of recorded history every half decade or so. In 1765 a party sought for gold that Tonty was supposed to have left buried on Starved Rock. In 1773 one Pat Kennedy visited it looking for copper mines. His journal speaks of the town and its fort. In 1776 a trader on a large scale, Pierre de Beuro, established himself on Bureau Creek, married a chief's daughter and lived very well. So well, in fact, that other traders became jealous and had him killed. But only an occasional moment of violence interrupted the quiet in which Au Pé was wrapped for decades at a time.

Reference to the year 1776 can be counted upon to quicken interest in almost any historical record of American life. Echoes of oratory and the roll of drums seem to sound through the very mention of the date. But the people of Au Pé knew nothing of its significance. George Rogers Clark had been conducting his conquest of the West for two years before any echo of his campaigns reached their ears. In 1778 when he had taken possession of Illinois, he sent three soldiers, along with two Frenchmen to act as interpreters, to tell the people that they were no longer under British rule. These visitors found a large, comparatively prosperous-looking town, complete with wine press, windmill, and church with gilt lettering over the door and wooden cross above.

News that their allegiance had been changed for them yet another time may very well have brought only a smile and a shrug from the French. In all the years of being subjects of King George they had not found it necessary to recognize their altered condition by so much as learning to speak English. Overlordship meant little in their lives. They survived in spite of it rather than because of any benefits that it conferred.

This was perhaps not true of Jean Baptiste Maillet. He had always been a leader in his community and that leadership was now acknowledged officially by his being made a captain. Since captains must serve their country, Maillet went to the aid of the one he had just acquired. As his company proceeded through the woods, one of his men fell ill. It was important that the Indians, who were now the allies of the British, should not know of his movements. Maillet could not send the man back. Nor could he carry him forward. So with characteristic firmness of purpose the captain sank a tomahawk deep in his sick neighbor's head, buried him hastily, and went on.

Then isolation settled down once more upon Au Pé. It was twenty years before the world's agitation again began to affect it. In 1810 Tecumseh, splendid in white buckskin and eagle feathers and mounted on a spirited black pony, visited the town. He was serving as advance agent and propagandist for a war against the frontier settlements, trying to draw all the tribes together. What precisely he hoped to gain by visiting the French is not clear. But whatever he wanted he did not get, and the French sent him politely on his way.

In the winter of 1811-12, the Indians living near Au Pé heard that the Americans planned a campaign against them. There had been some isolated acts of violence on the part of lawless individual Indians for which the settlers were demanding revenge. Captain Maillet went as emissary for the savages and carried to Governor Ninian Edwards at Kaskaskia their touching proposal. The mischiefmakers, the chief declared through Maillet, were no longer of his tribe. But to make amends he would choose young men to pay, with their lives, for all the crimes the white man wished to charge against the tribe. Governor Edwards could not, of course, accept the proposal, but the feeling against the Indians persisted.

Now, as the War of 1812 began, the French at Au Pé fell under the hysterical suspicion of the Americans. In time of war the improbable is always the easiest thing to believe. When a vagabond named Elijah Bruce, who had been driven from Au Pé for misconduct, hurried off to Kaskaskia with tall stories against the French, his tales were believed. One was that the French were passing on to the Indians supplies from the British. Another was that Captain Maillet had stolen cattle to feed the warriors. There was no tale too offensive to give the ears of the good folk at Kaskaskia a pleasant shock.

So, for still another time, the French were to suffer at the hands of a third government which had no very clear idea of what it wanted to do for them but expected much of them in return. The residents of Au Pé had been under the jurisdiction of the United States government long enough for a whole new generation to grow up. Yet they had never been asked to take the oath of allegiance. Now, partly because they had been neglected, they were treated with the suspicion of foster children.

Governor Edwards had been persuaded to believe the worst of the stories about these foreign people and he allowed soldiers, sent out against the Indians, to perform a little side line of meaningless persecution.

On November 5, 1812, when the French were attending mass, four armed boats under the command of Captain Craig reached the wharf at Au Pé. By way of announcing their arrival, they fired off their cannon. The startled people ran out of the church with Father Racine at their head. The only one among them who spoke English was Thomas Forsyth, an agent of the American government whose official status was a secret. He demanded to know the meaning of the attack on the town, but his questions were evaded. Prejudice invited the soldiers to indulge in the worst of their impulses and at the same time cling to a sense of virtue. Virtuously they broke into a store and virtuously finished off two casks of Felix La Fontain's best wine. Drunkenness prompted them to still more audacious displays of their stanch loyalty to the flag; they robbed houses of gold pens and watches. After dark Captain Craig at last got his men on board once more, and the wind drove the ships a little distance downstream. The people, thinking that the incident was concluded, went to bed clucking their tongues over their losses. But there was still another act to be played in this tragic farce.

In the morning some men of Au Pé, trying to restore life to normal, went to shoot some beeves in the woods near the town. The reports of their guns woke

Captain Craig's soldiers and woke also their martial spirit. Fancying that they had been fired upon, they answered with their cannon. And now the self-appointed gods of vengeance really went to work.

Men were dragged from their beds and herded naked through the town to be made prisoners on board the ship. Houses were looted—thoroughly this time—and then burned. The windmill and all its store of grain were destroyed. The church was robbed of a valuable crucifix, the gift of the Bishop of Quebec.

When the ships had been filled with as many prisoners as they could conveniently carry, they sailed away. Two miles below the present site of Alton the prisoners were herded once more onto land and left in the freezing weather without clothing, food, or shelter of any kind.

Some of the women and children had been left behind in the village. As they wandered through the woods in a desperate effort to follow where the boats had gone with their men, they came upon an Indian, Gomo. And it was the savage who treated these helpless people with tenderness. He put them into canoes and took them down the river where at last they rejoined the others of their now completely lost village.

In the spring the refugees sent from Kaskaskia for their cattle which had run wild ever since the attack. Some of them were recovered; but the early citizens of the state of Illinois believed that the wild hogs that ran through the country, often attacking farmers in their homes, were the offspring of the hogs that the citizens of Au Pé had lost.

Romance of the liveliest kind springs out of every violence. One of the residents of Au Pé at the time of

Captain Craig's attack was a certain Mme. La Croix. She was alone in her house with several small children when the soldiers swaggered in. Her husband was a respected citizen who had gone to Au Pé in 1805 to engage in fur trade with the Indians. At the time of Captain Craig's visit he was on his way to Canada in his two-masted batteau.

The next news that M. La Croix had from home was that his wife and children were dead, his home and livelihood gone. In an understandable fury he joined the British Army, determined to be, in his own pitiful and hopeless turn, a god of vengeance.

When the war was over at last, he heard that his wife had not died, after all, in the attack; that his children were well; and that the whole family was established with a reasonable degree of comfort at Cahokia. There is no ironic fillip to this romantic story. M. La Croix rejoined his family and died in their midst a few years later. After his death his widow married the young lawyer, John Reynolds, who was later to be governor of the state.

The French did not return to their village. But the successful claims which their descendants made against the government left Robert Forsyth, son of Thomas, and René La Croix, son of Mrs. Reynolds, prosperous members of the communities to which they went.

The French were not, however, slavishly forgiving. Hippolyte Pilette, who had seen his mother driven from her house, shaken with ague, a newborn child in her arms, did not forget the scene. Even when he was an old man, given to jollity under any favorable circumstances involving gossip and a glass of wine, he grew savage at the mention of that moment in the past. He knew few words of English but "I hate Yankees" were among the ones he spoke with eloquence.

There are a few other scattered incidents of pioneer history before the continuous modern development of a community on Peoria lake began. In 1813 the Indian, Black Partridge, heard that the Maillet fort was being rebuilt by American troops. He attacked the forces, commanded by Captain Nicholas, and was repulsed. The fort was completed and named for the American conqueror, George Rogers Clark. Later when the country became quiet and orderly once more, Fort Clark was abandoned. In 1816 Antoine Des Champs became general agent of the American Fur Company in Illinois. He visited Fort Clark and found that it had become the lair of deer and the roost of wild turkeys. In 1818 Des Champs, descending the river toward St. Louis, saw the fort in flames. Indians, having no more satisfying means of expressing their ill-will toward the white settlers, had set it on fire. The act was perhaps by way of a practice maneuver just to keep the troops from getting rusty in their technique.

In 1819 Captain Abner Eads, Isaac and Josiah Fahlon, and J. Hersey came to the site of Fort Clark on a hunting trip and pitched their tent against the stockades. In 1832 the fort was rebuilt during the Black Hawk War. By then the community on the lake was large once more and was called Peoria as it is today.

For a century and a half white men had been living, struggling, laughing, dying on the shore of that lake. As American communities went, it was already old and experienced in the pageant of building, destroying, and building again to which our human nature, in its alternate moods of patient creativity and mad, passionate destructiveness, is so strenuously devoted.

CHAPTER NINE

Dress Rehearsal for a Battle Scene

W HEN the pyrotechnical distractions of the War of 1812 were over, the drama in Illinois began to undergo a significant change. The cast of characters was different. The Indians ceded their lands to the government and moved westward. When they returned, during the Black Hawk War, for a final frenzied protest at being disinherited, they were no longer a serious threat to the white man's security.

The French no longer dominated the center of the stage. Their number was overwhelmed by the rush of settlers who came out of Kentucky, Tennessee, and Pennsylvania, bringing a sharper tang of personality and a firmer kind of resolution. Though their thinking was partly conditioned by previous residence in the southern section of the country, they were not deeply committed to its social philosophy. Indeed, they were committed to nothing but a love of the frontier. Morris Birkbeck, one of the English settlers in Illinois, said of his neighbors: "To struggle with privations has now become the habit of their ~~lives~~, most of them having made several successive plunges into the wilderness." George Flower added the testimony that they lived by "the old hunter's rule: when you hear the sound of a neighbor's gun, it is time to move away."

Restless, tough, and independent, they did not mind solitude overmuch, though they enjoyed offering a certain kind of bluff, humorous hospitality. They were mostly of Scotch-Irish, German, or Welsh extraction, with the Scotch-Irish strain predominating. This background accounted for the contrasts and contradictions of their temperaments. As a wit once said of such a man: "He is just Irish enough to know a joke; and just Scotch enough to keep it."

The French were not totally unable to make their pleasant voices heard in the new Babel. Here and there one like Pierre Menard was still noticeable. Canadian-born Menard had done well in trade. He was destined to have his name given to an Illinois county and also to have his person squatly immortalized in statuary about Springfield. But he is chiefly remembered for his abundant goodwill.

Once, when there was a shortage of salt in all the neighboring country, a group of men went to him to beg the supply he was known to have. "You got money?" he asked each man in turn. Some disconsolately admitted that they had no money and would have none till they had killed their hogs; others, feeling triumphant, boasted that they had come prepared to buy. Pierre Menard separated the sheep from the goats, putting the moneyed men on one side of the room, the indigent on the other. The men in whose pockets money jingled looked more complacent than ever, sure now of getting what they had come for. Suddenly Pierre Menard announced:

"You men who got de money can go to St. Louis for your salt. Dese poor men who got no money shall have my salt, by gar."

As lieutenant governor, Menard was delightfully innocent of parliamentary procedure. Measures that he disliked he blandly refused to put to a vote. One such concerned a provision to allow settlers to pay for land in the dubious bills of the bank of Edwardsville. Menard considered it a scheme to defraud the government and wanted nothing to do with it. Persuaded at last that he was obliged to put the matter before the legislators, he said:

"Gentlemen, if I mus', I mus'. You who are in favor signify by saying 'aye,' but I bet you ten thousand dollar' Congre' never make him land office money. You who are opposed say 'no'."

They might better have let Menard rule, for the government did lose $40,000 by failing to follow his sound trader's sense.

Limitlessly hospitable to Indians or whites who came to his door, Pierre Menard left a memory like a cheerful laugh.

The settler lived humbly, but proudly nonetheless. He did not "curse the bread" that was on his table but defended it against the ridicule of the finicky, superior visitor. Such a tactless guest in a tavern once nearly got his head cracked open when a robust son of Illinois, having listened to his belittling talk, approached him with threatening severity.

"See yer, stranger," he said, "I don't know who

you are and I don't keer a durn nuther, but I'll have you understand that the man that makes fun of corn bread makes fun of the principal part of my living."

To this "principal part" he added very little butter. Bacon was a mainstay of diet. Potatoes were unknown, and when at last they were introduced they were unpopular. People who succumbed to the temptation of eating them, as being better than nothing, were social outcasts who had to live down or endure the insult of being called "Irish."

The men of Illinois traveled over roads that were of a singular and incredible badness. To cover his annoyance with this handicap, the settler made jokes at his own expense. A typical story was told of a traveler who saw a fine beaver hat lying in the mire. Thinking he had recovered a lost prize, he picked it up. From beneath it came an indignant voice saying, "Hello, stranger. Who told you to take my hat off?" Discovering that there was indeed a wearer under the hat, the traveler hastily apologized and volunteered to pull the unfortunate fellow out of the mud. That was not at all necessary, the wearer of the hat blandly announced. He was riding, he said, a competent horse which had pulled him out of even worse places.

For obvious reasons, the settler stayed at home a great deal of the time. He was not greatly interested in politics. If he demanded anything of the territorial government it was a dam, a road, something quite practical that might improve his property or make his way of life just a little less hard.

If this self-sufficient settler had not been too weary at night after he had pulled off his boots and his jeans (he wore no underwear) and crawled into bed, he might have made this brief survey of the recent political history of his community. In 1787 the Illinois country had become theoretically a part of the United States by the ordinance which bestowed a certain body of laws, including one against slavery which everyone nonchalantly ignored. In 1790 a real territorial government had been set up with headquarters at Kaskaskia. Until 1800 the Illinois country was part of the Northwest Territory; from 1800 to 1809 it was part of Indiana Territory; in 1818 it became a state. By 1819 the rush of settlers had begun. The newcomers went in the largest numbers to the southern part, which soon became dotted with settlements. The sturdiest spirits who did not mind being on the extreme outpost of the wilderness went to Alton, just below the mouth of the Illinois River; to Jacksonville, a short distance north in the river valley; to Springfield, thirty miles east; to Peoria in its pleasant site directly on the river. In 1819 Jacksonville had a population of nineteen souls; in 1823, it had a thousand; and in 1825, four thousand. The drama of modern Illinois was ready to begin.

By that curious rhyming trick of fate, the first great political event of Illinois history forewarned of a greater political event which was to come. During the years between 1818 and 1824, Illinois was dealing with the problem of slavery exactly as the nation was later to have to deal with it. What happened during that time was like a rehearsal for a battle scene. The ardent, charming, unappreciated Daniel P. Cook played a role which Lincoln was presently to take over and interpret with no more sincerity, though with greater significance. There is a curious parallel between the pattern of the first fight against slavery and the second. The mystic might find in it a demonstration of the Dunne theory of the fluidity of time, which permits, to the man of wisdom, an anticipatory glimpse of what is to come. The realist will simply recognize once more, with a kind of sadness, that all excellent things must be fought for again and again. Lives like those of Cook and Lincoln make one aware that men of goodwill must always be the victims of their principles. In the bitter struggle to hold a little ground for decency against those who feel the dark impulse to drag the world back to savagery, they sacrifice themselves with casual gallantry.

The Ordinance of 1787 which forbade slavery in Illinois had been largely offset in principle by the provisions with regard to indentured servants. These regulations legalized conditions which were so bad that actual bondage might have been an improvement. The constitution under which Illinois entered the Union as a state in 1818 was deliberately confused. It seemed to declare against slavery because the framers knew that no other attitude would be acceptable to Congress. However, the code of laws, established under the constitution, was extremely harsh in its treatment of the Negroes. This sly sabotage of the principle of freedom, to which Illinois was supposedly committed, looked toward a revision of the laws and, eventually, toward the legalization of slavery. That was what a great majority of the representative citizens in the towns like Jacksonville really wanted. The right to hold slaves seemed to them a sacred one and they did not propose to let any "blue-bellied Yankees" take it from them. They were just biding their time to get it back.

The so-called "French slaves" provided a precedent for slavery in Illinois. They were the descendants of the

Negroes whom Philippe Renault had brought to work the mines a century before. When Renault had gone home he had disposed of them to other French settlers. In the heated, and largely hypocritical, discussions of slavery which took place in early Illinois the right of Negroes to be considered as human beings, worthy of the protection of the constitution, had been cynically overlooked.

In 1820 Missouri was loudly clamoring for admission to the Union as a slave state. The nation was ready for a full discussion of the problem. To the Congress which was to consider it went Daniel Cook.

He was young and frail and in a touching, unearthly way extremely handsome. Drawing, in lieu of health, upon that limitless supply of ardor which is always at the disposal of the imaginative, he had at twenty-five held many posts of honor and responsibility. An account of his activities would sound like an explosion of energy were it not for the obvious orderliness of Daniel Cook's routine. He had been, all within five years, a businessman at Kaskaskia, a student of law, a practicing lawyer, the joint owner and editor of the *Illinois Intelligencer*, a propagandist against slavery, an auditor of public accounts, a special emissary between President Monroe and John Quincy Adams at the Court of St. James's, a circuit judge, legislative attorney general, an unsuccessful candidate for Congress, and finally, a successful candidate for Congress. His personal popularity was enormous. It was sufficient to keep him as the sole representative of his state before the national government for seven years despite the fact that he persistently followed his own conscience and often did things which irritated the people at home. His contemporary, John Reynolds, said of him that he was "the darling of the people," and he well might be because, in addition to having charming manners and a genuine gentleness of spirit, he was always ready to lend or give money to anyone who asked for it. A ceremonious unknown gentleman, with whom he was traveling by steamboat, once had the temerity to ask him for $50. Probably to his own intense amazement, the adventurer got it.

The parallel between Cook and Lincoln announces itself astonishingly in the prelude to Cook's political career. As a candidate for Congress, he and his pro-slavery opponent, McLean, appeared before the people in a series of joint debates. When Lincoln and Douglas did the same thing in 1858, there were men still alive who had heard the earlier discussions. To them Cook seemed still as impressive a figure as Lincoln himself.

Indeed, it is Lincoln's own intonation that one catches in an excerpt from a speech in which Cook denounced the Missouri Compromise. By its provisions, Missouri was to be admitted as a slave state, but slavery was to be forbidden, thereafter, north of latitude 36 degrees, 30 minutes.

"Away with your compromise," Cook protested. "Let Missouri in and the predominance of slave influence is settled and the whole country will be overrun with it. Indeed I am opposed to any compromise on the subject. I consider it my duty to aid in arresting an evil and a duty of so high a nature as to amount to a constitutional duty, embraced within the oath I have taken to support that instrument."

A generation later, Lincoln fought this battle all over again. The Missouri Compromise was again directly involved in the struggle. Like Cook, Lincoln said that he considered it a moral duty to arrest the evil of slavery. Like Cook, he considered that the Constitution stated that obligation in no uncertain terms.

When the question of admitting Missouri as a slave state was put finally to a vote, Cook was among the "nays." It would have been convenient and advantageous, he said, to have been able to vote for admission. He knew that the people at home in Illinois were going to be angry with him, and they were. But he continued:

". . . while I consider the Constitution the rock upon which our temple of liberty must stand . . . I feel myself called upon to forego all such considerations and defend it from infringement."

In 1822 Daniel Cook married Julia Edwards, daughter of Ninian Edwards, the early territorial governor. Again, chance was contriving to draw Cook close to Lincoln. For by his marriage to Mary Todd, Lincoln later became a brother-in-law of the younger Ninian Edwards.

In the same year, the antislavery men of Illinois took their courage in their hands and offered direct defiance. Governor Edward Coles, a Virginian by birth but before all else a man of conscience, suggested freeing the French slaves. To the proslavery men this seemed like a flagrant assault upon their dearest tradition and they prepared for an active fight to legalize slavery. A fine, lusty campaign of bribery and corruption succeeded in forcing a bill to do so through the House and in this the Senate concurred. In the election of 1824 the issue was to be put before the people.

It was a moment of great tension in the history of Illinois. Governor Thomas Ford gave a little of his fine gift for contempt to this description of the revealing moment:

"Newspapers, hand bills and pamphlets were scattered everywhere and everywhere they scorched and scathed as they flew. Almost every stump, in every county, had its bellowing, indignant orator on one side or the other and the whole people for the space of months did scarcely anything but read, quarrel, wrangle and argue with each other. . . ."

Governor Reynolds makes this prophetic comment:

"Men, women and children entered the arena of warfare and strife and families and neighbors were so divided and fierce and bitter toward one another that it seemed a regular Civil War might be the result. Many personal combats were indulged in, upon the question, and the whole country seemed at times to be ready and willing to resort to physical force to decide the contest."

Reynolds remembered also that the cripples, the sick, the old were carried to the polls to vote. Cook was by far the best orator on either side, but he and his fellow believers in freedom did not count wholly on their eloquence. They were admirably organized. When the votes were counted, slavery was found to have met with an unmistakable defeat.

The significant thing is that the issue had been settled on principle. If prejudice alone had been operative, slavery would have won, for it was in the beginning vastly stronger. In towns, many of the leaders shared with the majority of the people a powerful belief in the rightness of slavery. Truman Post points out: "In Jacksonville, there was a collision between two antagonists, one born directly or indirectly of slavery, and the other of freedom. Antagonistic principles had slept side by side in unconscious or timid procrastination of the inevitable. These principles were now in direct encounter, in the same field, confronting one another, in struggle and each conscious of the one as its mortal foe."

The decision at the polls did not, of course, kill off prejudice at a blow. What Post calls "the relentless and sleepless inquisition of slave power—its espionage and censorship" went on. But these efforts at defiance were fatuous and impotent. The issue was closed.

Illinois has other reasons for remembering Cook more vividly than as merely the donor of his name to Cook County. He was in many ways a brilliantly effective legislator in Congress. As member of the Committee on Public Lands, he helped to clear up the Homeric confusion in that important department of government. The affairs of individuals and government alike had been thrown into chaos by the system of credit which had prevailed. Through Cook's influence, the old system was abolished and the price of land fixed at $1.25 an acre, a rate far more considerate of the pioneer's slim purse.

The river itself owes him a particular debt. In 1822 he championed the project of building a canal which should join the Illinois to Lake Michigan. It was his hope to obtain help from the federal government. All he succeeded in getting was a grant of land, ninety feet wide, through the public domain. With tight-lipped, tight-fingered decisiveness, the federal government declared itself otherwise liable for no expense in the matter. Illinois's request for financial help was dismissed with a kind of spinsterish finality as though it were the demand of an importunate, selfish child.

But Cook continued to importune, resolutely.

"This is a work," he said, "in which the nation is interested and which the government should therefore aid in executing. As a ligament to bind the Union together, no work of the same magnitude can be more useful."

He wore them down in the end. In 1827, just before he left Congress for the last time, he secured passage of a bill which made the canal a national project. His success established solidly, for the first time, the principle that the public domain should be used for public purposes.

In a small way, which became his size, Cook was a martyr too. He had always voted as his very reliable intelligence and still more delicate conscience ordered. Several times Illinois had been annoyed at him and each time she had forgiven him. But Cook disobeyed once too often. When, in 1824, the presidential election was thrown into the House, Illinois had chosen Jackson as its candidate. Cook cast his vote for Adams. The resentment against him at home was strong. When he himself was again a candidate for re-election, his opponent was Joseph Duncan, an almost unknown man. But Duncan won.

Most shocked by this outcome were a large number of men who had voted against Cook.

"We did not intend to defeat little Cook," they said, "but to lessen his majority so as to make him feel his dependence upon us."

But inadvertently they had killed him, besides defeating him. He had lived for many years on vitality borrowed from his imagination, and now without a job to do he was lost. Before the year was out charming little Cook was dead.

He had lived much more triumphantly than he knew. For by destroying in Illinois the inclination to make slaves of men he had prepared it as a testing ground where, later, it could be dealt with as a national issue.

The New England states had never been tempted by slavery. Their purity of motive in wanting to be rid of it seemed to the impartial observer a little smug and objectionable. The southern states believed that slavery was a right which was somehow guaranteed to them as inalienable by a very flexible Constitution of their own interpretation. But Illinois, having been through the struggle once, knowing all the arguments and all the answers, being neither self-righteously smug in its denunciations of slavery nor inclined to hug it hysterically to its heart, was the ideal and inevitable place to become a forum of freedom.

In that service "little Cook" had his dignified and enviable share.

CHAPTER TEN

Tourists Accommodated

"OUR far west is improving rapidly, astonishingly. It is five years since I visited it and the changes within that period are like the work of enchantment. Flourishing towns have grown up, farms have been opened, comfortable dwellings, fine barns and all appurtenances in a country in which the hardy pioneer had at that time sprinkled a few cabins. The conception of Coleridge may be realized sooner than he anticipated. The possible destiny of the United States as a nation of a hundred millions of freemen, stretching from the Atlantic to the Pacific, living under the laws of Alfred and speaking the language of Shakespeare and Milton is an august conception—why should we not wish to see it realized?"

This striking, if flamboyant, prophecy was made during the teeming thirties when Illinois was, indeed, strenuously busy in creating a new world. It was not, to be sure, the ideal society of which Coleridge and

Southey dreamed, the "pantisocracy" which they hoped to create on the banks of the Susquehanna River. It is, perhaps, just as well that Illinois fell into tougher hands. For all that poor Coleridge got out of the pantisocracy was the dull marriage into which Southey rushed him, as a preliminary maneuver, and an increased need to escape to the comfort of drugs.

The nameless prophet, quoted above, who talked so glibly about a nation of freemen shared the ideas of his time and one thing which made him love Illinois was the thought of the profit that could be made from it.

"The state of Illinois," he went on with unabashed candor, "has probably the finest body of fertile land of any state in the Union and the opportunities for speculation are numerous . . . property will continue to advance . . . admirable farms and town lots may be purchased with the certainty of realizing large profits."

So it was the shrewd-eyed men who came to America to build its towns, instead of the poetic idealists, like Coleridge, who found it easier to stay at home and have vague love affairs and take laudanum.

The travelers give us vivid, detailed pictures of what Illinois was like in those days when everyone was creating, if not a new heaven, at least a new earth. Mostly they agreed with Touchstone that when they were at home they were "in a better place." Few of the visitors from England wrote to their friends the nineteenth century equivalent of "having a wonderful time; wish you were here." But they did respect the citizenry for the energy with which, during a quiet period of the state's history, they got on with the job of building houses, churches, schools, roads, of harvesting the wheat and making clothes. They even took a moment out, now and then, for family life and a joke or two.

James Stuart came in 1830. He was a haughty creature, very much the aristocrat. Though he wished to see the "state of common life," he drew instinctively away from its more pungent realities. At Lower Alton he stayed at Mr. Miller's hotel, "quite a second rate house of entertainment." It was necessary to pass through the room where Mrs. Miller lay in bed in order to get to his own room. This he forgave because Mrs. Miller straightway arose and got him some excellent ham and eggs. He visited and admired the view from the heights above the mouth of the Illinois River, observing that most of its length was accessible to steamboats. He thought the prairie ground eminently beautiful and said respectful things about the fine black loam.

He liked the Reverend Mr. Picket, with whom he stayed one night, because that rugged gentleman lived by farming and performed all his ministerial duties gratis. Mr. Picket and his sons plowed their hundred acres while his wife and daughter managed the eight cows. It seemed to Mr. Stuart very droll that one of the Picket daughters should be called Minerva and he made many pleasantries about it, all of which were answered with good humor. Mr. Picket charged sixpence for supper and sixpence for a bed.

Mr. Stuart was less happy at Bentley's hotel in Jacksonville, partly because "the young ladies who acted as waitresses . . . having cleared the table and again covered it with the necessary articles sat down to their meal with me on a footing of the most perfect equality." He spoke to Squire Bentley firmly about the matter but found him such a barbarian that it was not worth the trouble to try to improve him.

He visited the Illinois Academy at Jacksonville (Illinois College) and found that "the annual expense for the teachers is for English alone twelve dollars, and for the languages, mathematics, philosophy, etc., sixteen dollars."

Of all the people whom he met he most heartily approved Mr. Kerr, a hospitable Scotsman, whose wife gave him an abundant breakfast, when he went to call, consisting of "tea, coffee, eggs, pork steaks, peach preserves, honey and various sorts of bread." Mrs. Kerr asked her guest if he did not consider the view from her door equal to that from Hopetoun House, the finest place in the neighborhood of Mr. Kerr's birthplace at Queensbury. Mr. Stuart deliberated soberly and found that he could not, in all honesty, say that it was as fine. For, after all, the Firth of Forth did make a considerable difference.

At Springfield Mr. Stuart met other farmers of whom he approved. There was, for example, Mr. Strawbridge, formerly of Donegal, who farmed 640 acres of land which produced "forty bushel of wheat to the second crop without sowing." Mr. Strawbridge made a good side line of selling wooden posts to the mines at Galena. He had sold 8,000, during the year before, at $3 per hundred. Mr. Stuart and Mr. Strawbridge discussed the servant problem and agreed that the dearth of domestic help had made those that could be secured unbearably saucy.

Mr. Stuart wanted very much to be generous. The Illinois landscape had his unqualified endorsement. The economy of that isolated society seemed to him to

be admirably administered by his former fellow coun-
trymen. The life was simple but orderly and when
occasionally Mr. Stuart found a planter who looked
inadequate to his job it was occasion for remark. He ap-
plauded the vision of settlers whom he saw arriving
daily in great caravans. Their wagons were loaded with
furniture and children; their cows, horses, and dogs
were driven before or followed after.

And Mr. Stuart admired the tenacity with which
the people of Illinois adhered to democratic principles,
"retaining in their hands every power which can be conveniently withheld from the rulers." He thought it extraordinary that in Vandalia where there had been not
a single dwelling until 1821, "three meetings of an
antiquarian and historical society had already taken
place." He thought the quality of the *Illinois Magazine*
as good (incredible concession for a Scotsman!) as that
of *Blackwood's* in Edinburgh.

But he definitely did not like sleeping two in a bed,
in a room containing several other beds. He was woefully offended when, after sleeping for a night under
a roof that leaked, he asked for water and a towel and
"to my horror, instead of the latter, a part of an infant's
paraphernalia was given me—the name of which . . .
it is well not to mention!"

And there were always and everywhere those saucy
girls! One of them sat, after serving the guests, "at
the end of the table and at some distance from it, much
more intent on placing one leg above the other in a
proper position for showing her foot and ankle than in
giving the necessary attendance to the table."

The utter lack, in Illinois, of any feeling for the
social proprieties continually stirred Mr. Stuart's resent-

ment. One cannot help feeling that he should have stayed at home to indulge in the good old Scotch passion for discussing theology, while he let someone just a little more like Robert Burns come to America in his place.

Mr. Stuart left in time to avoid the incredible winter of 1830-31. The story of the "great snow" belongs to the record of social history, because time was reckoned by it for many years after. An observer at Beardstown remembered:

"The snow fell at first about thirty inches deep then the weather settled and another drift fell and another and another until it was four to six feet deep. In drifts it was much deeper. Fences were covered and lanes filled up. There was much suffering everywhere. Stock died for want of food. Deer stood in their tracks and died. Prairie chickens and quail having alighted in the snow could not get out. Man was the only animal that could walk, and game alone, of the food kind, was all he had in plenty. That could be had for the picking up from the snow for it was helpless. But finally even the game became so poor from starvation that it was unfit for food. The snow staid [sic] on the ground nearly all winter until March and people ran short of everything particularly fuel.

"Mr. Beard [founder of Beardstown, and its patriarch], recollecting a widow with a small family living at the bluff walked out there and found her and her family on the verge of starvation, hovering over the last remnants of a fire, she having used all her fuel. Mr. Beard tore up some fencing and chopped a large pile of wood for her and afterwards carried provisions to her through the snow, a distance of seven miles, as a horse could not walk."

It is fortunate for people who had to face such rigors that whisky sold at 48 cents a gallon.

The necessities of life were not always obtainable but the price was gauged to the economy of the time. Butter was 10 cents a pound; beef, 2½ cents a pound. Cigars sold at $1 a thousand.

In 1835 a more jovial and adaptable traveler went to Illinois from New York. C. F. Hoffman possessed humor and a sense of irony which made him more aware of men than of their economy. He liked to listen to stories of the settlers and of their relations with the Indians.

"Why, sir," an Illinois man said to him of one crisis, "those Indians behaved most ridiculous. They dashed children's brains against the door-posts; they cut off their heads; they tore . . ." Complete details to which the quaint epithet "ridiculous" had been applied were too offensive for the delicate-minded Mr. Hoffman to give. It relieved him to know that in 1835 the Indians were "dispersed . . . over the neighborhood" and "perfectly harmless."

Mr. Hoffman traveled down the river, looking for Starved Rock. He failed to find it even after he had had directions from a "sickly-looking but rather interesting woman" who came out of "a miserable log hut beside which housed under a few boards, stood a handsome barouche." His eye was for the landscape chiefly, though he preferred to have it fitted out with figures. He liked to descend to the ice of the river, "a broad and noble stream," to sit "upon a fallen log among the tangled vines of the rich bottom opposite to Hennepin and watch a flock of green parroquets fluttering among the wych elms . . . while the sun, for a moment piercing his murky veil, touched with gold the icicles that glazed their drooping branches."

He felt an intense admiration for Samson, his driver, both of whose feet were frozen on one occasion. He would have lost them had there not happened to be a doctor at the house where the party stopped. "The good humored little patient was removed without delay to the back room and we commenced pouring water into his boots until they melted from his feet, the temperature of the water being gradually heightened until it became blood warm." Next morning, Samson wrapped his still swollen feet in horse blankets and went back with his team.

Mr. Hoffman, whose business was simply to observe, stayed on with the farmer "whose sturdy frame, bold features and long black hair would, with his frank address, afford as fine a specimen of the western border as one could meet with and never allow you to suspect that ten or fifteen years ago he had been a New York tradesman."

At Galena, Mr. Hoffman recorded one more glimpse of the scene and he chose a memorable one:

"The intervening prairie for the first six miles was high and level with not a stick of timber—one broad

snow-covered plain where you could see the dark figure
of a wolf for miles off as it stood in relief against the
white, unbroken surface."

Mr. Hoffman found, however, that there had been
no improvement since Mr. Stuart's time in the matter
of beds. One night at Boyd's Grove, he and his companion had taken possession of the two beds available

in the farmhouse when other travelers came wanting
accommodations. "My companion pretended to be in a
sound sleep and I intimated that I should betake myself
to my buffalo robe and the floor in case a bedfellow were
thrust in upon me: whereat the kind lady was exceed-
ingly miffed; and we could hear her through the parti-
tion a moment afterward expressing herself after this
amiable fashion: 'Ugh! great people, truly! a bed to
themselves, the hogs! They travel together—and they

eat together—and they eat enough, too,—and yet they can't sleep together.' "

In 1837 the Reverend Mr. John Mason Peck took the grand tour of Illinois to write a gazetteer. He found that "wolves, panthers, and wild-cats are still numerous . . . wild horses are found ranging the forests." The sketchiness with which civilization had tamed the country was, however, an advantage to the settler. Mr. Peck wanted it "distinctly understood, once for all, that a poor man can always purchase horses, cattle, hogs and provisions for labor either by the day, month or job."

There had evidently been acrimonious talk in the reverend gentleman's hearing about the way in which eastern speculators were exploiting the land and its men.

Mr. Peck had a wealth of information to offer about social conditions all of it expressed with the same air of belligerent firmness.

"The people of the west and of Illinois," he says, "have much plain, blunt but sincere hospitality. Emigrants who come amongst them with a disposition to be pleased with the people and the country—to make no invidious comparisons—to assume no airs of distinction, will be welcome."

He did not have the best possible opinion of his confreres in the ministry.

"Some are very illiterate and make utter confusion of the word of God. Such persons are usually proud, conceited, fanatical and influenced by spirit far removed from the meek, docile, benevolent and charitable spirit of the gospel."

It is just possible that he himself was not altogether meek.

His judgment against the clergy did not, of course,

apply to such a gallant person as the Reverend Edward Beecher, of the great Beecher family, who headed the faculty at Illinois College. Mr. Peck was much impressed with that institution both for its social and for its educational system.

"Students who choose are allowed to employ a portion of each day in manual labor either upon the farm or in the workshop. The library consists of some 1,500 volumes. There is also a valuable chemical and philosophical apparatus."

It should, perhaps, be mentioned that in the early nineteenth century, "philosophical apparatus" meant equipment for the study of the physical sciences. It would be too bad (though it is rather a tempting notion) to leave the false idea that the faculty at Illinois College had invented a machine to measure the driving force of the "categorical imperative" of Kant.

Mr. Peck shared the enthusiasm of the state for the plan to improve the Illinois River. "From this imperfect sketch of the obstructions," he observed, "it will be seen that with the comparatively trifling expense of $100,000 which the legislature has provided, the navigation of the Illinois River may be good at all stages of water."

Thus he announced a theme upon which there were to be tragic and ironic variations for many years to come.

His gazetteer described the town of Ottawa as having 10 stores, 2 taverns, and 80 families. The steamboats reached it in the spring. New Salem had 3 or 4 stores and 30 families. Springfield was becoming magnificent. It had 19 dry goods stores, 6 retail stores, 4 public houses, 1 bookstore, 18 physicians, 11 lawyers.

He did not say that one of those lawyers was called

Lincoln. It would have taken a man of keener prophetic vision than the Reverend Mr. Peck to have foreseen that Springfield was destined to warm itself forever in the radiance of that name.

BOOK II

In the Shadow of a Giant

CHAPTER ELEVEN

Riverman

HALFWAY toward the end of its journey, the Illinois River is joined by the Sangamon and this confluence brings together two important streams of history. For it was this waterway system that linked the state to the outside world. Along the rivers moved the men who in their turn moved destiny.

In the 1830's the rivermen were the visionaries and the leaders. La Salle's dream of empire was reborn in their imaginations and they saw the importance of the part that their rivers might play in such an enterprise. One of the more exuberant of them put his faith into verse, singing:

> For I will make our Sangamo
> Outshine the glory of the Po.

Sentiments like tnat must have warmed the spirit of a man like Denton Offut. He had reached Illinois in 1831 with no past worth bothering to talk about but

117

with the brightest visions of the future. He was the complete riverman, big, buoyant, and bombastic; fond of company, of yarning, of liquor. His imagination served him ardently but not always well. The beginning and the end of his story reveal, against a humble background, the familiar pattern of the empire builder's rise and fall.

He was a fine swaggering fellow when, in the spring of 1831, he persuaded a group of young men to take a boatload of stock and provisions down the Sangamon River, down the Illinois, and finally down the Mississippi to New Orleans. He was willing to pay them 50 cents a day and an extra $60 to make the trip. Denton Offut was to supply the boat. The young men agreed. Their names were John Hanks, Abe Lincoln, and John Johnston.

In March they made their way down the Sangamon to a place called Judy's Ferry. Springfield was later to spring up on that site, but when the party of young men reached it there was only a cluster of shacks. The most noticeable of these had before its door a sign on which a buck's head was painted to indicate that it was a place of public entertainment.

Behind the door was Denton Offut, mellow and cheerful in his cups, jovially indifferent to the fact that he had promised to supply a boat upon which to move his stock.

It is the principal gift of the promoter to be persuasive. Denton Offut, sitting in the Buckhorn Tavern at Judy's Ferry, postured and made promises, talked in terms of world power, and finally sent the young men away to build the boat for him. They got lumber from

Congress land, arranged for the use of machinery at Kirkpatrick's mill, and set to work.

They dragged Denton out of the Buckhorn long enough to see the boat launched. He was lavish in his praise of the sturdy young rivermen who had worked so quickly and efficiently for him.

By April 19th, pork in barrels, corn, and hogs had been stowed on board and the journey was begun. There was another unfortunate interruption at New Salem, where the boat was stranded on Rutledge's mill-dam. A huge crowd gathered on the steep bank overlooking the river hoping, in the casually malicious way of crowds, to see disaster. But the young man named Lincoln was not baffled for long by this caprice of the river. He unloaded the goods, bored a hole in the end of the boat which extended over the dam, released the water, floated free, plugged the hole, and reloaded.

Denton Offut, potential empire builder, was rapturous over the discovery of so able an assistant. With the presence of mind of the born booster, he called the assemblage on the bank to order and delivered an impromptu oration on civic responsibility and opportunity. He would, Offut promised, build a steamboat to "plow up and down the Sangamon." With young Lincoln as her captain, "By thunder, she'd have to go."

Then with an uplifting sense of duty done he got on with his drinking while Lincoln got on to New Orleans.

While his boat was gone, Offut made a trip to St. Louis and laid in stock for a store which he made haste to establish in the village of New Salem. He chose an excellent site just above the Rutledge dam. Here was one of the chief centers of community life. All the farmers from the country about sent corn to the mill to be ground into meal. Their boys would ride into town carrying two bushel sacks. The horses would be tethered to trees and saplings. Sometimes there would be as many as forty of them waiting patiently on the steep bank, while down below the boys shouted noisily to each other as they swam in the river or played fox and geese in the tract called Miller's Half Bushel. Then as the wheel slowly ground out the meal, bushel by bushel, the children in the river would reluctantly become responsible members of society once more, reload their horses and start toward home.

Six days a week the people of the Illinois valley ate what they called corn dodgers. These were cakes baked in a skillet to so hard a consistency that a wit of the period once observed, in a mood halfway between affectionate awe and fierce resentment, that "you could knock down a Texas steer with a chunk of the stuff or split an end-board forty yards off-hand." Only on Sunday, if all the children had been good, was there any variation in this item of diet. The Lord's day brought biscuit and preserves to the righteous.

Denton Offut, who wished to serve wherever service was profitable, lost no time in acquiring the mill which ground out the corn meal.

Partly because of its teeming activity, the quarter of the town where Offut's mill and store stood was held in least esteem by the villagers. It was the scene of the activities of the wild Clary's Grove boys, the powerful young adults who distracted themselves from the lack of other entertainment by blacking each other's eyes and rolling complaisant drunkards downhill in barrels.

Through this quarter, too, came and went the other

picturesque figures of the period, men like Daddy Boger who had fought in the Revolutionary War and who now made baskets and sold them for a living; and women like Granny Spears who at ninety still rode about on horseback to every house where a birth was expected. Granny had been caught by the Indians in her youth and had learned their remedies for all the ills of the flesh. Crouched on her horse, her long nose nearly meeting her pointed chin, she might easily have suggested witchcraft to a people less healthy and uncomplicated than those of Illinois.

When young Lincoln had returned from the south, Denton Offut demonstrated his generous intentions to him once again by putting him in charge of the store. With the mill and half a dozen other projects added to his constantly broadening program, more and more responsibility was delegated to the clerk. Offut was enormously proud of his assistant. He sensed unusual qualities in this variable young man who could match and overcome the strength of the strongest bully among the Clary's Grove boys without losing his own attitude of humorous goodwill toward all mankind.

There are two ways of being at home among roisterers, Denton Offut knew. One was his own, that of a brother in exuberant extravagance. His red cheeks would puff out with easy appreciation of any episode of village comedy, however brutal. Yet he admired his young clerk's subtler and more profound way of identifying himself with the people among whom he lived.

Unconsciously this lanky young man was training himself for the task to which his life was to be devoted. It was that of lending eloquence to the wisdom of the race. Living among the men and women who brought their simple daily needs to the mill and to the store, he saw human experience reduced to the lowest common denominator of need. He loved folkways for themselves. He wrestled with the Clary's Grove boys not merely physically but in spirit, and received a kind of blessing from them. What they gave him was an appreciation of their robust sanity, their earthy vigor, the tang and savor of their speech. His mind became the repository of their ribaldry, their wit, and also their wisdom. Among his contemporaries, Lincoln was famous for an inexhaustible store of anecdotes. Yet he himself once said that he had invented only one story in all his life, the least typical of his repertory. The rest were adaptations of the folklore of the backwoods people and the river people to whose speech and thought his mind and ear were so subtly attuned. He heard their parables when he worked for Denton Offut in the store which was also a saloon and a social center.

Another thing that Denton Offut admired in his clerk was that, while he himself became more and more interested in the store as a place of relaxation and entertainment, Lincoln was not even aware of temptation. On a bet he could lift a cask into his arms and drink from the bunghole, but he spat the liquor out of his mouth when the exploit was concluded. This was a masterpiece of stoicism which Denton could admire without being able to copy.

And so, all at once, it happened that the Offut empire crumbled. Debts accumulated in place of gains. Offut lost the lease of the mill and finally as difficulties mounted he copied the example of many another pioneer merchant and ran away.

There is an amusing postcript to his story. It was

not to be expected that he would end his days in chagrin over lost opportunity and lost integrity.

He appeared for one final glimpse in the city of Baltimore where he had assumed the role of veterinary surgeon and horse tamer. The charlatan had claimed the upper hand in his temperament as his dress fancifully proclaimed. The very noticeable austerity of the black which dominated his costume was even more noticeably interrupted by the bright red sash which he wore across his shoulder, fixed with a huge rosette. Denton Offut was not a person for half measures when he started out to be conspicuous.

The service with which he was attempting to recommend himself to the citizens of Baltimore was that of subduing unmanageable horses. He professed to have a secret which he whispered in the animal's ear. To the unwary he offered the sale of this formula for a mere $5. The comedy was further enlivened with a scene in which the recipient was put under oath not to divulge the secret.

It is curious that two rivermen so different as Offut and Lincoln should have been brought so dramatically into contrast. Denton was the busy, blustering, energetic man of many plans. His grasp upon the reality of his world was nervous and fleeting. He was the promoter who, without fully understanding his own purposes, really intends to exploit. He began as the creator of a new world but, because there was no grandeur in him to hold him to his purpose, he ended as a clown.

Much more truly the river belonged to Lincoln. He was a worker on the water and he learned all the tricks of survival in a contest requiring constant watchfulness, ingenuity, and adaptability. The river taught him its way of achieving a goal. Lincoln learned to let his life flow as it must: over the deep places, over the shallows, around obstacles, through hazards. Like the river, his life moved on irresistibly toward its objective. The

movement of his career was sometimes sluggish, sometimes swift. Toward the end, it tumbled with turbulent speed. But one sees in it the steady reliability of the Illinois itself, knowing unconsciously the way in which it must go.

CHAPTER TWELVE

Part-time Politician

P ETER CARTWRIGHT spent his life wrestling with
the devil. As a spiritual leader of the Methodist Church
he made no soft, mystical interpretation of his duty. In
his vigorous and dramatic theology, a principal item of
belief was that the devil took up a tenacious tenancy in
the body of frail man. So, quite literally, Peter wrestled
with the man to drive out the devil.

From an improvised pulpit in the rude meeting-
houses of the Illinois river towns he would recklessly
demand of some sturdy young brave that he come forward and be saved.

"I mean that young man there, standing on the
seats of the ladies, with a ruffled shirt on," he would
shout. And then his bluff dramatic sense, which always
took the form of making worldliness ridiculous, would
prompt him to add: "I doubt not that ruffled shirt was
borrowed."

If the young sinner proved defiant, Peter would

THE WILD CLARY'S GROVE BOYS DISTRACTED THEMSELVES

ROLLING COMPLAISANT DRUNKARDS DOWNHILL IN BARRELS.

stride down to where he stood, take him by the scruff of the neck, fling him down in front of the congregation, and hold him there by force while he exhorted God to save this erring child.

Peter had the physique to lend authority to such direct-action campaigns for redemption. Though he was only of medium height, his build was massive. His chest was broad and his arms were powerful. Straight through his maturity his strength seemed to increase. It had to, for when he was traveling his circuit it was often necessary for him to fight his way through a forest and swim a swollen river.

His brow was broad and over it tumbled a mass of shaggy hair. In the early days of his ministry it was coal black; later it turned iron gray. To the end, its thickness hinted at a kind of excessive vitality. His head was crowned, winter and summer, with a broad-brimmed Quaker hat of white. Peter appears to have had an innocent aptitude for being picturesque.

The eyes were small, but set deep in his head. Men remembered them long after his death as "piercing and radiant." Despite the ruthlessness of his attacks on sin, he was remembered also for the generosity of his temperament. His was the sort of goodness that people of the wild could understand. He represented the church militant in a community where life itself was an uninterrupted battle.

Peter came by saintliness in the traditional way. After the innocence of infancy, he made, as a boy, a long detour along the paths of unrighteousness before he zigzagged back to virtue. A traveler once stopped at his childhood home in Kentucky and, entering the cabin, found a large family of boys and girls tied to bedposts and other pieces of heavy furniture. He asked the reason and was told by young Peter that his parents on leaving home had taken this precaution to keep the children from fighting. "If I set you free," the visitor asked, "will you behave yourselves?" "You try us once," Peter answered cryptically.

Prompted by the irresistible impulse of the adult to study juvenile psychology in all its unpredictable manifestations, the visitor untied the ropes. Straightway the Cartwright young began blacking each other's eyes with a quiet frenzy of resolution.

But long before he reached Illinois, Peter had had a moment of illumination and ceased being a "wild, wicked boy." His apprenticeship in the ministry had been served in Kentucky, but Peter seemed to invite the challenge of the newest, rawest world he could find. He settled his wife and children on a farm in the Illinois valley and from it set out, for periods of six weeks at a time, to preach the gospel to his tempestuous, yet susceptible brethren.

His successes were rather astonishing. In his autobiography he sketches a dramatic picture of the effect that his words had upon the people who sat at his feet. With proper modesty he regards himself merely as the medium of divine influence. Yet it is with a kind of professional pride that he sets down the record.

"In about thirty minutes, the power of God fell upon the congregation in such a manner as is seldom seen. The people fell in all directions, right and left, front and rear. It was supposed that not less than three hundred fell like dead men in a mighty battle; and there was no need of calling in mourners, for they were strewn all over the camp ground."

To achieve such spiritual triumphs, Peter Cartwright labored with more physical steadfastness than was exacted of the ordinary pioneer. Periodically he must set out from his comfortable and prosperous farm to cover his large circuit. He traveled a hundred miles north, crossed the Illinois River, moved on as far as Galena, turned back to Galesburg, then to Canton and Beardstown, across the Illinois once more, and so home.

At the river he would dismount, strip himself, swim across holding the bundle of his clothes and riding equipment high above his head, swim back to take his horse across, dress and proceed on his way. It seems never to have occurred to him that there was anything heroic about these journeys. They were made all alone across prairies where he might travel for a day at a time without seeing a single cabin. They took him deep into forests through which he must make his way by following the trail blazed in the bark of the trees. Yet satisfaction came to him in the thought that he was following the command of the old hymn:

> Oh whip the devil around the stump
> And hit him a crack at every jump.

There was plenty of defiance among Peter Cartwright's sinners. He was forever being threatened with whippings. From most of these embarrassments he extricated himself by his wit. Once the soldier-father of a boy whom he had rebuked challenged him to a duel. Told that he might make the choice of weapons to be used on the field of honor, Peter selected cornstalks.

But in a real emergency he was able to meet any threat to the effectiveness of his work. There is an almost Homeric quality to the description which Peter gives of the fight which followed an attempt on his part to discipline an unruly, but popular visitor to a large camp meeting. It reaches a climax in this stirring scene:

"An old drunken magistrate came up to me and ordered me to let my prisoner go. I told him I should not. He swore if I did not he would knock me down. I told him to crack away. Then one of my friends, at my request, took hold of my prisoner and the drunken justice made a pass at me, but I parried the stroke and, seizing him by the collar and the hair of his head and fetching him a sudden jerk forward brought him to the ground and jumped on him. I told him to be quiet or I would pound him well. The mob then rushed to the scene; they knocked down seven magistrates, several preachers and others. I gave up my prisoner to another and threw myself in front of the friends of order. Just at this moment the ringleader of the mob and I met; he made three passes at me; by the force of his own effort he threw the side of his head toward me. It seemed at that moment, I had not the power to resist temptation and I struck a sudden blow which dropped him to the earth. Just at this moment, the friends of order rushed at hundreds of the mob, knocking them down in all directions."

It was his ability to dramatize the power of God in his own sturdy person that made him so effective with the men and women of the Illinois valley. Once when he was staying overnight in the cabin of a stranger, he was deeply antagonized by the unruly spirit of his host's termagant wife.

"Madam," he said to her at last with a characteristic mixture of righteous wrath and personal irritation, "if you were my wife I would break you of your bad ways or I would break your neck."

Buoyed up by her memory of past triumphs, the shrew made the grave mistake of defying Peter Cartwright. Feeling at once the strength of his mission, he put the wife outside the cabin door and bolted it against her. The scene that followed was one of operatic quality. A storm provided the orchestral accompaniment while Peter and the termagant conducted a striking battle of wills.

"While she was raging and foaming in the yard around the cabin, I started a spiritual song and sang loud to drown out her voice as much as possible. I sang on and she roared and thundered on outside till she became perfectly exhausted."

He took her in at last, a chastened, dutiful woman. At least Peter, who had a harmless fondness for dwelling on his triumphs, ends the record at a moment when the prognosis seemed hopeful.

Like many other godly men, Peter seems to have been least successful in disciplining his own family. His wife bore him nine children and though some, who came to maturity, led lives that did his example credit, others gave him difficulties. There was a more than half-attractive defiance, for example, to the daughter who ran off with a famous rowdy named Patten Harrison. Peter was not pleased. He pursued the eloping couple, swearing that he would "break that up if I have to follow them within two jumps of hell." But he took the wrong road in his pursuit and before his great firmness of character could express its protest effectively, the young people were married.

"I have beat the devil," Peter Cartwright's daughter exclaimed in triumph.

Her new husband asked her what she meant. The look of satisfaction which her father had worn so often must have been reflected in her face as she replied:

"I have headed off Old Peter and the devil never could."

In the perfect Cartwright anecdote, however, it is Peter himself who has the shout of victory. Typical of his robust, backwoods wit is the story of the boy who annoyed him one night during a camp meeting, by standing in the bushes near by and braying like a donkey. Peter seemed curiously meek about accepting this outrage. His tormentor should have been warned by that portentous silence. Peter had thought of a better way of evening the score. In the next night's sermon, he returned to the subject of the wild riverboy's comedy, saying:

"I rather think his braying was the most sensible and honest thing he ever did in his life for it shows he has just found out what class he belonged to and was determined like an honest man to let everyone know it."

His talent for bluff satire was the source of his strength. As one friendly critic has written: "Fortunately for him, most of his ministry was in the midst of a population who believed that anything which could be made ridiculous must be false."

"Uncle Peter" he came to be called as the years piled on his grizzled, shaggy head. He became a part-time politician, urged into this new role by the neighbors who had every reason to respect both his ability and his integrity. He contended several times for a seat in the legislature, campaigning as vigorously in defense of the state's honor as he had campaigned in defense of the kingdom of God.

The light of prophecy (after the event) finds a special interest in the year 1832. It was then that Peter Cartwright ran against the lanky, young political amateur, Abe Lincoln of New Salem.

Peter knew the inhabitants of Salem well. He had close friends among them, and enemies too. With Samuel Hill he had a standing feud. This was partly because Hill, the aristocrat of Salem, was also its autocrat. He had a way of hiring stout fellows to whip those of whom he disapproved. But he never had Peter molested despite the fact that his patience must often have been tried. Peter, the able rhetorician, made a neat little side line of insult. He loved to remark in Sam Hill's hearing that he had often doubted whether the storekeeper had a soul until one day he put a quarter on Hill's lips and his soul came "guggling" up to get the silver.

Cartwright must have known Lincoln in the earliest days at New Salem, for he listened to gossip about him and repeated in some of his campaign talks that Lincoln was an infidel who had written an atheistic book. Later, when he learned that he had been tricked into repeating a lie, he was disgusted with himself and with the sly ways of politicians.

Probably he knew also that Abe Lincoln was a much-loved young man who enjoyed playing with children; who gave his own leisure to chopping wood for little boys so that they might have money with which to buy shoes; who was quixotically honest and kind. There may have been rumors about Abe and Ann Rutledge, the prettiest and best educated girl in Salem. She believed herself to have been jilted by a luridly attractive adventurer. And Abe, who was so shy of women that he had never dared to think of courtship before, took her under his protection exactly as he might have taken a baffled child. Salem thought no more of the affair than that. It was later to be blown up into a great, but largely imaginary romance.

Certainly Peter must have known that Lincoln had been to the Black Hawk War; that his comrades had elected him captain of their company; that he had served with his usual goodwill and good sense, though, as he said of his contribution to the nation's glory, no blood of his had been spilled in the campaign other than that spilled by mosquitoes.

Despite his personal popularity, Abe Lincoln was not elected to the legislature in 1832. Peter Cartwright was and had no admiration for the ways of politicians as he saw them in operation at Vandalia, then the capital of Illinois. He once commented:

"I say without any desire to speak evil of the rulers of the people that I found a great deal of corruption in our legislature and I found that almost every measure had to be carried by a corrupt bargain and sale which should cause every man to blush for his country."

It was a busy, useful life that Uncle Peter led. There were his six hundred acres to cultivate with the aid of his sons; and some eight thousand sermons to be preached as he rode and swam and fought his way from town to town; and the glory of God to be defended with his fists. Under these stresses he never parted with either resolution or wit. Once he was prevented from reaching Springfield in time for a service at which he was to preside. He sent a characteristic message to the waiting congregation:

"Dear brethren, the devil has foundered my horse which will detain me from reaching your tabernacle until evening. I might have performed the journey on foot, but I would not leave my poor Paul especially as he has never left Peter. Watch and pray and don't let the devil get among you on the sly before candlelight when I shall be at my post."

The shadow of Lincoln's long figure crossed Peter's path many times. In 1846 the occasion was the contest which they fought out as candidates for Congress. At one of Peter's meetings, he mixed politics and religion by calling on sinners to come forth and be saved. Lincoln rose to leave the hall. "Where are you going, Mr. Lincoln?" Peter called out. "To Congress, Mr. Cartwright," Lincoln answered. And to Congress he did go, leaving Peter to lick his wounds and say, "I hope the good Lord will forever save me from getting any more political bees in my bonnet."

And there was the tragic occasion when Lincoln defended Peter's grandson on a murder charge. "Peachy" Harrison, child of that marriage which Peter had so dramatically tried to prevent, stabbed and killed a man in a brawl. Lincoln, at the trial, pointed to the excellent old man whom all the valley respected and persuaded the jury to let the boy off.

But that was not quite the last scene in which Lincoln's figure loomed large in the background of Peter's life. An eloquent epilogue occurred at a dinner in New York where Peter Cartwright was the honored guest of the great ones of the city. The time was the Civil War and Peter heard his fellow guests grumble at the annoyances which the struggle brought them. With suave scorn, the elect derided the president. Peter rose to his feet.

"I am an old man," he said. "If I had known I would meet such a nest of traitors and tories I would not have put my feet under your table. You are accomplishing more for the secessionists here today by your criticisms and lack of sympathy with President Lincoln's noble labors for the Union than you could do were you down South at this hour enrolled in the ranks of Jeff Davis' confederacy."

He scolded them roundly for a minute or two and he concluded:

"I am through. I may have said too much and said it too harshly. I am not a man of smooth soft words. I was born in a canebrake where my mother was hurried to escape the tomahawks of savage Indians: I was rocked in a beegum for my cradle and my graduation degrees were taken from life's thunderstorms. I may be considered a very rude guest . . . but I could not go sneaking away feeling that I had been a coward and false to my country.

"In a last word, I give you a toast, Liberty and Union—one and inseparable."

He died in 1872, but the valley remembered him long afterward. He spoke of righteousness, of sin, and of redemption in terms which the river people could well understand. He used figurative language, as Lincoln was later to use it, with a poet's instinctive understanding of suitability to the occasion. In a single sermon, you might hear "the thundrous tread of the buffaloes as they rushed wildly across the prairie; the crash of the windrow as it fell smitten by the breath of the tempest, the piercing scream of the wildcat as it seared the midnight forest . . . the rhythm of the . . . river, the whisper of the groves . . ."

He was the kind of saint—and the only kind— that the Illinois valley would have received: a sharp-tongued, keen-witted, heavy-fisted fighter for righteousness.

CHAPTER THIRTEEN

Duelist

THE career of James Shields had such an affinity
with pleasant surprise and with gallant climax that it
seems somehow incomplete without a sprightly musical
setting. Showing a proper respect for the tradition of
romantic opera, it began with birth in the village of
Altmore, County Tyrone, Ireland. It proceeded through
many strenuous years during which, as a citizen of the
United States, Shields served its interests as soldier,
jurist, legislator. With a thoroughness characteristic of
his executive temperament, he seems to have done everything in triplicate. He fought in three wars and represented three different states as United States senator.

In his later years, the general took quite naturally
to the lecture platform. He liked, in those nostalgic
days, to give this picture of himself at the beginning of
his life:

". . . On the hills of Tyrone there roamed an Irish
lad—wild as any hare that ever skirted them—born

amid wars and rumors of wars, with a love of liberty innate in the Irish . . ."

He was probably a great deal less free and faunlike than that description suggests. For he had a mother who took with intense seriousness the responsibility of rearing a child. It was hers alone, for she had been a widow from the boy's sixth year. At a time when the British so disliked the idea of education for the Irish that the government offered a bounty for the head of a schoolteacher, which was the same as for that of a wolf, she insisted upon his being thoroughly instructed. He attended the "hedge school" from which pupils could be hastily dismissed at the first sign that authority was drawing near. Later he was privately tutored by a priest.

He had also his own spectacular ways of picking up instruction. His gift for quarreling introduced him to one of the important influences of his life. Ireland was then full of veterans of the Continental Wars. Tangling with one of them in argument, young Shields found himself committed, at the age of fifteen, to a duel. The pistols of both contestants misfired and in the laughter and relief which followed this opéra-bouffe climax, the soldier became the boy's friend. Later he was also his instructor in French and in military science.

Heroes are not by nature adaptable, but Shields's heroism, being of a comfortable, secondary sort, was ever ready to do the job that offered. When the ship on which he had started to America was wrecked off the coast of Scotland, he improved his idle time by serving as tutor to the family of a Presbyterian minister. On the transatlantic voyage he paid for his passage by doing himself over into a sailor. He proved to be a good one.

The first of a long series of accidents, which demonstrated that he was all but indestructible, occurred when he was blown from the topmast. Shields survived with a minimum damage of two broken legs. Arrived in America, he discovered that the crying need of the moment was for Indian fighters and hurried off to the Seminole War.

All this is the prelude to the significant period of his life, which began with his twenty-first birthday in Illinois. Kaskaskia, at the moment of Shields's arrival, was not in need of sailors or soldiers, but it was able to use a teacher who knew both English and French. Shields stepped into the job.

This was a fine moment in the making of a new world, when the rigidities of tradition had not yet fixed their pattern on anyone's way of life. A young man of spirit could improvise almost any career that a bold imagination might suggest. Shields was lacking in neither spirit nor imagination. He trained himself for the law and was admitted to the bar in 1832. Four years later he was elected to the legislature; in the midst of his second term he was appointed state auditor by Governor Ford.

Shields's contemporaries have recorded that he was, during this period, a man of fine appearance. He was above medium height, strong and well-proportioned. He had thick black hair and piercing eyes. The bristling aggressiveness of his mustache supported his chosen role of military man in genteel retirement. He spoke with a soft Irish brogue. Usher Linder, long after, remembered Shields's calling to him on the street of Kaskaskia: "Linthur! Linthur!" It was his usual manner to be gracious and affable, but when he was elbowed by frontier pugnacity or even by frontier jocularity he could quickly square his shoulders for a fight.

He was once involved in a curious feud with another Illinois lawyer and legislator, Abraham Lincoln.

The two men were political rivals who disagreed on all matters of abstract principle. Shields's service as auditor coincided with a difficult time in the history of the state. The poor were feeling the pinch of hardship following the collapse of a too-ambitious program of state expansion. Despite the panic, Shields insisted upon the payment of taxes in silver or gold rather than in the depreciated paper money. His intention was the estimable one of keeping the state's credit steady, but his regulations were unpopular and he became the object of vigorous attack.

One of the Whigs who opposed this grimly conscientious Democrat was Lincoln. His method of undermining Shields's authority was one which he used frequently in the early days of his political life, that of ridicule. To his favorite mouthpiece, the Springfield *Journal,* he contributed a letter written, not under his own signature, but in the name of "Rebecca," a poor countrywoman "of the lost townships."

Expression, in early Illinois, was free to the point of recklessness. Lincoln's "Rebecca" letter suggested that the rules which Shields had made were forcing upright citizens to commit perjury. The auditor was creating candidates for the "greedy gullet of the penitentiary."

This attack on Shields did not stop with one letter. It lengthened out into a series and the story of how James Shields was tormented by Whig doubters rhymes curiously upon an important theme of Lincoln's life.

A year earlier the tall, ungainly lawyer had been

made welcome in the gayest homes, of which Springfield
had many. Liveliest of all was that of Ninian Wirt
Edwards, an aristocrat who was said to "hate democracy
worse than the devil hates holy water." Mrs. Edwards's
sister, Mary Todd of Kentucky, also lived under this
roof as assistant hostess. She found Lincoln's conversation amusing and stimulating and allowed his conspicuous intellectual gifts to make amends for his lack of
other social graces. Presently Mary Todd's engagement
to Lincoln was announced, but, not at all to knowing
Springfield's surprise, it was later broken.

What the wise old ladies of the time said was that
the well-born Edwardses and Todds had not been able,
after all, to countenance a union between one of their
number and a man who had no family background, no
money, no obvious eligibility of any kind. They felt
sure that Lincoln had been jilted.

The wise old ladies were, of course, wrong. Lincoln
had little self-esteem of the kind that makes a man
confident in his relations with women. Except for the
episode in which he had taken pathetic, injured Ann
Rutledge under his compassionate protection, his affairs
with girls had always shown a curious pattern of advance and retreat. He retreated from Mary Todd because it was his temperament to do so. Maimed on the
emotional side of his nature, he never played with
any grace the role of the aggressor in love. But, first
with Ann Rutledge and later with Mary Todd, he revealed an inexhaustible strength in the role of the
protector in love.

Lincoln did ask to be released from his engagement to Mary Todd, but not in the way that present-
day biographers have allowed themselves to believe.

Contemporary Springfield did not even know that he was responsible for the break and would have been merely bewildered by the legend that he failed to appear at the house where guests had been invited for the wedding. The wise old ladies pitied Lincoln as a man who had flown high for a time and then been rebuked for his over-ambitious pretensions. Both Lincoln and Mary Todd were glad to have that version of their break believed.

At the time of the Shields controversy they were edging their way back into intimacy after a period in which Mary Todd had continued to be very gay and Lincoln had been a melancholy outsider, absent from Springfield's parties. Sprightly Miss Todd and her politically minded friend, Miss Jayne, thought it would be amusing to collaborate with Lincoln on the "Rebecca" letters. Without his assistance, they wrote more.

The fiery Irishman might have been able to endure the assault on his policy as auditor, but even his person was not immune from ridicule. For example, "Rebecca" wrote:

"I looked in at the window and there was this same fellow Shields, floatin' about in the air like a lock of cat fur where cats have been fighting. His very features, in the ecstatic agony of his soul, spoke audibly and said: 'Dear girls, it is distressing, but I cannot marry you all. Too well I know how much you suffer, but it is not my fault that I am so handsome and so interesting.'"

Prodded beyond endurance, Shields discovered the authorship of the original letter and challenged Lincoln to a duel.

As the challenged party Lincoln had the choice

of weapons. He selected "cavalry broadswords of the largest size" and made these further stipulations:

"A plank ten feet long . . . to be firmly fixed on edge in the ground as a dividing line between us, which neither is to pass or forfeit his life. Next a line drawn on the ground on either side of said plank and parallel with it at the distance of the whole length of the sword and three feet additional from the plank and the passing over such line by either party during the fight shall be deemed a surrender of the contest."

It was a little like planning to fight desperately with daggers at eighty paces, but the two parties dutifully set out for the dueling ground. Illinois was unsympathetic to those who wished to redress injury on the field of honor and the duelists had to travel across the Illinois River and then on toward Missouri. They met on an island in the Mississippi. There the duel, like James Shields's first attempt, collapsed into an opéra-bouffe affair. Shields said the terms of the contest were absurd. Lincoln said dueling was absurd. So they patched up the quarrel and went home whole.

Throughout the rest of his strenuous life, Shields moved in Lincoln's shadow. At first he seemed to have left his Whig rival far behind. When Stephen Douglas resigned from the state supreme court, Shields was appointed to his place. The following year he was elected to a full term. Later, President Polk appointed him commissioner general of the Land Office. Shields was getting on.

The Mexican War interrupted his political career. While Lincoln, as a member of Congress, was preparing himself for lonely leadership by denouncing the campaign as an imperialistic adventure, Shields got himself appointed a brigadier general of volunteers and rushed away to do active battle in a cause which, at the moment, had popular appeal.

He distinguished himself greatly. At the battle of Cerro Gordo, in a mountain pass, he was sent to intercept the main army of Santa Anna. He was in the forefront of the fighting when he was struck in the breast by grape shot which passed quite through his body. He was thought to be mortally hurt but, according to the stories of his contemporaries, an imaginative surgeon twisted a silk handkerchief about a ramrod and forced it through the wound. Thus cleaned, it caused the still indestructible general as little inconvenience as possible. Within six weeks he was in the field again.

At Chapultepec a bullet shattered an arm, but the general refused to retire until he had seen the American flag hoisted within the walls.

He was now authentically a hero. South Carolina voted $5,000 to provide him with a jeweled sword. Illinois, a little less extravagant with its own son, raised $3,000 for a similar piece of martial equipment. President Polk offered him the governorship of Oregon and he had accepted when Illinois persuaded him to go instead as its representative in the United States Senate. An ironic footnote to this episode in Shields's career is to be found in the fact that later, when the Whigs were in power, Lincoln would have been glad to be offered the governorship of Oregon. But he was not thought important enough to receive such a political prize.

Finally, it was Lincoln who drove Shields from the Senate. As a Democrat, the general's utterances on the approaching conflict over slavery had been discreet and gently oratorical. They called for compromise. Lincoln did not trust Shields any more than he trusted Douglas. When he and the general were once more rival candidates and Lincoln saw that his own strength was not great enough to win the senatorship, he threw his votes to Lyman Trumbull. Any outcome was better than that a Democrat should be returned to the Senate from Illinois.

Shields was hurt and disappointed. He packed up his jeweled swords and started wandering. The new state of Minnesota seemed to offer opportunities for a man who was still anxious to improvise a great career. He joined relatives near Faribault and the infant community, dazzled by finding so distinguished a hero among its citizens, promptly sent him to the United States Senate. But Minnesota was not sufficiently grateful to keep him there. Remembering the great days in Illinois and unwilling to accept lesser distinction, Shields started wandering again. He went to California and then traveled in Mexico, looking hopefully for mines.

There the onset of the Civil War offered him the opportunity for a new start. He offered his services to his old rival and Lincoln appointed him a brigadier general.

Again he proved himself much more than gallant and much more than useful. At the battle of Winchester he routed the hitherto invincible "Stonewall" Jackson. Though he was badly wounded, he continued to direct the battle until it was won.

In gratitude Lincoln elevated him to the rank of major general. The advancement was never confirmed. One of Shields's champions says that this was because, in executive session where the general could not go to defend himself, a member of Congress declared him to be insane. "I would like to have a few more such crazy generals," Lincoln is said to have commented.

Shields now saw himself as a soldier of misfortune. He resigned his commission and went to live on a farm in Missouri. There he consoled himself by marrying and trying to forget politics, but he was still to enjoy a brief epilogue to his career as a legislator. He became a representative in the Missouri General Assembly and then for another happy interval he was sent back to the United States Senate.

The general was the sort of person to whom legend clings. A popular story of his own day made him the "very perfect knight" whose chief duty was the defense of womanhood. During the Mexican War, we are told, a lady of unchallengeable virtue fell into the hands of the soulless Mexicans. General Shields rode to her rescue. A "sweet singer" of the period celebrated this crowning act of heroism in a long, long poem which concludes with this stanza:

> But not a braver deed was done
>   The conquering siege will show
> Than General Shields for woman wrought
>   Defying Mexico.

Alike in his periods of good fortune and in his intervals of lucklessness, he was a dramatic figure. No irony could be more touching than his largely unrequited love of the United States Senate. When he was old and poor and no longer capable of brilliant audacities, he applied for the post of doorkeeper to the Senate. He was refused.

But he is back in the national capital at last. His statue stands in the Hall of Fame. It was the people of the Illinois valley who put him there. And this time his tenure is secure.

CHAPTER FOURTEEN

Hermit of Eternity

IN a stiff, correct and sentimental poem written in his youth, Elijah P. Lovejoy declared that when he was dead he hoped to be allowed to retire to an obscure little star that had taken his fancy. He concluded:

> And I will live unknown, for I would be
> The lonely hermit of eternity.

The temptation is great to echo his own sentimentality and say that he has had his wish. Certainly it is a lonely immortality that has been meted out to Lovejoy. He fought for the cause of Abolition in Illinois, quite alone at first, far away from the support of the New England brotherhood of antislavery men. Personal security enveloped them as they fulminated so righteously. Lovejoy, living in the midst of enemies, had to have the courage of his eloquence in day-by-day encounters with neighbors whose philosophy he undertook to rebuke. Though he was a man of goodwill, he had to face the knowledge that he inspired fear and hatred. When those two passions had rubbed together long enough to produce their usual form of spontaneous combustion, Lovejoy was murdered. Even after his death he was hated for years and years, getting none of the posthumous glory that was assigned too generously to the other abolitionists. He had the misfortune to stage his martyrdom at a moment when it could earn him only a grudging sort of recognition.

He was born in 1802 at Albion, Maine, to one of those New England families which produced clergymen as naturally and exuberantly as an apple tree bears apples. His father was the Reverend Daniel Lovejoy, a Congregational minister. Elijah himself became a clergyman and so did two of his brothers. He was a precocious child who at four taught himself to read so that he might enjoy, quite independently, the solace of the Bible. He also "drank poetry like water" and Latin like an invigorating strong wine. After two or three weeks' study he was able to pass an examination in the intricacies of Cicero.

He did not at first intend to enter the ministry but, having been graduated from the academy at Monmouth, took up teaching as a career. In 1827 he went west following the irresistible impulse of the time, and established himself at St. Louis. Later he turned to newspaper work, editing a journal, the *Times,* which was eloquent in its support of Henry Clay. To his "dear, dear parents" he wrote home letters which were full of excellent sentiments but had curiously little news value. They do, however, reveal him as a healthy, happy, wholesome creature. One of the few explicit comments he makes about himself is that he has come

to weigh 180 pounds, which is more than he has ever
weighed before. This must be mentioned to dispel the
image of the pale ascetic with a predestined passion for
martyrdom. Lovejoy was a good swimmer, a vigorous,
cheerful, social person who would much rather have
gone on living. He did not woo martyrdom but accepted
it simply as the fate of a man who loves principles even
better than comfort and who respects the lives of all
men more deeply than he respects his own.

Piety was the family language of the Lovejoys. It
had a distinctly regrettable effect on their spontaneity
as letter writers. When Elijah suddenly heard the call to
enter the church, he was thirty years old. After a
precocious start, he had come to full flowering of his
mental life rather unusually late. This fact gave him
more than ordinary spiritual exuberance and he wrote:

"Oh, my dear parents are not the ways of Providence inscrutable? How long and how often did you
pray that your first born son might succeed his father
in preaching the gospel?"

The news made the parents as austerely joyous as
Elijah had hoped it might. The father, answering the
welcome letter, declared: "I read and read it and then
we sang the 101st hymn, first book." Clearly the son
was expected to know just which that hymn would be
and probably to burst straightway into a joyous echo
of its triumphant roll. The mother happily, but just a
little lugubriously, confided: "I really believe that God
has given you a broken and a contrite heart and that is
where the Holy Spirit delights to dwell."

Elijah himself was adept at offering this kind of
solemn comfort. When his sister's baby died, he wrote
her: "You weep for your child and I would not ask

you to refrain from weeping; for nature will assert its supremacy in the bosom of a mother."

When his father died, Elijah urged his mother to "kiss the hand that smites" and made this astonishing contribution to the literature of condolence: "And Mother the time is short. You will soon join your husband in Heaven."

It is surprising that a man who could be capable of such barren, chilling pieties should, when he had passed thirty, outgrow them. It was his devotion to a cause that finally warmed his heart within him and taught him to speak and write with a beautiful, desperate urgency of feeling.

In April, 1832, Lovejoy went to the Theological Seminary at Princeton. Just a year later he was licensed to preach. Short periods of service in Philadelphia, in Newport, and in New York City followed. But the West had become his home and to it he returned, this time to combine journalism and the work of the ministry as editor of a religious paper.

The *Observer* first appeared in November, 1833. An introductory editorial declared:

". . . While the *Observer* will seek to win its way to the hearts and consciences of men by the kindness of the sentiments it breathes, it will not temporize as it goes."

It did not temporize until Lovejoy was in his grave.

At first he wrote pious pieces like the improving letters he had been writing to his "dear, dear parents." He wrote about Truth and Faith and Vain Philosophy. He was a man of superior insight and education, of course, and occasionally he tried to interest his public in such things as the significance of the discoveries of Sir Isaac Newton.

But presently he found his theme and thereafter all that he wrote was really directed toward a demand for a solution of the problem of slavery. His ideas seem at first to have been astonishing only in their moderation. He rejected the idea of the infallibility of the abolitionist's judgment. He did not want to stir up prejudice and bitterness. In 1835 he was saying simply:

"With no decided advantage in soil, climate, productions or facilities, the free states have shot far ahead of those in which slavery is tolerated."

And again:

"Gradual emancipation is the remedy we propose."

In March of 1835 the humanizing process was greatly accelerated by Lovejoy's happy marriage. Having been a solemn old man up to the age of thirty-three, he suddenly became authentically boyish when he wrote to tell his mother about his bride. Celia Ann French, he said, was twenty-one, tall, well-shaped. The "lady" sat beside him as he wrote and he must have looked at her often as he catalogued her attractions: "Light complexion, dark flaxen hair, large blue eyes." Then he was completely overcome and broke off: "In short she is very beautiful."

Their life together was so short and so tragic that one longs to believe that rich rewards were crowded into its few years. Certainly Celia Ann Lovejoy was a woman of touching devotion. The time came when she must fight with her fists to defend her husband and her home. She did not hesitate to do it, and the picture of her trying to hold off a mob with no aid but her own resolution is one of the most pathetic in an almost unbearably moving story.

It was in October, 1835, that the first threats against Lovejoy began to be made at St. Louis. The "respectable citizens" suddenly discovered that the stress of the times called for a "new code," which was their fancy way of saying that they proposed to establish mob rule. They got together and passed hypocritical resolutions leveled at the head of Lovejoy, who had dared to write openly against slavery. They found this truth to be self-evident:

". . . freedom of speech being a conventional reservation made by the people in their sovereign capacity does not imply the moral right on the part of Abolitionists to freely discuss the question of slavery. . . .

"Slavery as it now exists in the United States is sanctioned by sacred scriptures."

In short, Lovejoy was to give up writing against slavery if he knew what was good for him. He wrote home to his brothers:

"I expect I shall be lynched, or tarred and feathered, or it may be hung up." With a touch of the old family habit of sermonizing, he added: "If they content themselves with whipping, I will not run until I have been whipped as many times as Paul was—eight times."

In another letter, he wrote: "They have whipped two men nearly to death. . . . Never in my life did I feel so calm, so composed, so tranquil."

That was not bravado. He felt, as he was to feel during two more turbulent years, the stabilizing authority of the job he had to do.

Lovejoy's financial affairs were involved in all the confusion of this campaign against him. His loyal backer refused to allow him to be crushed by debt but did insist that he move the base of his operations to Alton, across the Mississippi, where it was hoped he would have a more generous reception. An announcement of the plan for removal was publicly made and the mob, seeing that it was soon to lose its victim, made one last holiday by attacking his printing shop and tearing it down.

The beginning of the enterprise in Alton was not encouraging. The officers of the steamboat violated their agreement and landed his press at Alton on Sunday. Since it was against his religious scruples to see to it on that day, Lovejoy allowed it to stand on the bank, inviting the mob which presently smashed it to bits. The sober men of the community were outraged and promised to make good the loss. Lovejoy, nervously shaken, fell victim to "bilious fever" just as he started off to Cincinnati to replace his press. But he went anyway. In a letter to his mother he says that, when he had had to tell his wife of the destruction of all their property, she responded with unwavering concentration on the main point: "No matter what they have destroyed since they have not hurt you." He added (and one can still hear the accent of gratitude and awe) that not once had she ever rebuked him for prejudicing her chances of a serene domestic life by his public conduct.

In Alton, the *Observer* continued to be published until August, 1837. The first excitement quieted down. Lovejoy's editorial tone returned to that of moderation. He was even gently humorous. When the *Baptist Banner* solemnly announced that abolitionists had thrown off their masks and were openly advocating intermarriage between blacks and whites, Lovejoy responded:

"Now, brother of the *Banner*, stop a moment and do not go off at half charge as you are somewhat apt to do. Let us reason together for a moment—only a moment."

Then the poison of fear began to come to a head again. Fantastic stories were told against Lovejoy. Decent, reasonable men required him to defend himself against ridiculous charges. Gossip grotesquely accused him of saying from a pulpit, in Upper Alton, that if his wife should die that day he would be married to a black woman by the following Saturday night.

Once more there were meetings of the respectable citizens "to take in consideration the course pursued by the Reverend E. P. Lovejoy in the publication and dissemination of the highly odious doctrines of Abolitionism." They declared, more in sorrow than in anger, that when he had arrived in Alton he had given a pledge not to discuss abolitionism.

The truth was that Lovejoy had said simply that, since there was no slavery in Illinois, it might not prove to be a vital issue there. He had proceeded to say: "But, gentlemen, as long as I am an American citizen and as long as American blood runs in my veins, I shall hold myself at liberty to speak, to write and to publish whatever I please on any subject, being amenable to the laws of my country. . . ."

Attempts to bully Lovejoy had only one noticeable effect. They made him renounce the moderation of tone that he preferred and forced him to adopt the more strenuous accents in the eastern abolitionists. On the Fourth of July, 1837, he wrote:

"This day reproaches our sloth and inactivity. It is the day of the nation's birth. Even as I write, crowds are hurrying past our window in eager anticipation of the appointed hour to listen to the declaration that 'all men are born free and equal,' to hear the orator denounce in strains of manly indignation the attempt of England to lay a yoke on the shoulders of our fathers which neither they nor their children could bear. Alas! what bitter mockery is this? We assemble to thank God for our own freedom and to eat and drink with joy and gladness of heart while our feet are on the necks of our fellow men! Not all our shouts of self congratulation can drown their groans. Even the very flag of freedom that waves over our heads is formed from materials cultivated by slaves, on a soil moistened by their blood, drawn from their backs by the whip of the republican task master."

The people of Alton were infuriated. Utterances like that, they said, proved that only experience could teach Lovejoy "the full measure of the community's indignation which he had merited." He had "lost all claim to . . . protection." And so it happened that fifteen or twenty stern disciplinarians entered his shop, between ten and eleven o'clock in the evening, and destroyed his press, type, everything.

The hour was comfortably early for such a holiday and a crowd gathered to see the fun. Some brave souls protested that it might be better to wait until morning when all of Lovejoy's belongings could be packed up and, with his objectionable self, be put on a boat going down the river. But it was more amusing to let impetuosity rule. And it did.

There was exuberance enough left over, a night or

two later, to stage a little epilogue to the drama of violence. Overtaking Lovejoy on the street at night, a mob attacked him. He had been to the house of friends to marry a young couple and on the way home had stopped at "the apothecary's" to get medicine for his sick wife. When he saw that he must submit to the mob's play spirit, he asked that someone should take the

medicine to his home and deliver it to his wife without alarming her. Somehow that took all the spontaneity out of the boys of the town, and they let Lovejoy go.

Still he refused to turn away from the job he had undertaken. Sympathies ran with him for a time after the attack of the mob. He made an appeal for money with which to buy still another press. The response was prompt and generous and it came from all classes. With the funds raised by subscription in Alton and Quincy, he sent again to Cincinnati for supplies.

Then his most loyal friends began to waver. He

still tried to please them. Did they wish him to resign in favor of someone else? All he asked was that his debts be paid and that he be given money enough to take his family away. His backers plucked up their courage once more. He was not to resign. They would see him through.

On September 21st, the press arrived. It was taken to a warehouse and a constable set to guard it. But in crises of this kind the law sometimes finds it expedient not to use its full strength. When twelve men with handkerchiefs over their faces invaded the warehouse, no effective resistance was offered. The mayor appeared and asked the committee on righteous violence if they would not please go home. They said they would when they had finished what they had come to do. The mayor was impressed with what a gentlemanly mob they were and said so afterward. They rolled the press out of the warehouse, broke it to pieces and pushed it into the river.

They were not quite so genteel when they attacked Lovejoy in his house a few days later. It was then that Mrs. Lovejoy contemptuously slapped the faces of the men who were trying to drag her husband from the house. She stood before him with her fists raised. They should not take him without first taking her, she told them.

The mob, wavering between audacity and cowardice, dragged the torment out all night long. They went away and returned, went away and returned, until the nerves of everyone were shattered and even Mrs. Lovejoy collapsed in a faint. Once when reason threatened to prevail, an imaginative, drama-loving creature who had earlier struck Mrs. Lovejoy and

threatened her with a knife, shouted out that Lovejoy
had incited a Negro to violate a white man's wife. This
thoughtful observation offered the moment of last suspense before the mob finally reeled away.

It is strange how men stand their ground. Part of
resolution may be simply habit. A close acquaintance-
ship with misery weakens the impulse to try to throw
it off. Lovejoy should have seen by now that his work
was hopeless. But with a stubbornness containing the
beauty both of pride and of humility he sent for another
press.

Writing of his torments to his brother, he observed
sadly that "the pulpit with but one exception is silent."
At a session of the Presbyterian Synod, the Reverend
J. M. Peck charged the abolitionists with a lack of tact,
saying that they used abusive and unwarrantable
epithets against slaveholders. The Reverend John Hogan
declared piously that "it was the duty of Lovejoy as a Christian and patriot to abstain from the
exercise of some of his abstract rights under existing
circumstances."

But he was not quite alone even now. When his
fourth press arrived, forty or fifty citizens guarded it
through the first night. The second night only twelve
of the volunteers remained. Lovejoy was with them.
And the mob came.

They were armed with stones and pistols. The
stones were hurled first at the windows. "Give us the
press!" the mob shouted. The volunteers did not at once
surrender. There were shouts from the street and answering shouts from the warehouse. The resolution of
the guardians of the press weakened. They decided to
give up, if they were allowed to go free without being

molested. But fun was what the men of the mob now wanted. "Burn them out!" they cried. Someone brought a ladder. Several of the men scrambled to the roof and kindled a fire.

It was hopeless now to defy the mob. As Lovejoy came around the side of the warehouse, there was a series of reports. He was shot three times through the body. He fell and died.

The body was buried next day, furtively in an obscure corner of the cemetery. But the community was not yet quite sober.

"If I had a fife I'd play the dead march for him," one of the mobsters shouted to his cronies on a street corner.

The stone over the grave reads:

Hic Jacet
Lovejoy
Jam Parce Sepulto
(Here lies Lovejoy.   Spare him now that he is buried.)

But they did not spare him even in his grave. They continued to punish him by ignoring all duty, as a community, toward his helpless wife. The human impulse to forget whatever makes one ashamed took Mrs. Lovejoy for its victim. She died a few years later, still young, but looking like an old woman. She had never recovered from the shock of her husband's martyrdom. At the last she was poor and neglected and utterly betrayed.

Though perhaps he never heard of Lincoln, Lovejoy moved in the giant's shadow. The period of the martyrdom at Alton coincided with one during which the Emancipator heard no prophetic hint of his destiny. Lincoln was never an abolitionist. The caution which ran so deep in him made him distrust sharp conflicts. His only public reference to Lovejoy was one of bitter irony and disapproval.

Yet all the while his gifts of eloquence and of leadership were maturing. The principle of justice from which he would have been glad to turn away more and more unshakably took possession of him. In the end it was he who justified Lovejoy's sacrifices and ennobled his martyrdom.

CHAPTER FIFTEEN

Artist, In Spite of Himself

IN the year 1829 a young man named Joseph Gillespie returned to his home at Edwardsville from the lead mines at Galena. Like many another hopeful young man of the time, he had gone there to make his fortune. The final years of his teens had been spent sleeping on the ground, working long hours, carrying a spade with him wherever he went for killing rattlesnakes as well as for digging. But he had not struck it rich.

Indeed, by the time he reached a little community called Phillips' Ferry on the banks of the Illinois River his resources had been reduced to one dollar. The rest of the hundred-mile journey was made on foot, and as Joe Gillespie trudged from one river town to another, he met everywhere the noisy, jovial hospitality which in Illinois the sharers of each day's rough adventure offered one another. After a night's lodging or a meal, Joe would offer to pay for his entertainment, but this proved to be a merely formal gesture of pride and politeness. For in all the towns of the Illinois valley there was not one man who could change a dollar. It was not until he reached Carrollton that Joe encountered a man of property and of means who could take the ten or twenty cents due him and give Joe back the rest. Fortunately by that time he was close to home.

Gillespie was born in New York of Scotch-Irish parents. For several generations his ancestors had worked at bleaching linen for the Belfast market. But the passion for liberty was in their blood. The Gillespies were forever becoming picturesquely, sometimes disastrously, involved in Irish rebellions, and one of them had to flee the country with a price on his head. Joseph's parents chose emigration to America as the proper way of expressing distaste for tyranny. After twelve years in New York, they decided to penetrate deeper into the New World. David, the father, would have chosen Alabama; but Sara, the mother, firmly consistent in her somewhat austere love of liberty, refused to make a slave state her home. She was a woman whom the old settlers remembered with respect and awe as the ideal pioneer woman. The work of the farm never proved so arduous that she did not have time and energy to work at the education of her sons, Matthew and Joseph. Her sturdy athletic figure dominated their lives, supervising their labors by day on the farm and their perhaps grudging attention by night to the literature and theology of the Bible.

Joe became first a lawyer, then a lawmaker, and finally a judge. The love of scholarship toward which his resolute mother had inclined his imagination made him a superior citizen. He was better read in the academic background of the law than were most of his contemporaries. He acquired a knowledge of French and a passion for mythology. He helped to break down the pioneer's resistance to any claim of education upon his pocketbook and he had an honorable share in the framing of a plan for state schools.

He continued to think of his own taste in literature as being somewhat austere. Gillespie was fond of the poetry of Sir Walter Scott, but would read none of his novels because, as he said, he would give his time to nothing that was not true.

Yet Joe was an artist in spite of himself. He possessed an abiding interest in the infinite oddity of human nature. His mind recorded any dramatic or grotesque evidence of folly, and his ear was accurate in registering the idiom and accent of the time. An analyst of his gifts cannot avoid the conclusion that, though he may have done well not to read novels, he should have written them. For he was certainly an excellent chronicler of the day of small things.

He reached Edwardsville with his family when he was a boy of ten and already his eyes were wide open to dramatic contrasts. The town was full of them. It had lately become the headquarters of an Indian agency. On its streets rangers in homespun, naked savages, and the last of the colonial grandees rubbed shoulders in a vivid pageant.

Throughout his life the comedy of existence delighted this man who sternly forbade himself ever to see a play. He relished the incident of the pioneer who resolved to give up drinking. The man's forbearance lasted just long enough for styles in drinking vessels to change from the tumbler to the less obviously compromising wineglass. He was discovered one day by a friend occupying a public house floor in a woefully sodden condition. But drunkenness had not managed to drown his wit. Challenged to remember his resolution, this very typical man of Illinois still insisted, "I have given up drinking." Then borrowing the kind of inspiration that has made Rip Van Winkle a national hero, he held up his wineglass and added, "In large measure."

Better still was the significant kind of irony which the simplicity of early American life sometimes made luminously clear. Joe Gillespie watched the trek of slave-owners from Kentucky across Illinois into Missouri. The roads through Edwardsville were often lined with wealthy men followed by droves of Negroes. Pleasantries would be passed back and forth between the travelers and their hosts of the moment. "We'd like to stay in Illinois," the emigrants would say, "if we could keep our slaves."

One day Joe Gillespie saw bigotry and greed curiously personified. His memoirs describe: ". . . a great 'six footed' fellow, with one eye gouged out, barefooted, with nothing in the way of a wardrobe but a pair of tow trousers and a shirt, a rifle on his shoulder, his old woman mounted on an old gray horse the bones of which were ready to cut through the skin. . . . She was seated on a straw bed with a skillet and a big wheel tied on behind her and a frowsy, tow-headed youngster in her lap."

Like all who had gone before him in the procession, this dismal creature was asked hospitably why he did not stay in Illinois. Righteous indignation flared in his face as he answered:

"Well, sir, your sile is mighty fartil, but a man can't own niggers here, God-durn you."

Gillespie was an enthusiastic and conscientious

chronicler of the wit of other men. Once he and his
colleague, Usher Linder, spent the night at a tavern in
Kaskaskia. Neither had any money. It was a troublesome
question how they were to pay their bill. Hope stirred
within them when they discovered that their host was
badly in need of legal services. He had become involved
in one of those highly informal little affairs of honor,
so typical of the rugged times, in the course of which
his opponent had bitten out a piece of his ear. However,
he did not care to engage either Linder or Gillespie to
represent him, holding out for a better known lawyer,
Lyman Trumbull. Linder took the case of the other
warrior.

At the trial, he let his gift for fantasy get the upper
hand. His client, Linder insisted, had not intended to
injure his rival. Indeed, he had been intent to rendering
a much-needed service. He wished merely to trim the
ears of the landlord so that he might look less like a
jackass. So lively was the Illinois appreciation of gro-
tesquerie that Linder won his case.

Joe Gillespie's attention was always alert for the
memorable joke which, better than pages of analysis,
characterizes men and their times. He never forgot a
bit of pointed repartee like that in which John
Reynolds, when governor of Illinois, engaged with a
defender of the Little Giant, Stephen Douglas. Reynolds
did not like Douglas and said so. But, his questioner persisted, did he not think Douglas a strong man? That,
said Reynolds, reminded him of the dilemma of the
small boy who was trying to sell a yoke of oxen. "Boy,"
the potential purchaser asked, "are those steers really
strong?" There was a moment's hesitation and then

came the cautious response: "Yes, sir—devilish strong . . . in light work."

Joe Gillespie's personal history was not spectacular. He studied law with Cyrus Edwards; he rode the circuit practicing his profession; he was elected as a Whig to the legislature, served in the House for four years and in the Senate for ten years more.

The trip from Edwardsville to Springfield was made by sleigh. Swathed in buffalo robes, with heated bricks at his feet, a fur-lined cap on his head, he traveled up the valley with much more resolution than pleasure. The trip, he said, took as long as Jonah was in the whale's belly and he "would gladly have exchanged places with Jonah."

In 1861, just as Lincoln was being inaugurated as president, Joe Gillespie became a circuit judge and his last active years were spent on the bench.

He was Lincoln's warm friend. As he himself expressed it, with a lively mixture of figures such as the bold rhetoric of the time allowed: "I ever . . . followed his lead and regarded him as a rough diamond of the purest water."

The two men had met first in the Black Hawk War. Joe Gillespie had seen Lincoln wrestle and admired him both for his prowess and for his modest friendliness toward the man he had thrown. He and Lincoln served in the legislature together. They were Whig "regulars," good politicians. Lincoln's idealism had not yet taken its final form. His essential conservatism was leading him slowly, cautiously toward the set of beliefs for which he was at last to make so valiant a stand. But at the moment when he and Joe Gillespie were first lawmakers together, Lincoln was chiefly Springfield's bright young man, ready to do whatever its citizens thought would enhance its credit in the world.

Lincoln voted to move the capital from Vandalia to Springfield, though only Springfield profited by the change which put the state to heavy expense. He voted consistently for the protection of the Springfield State Bank, though its career was finally to end in disaster and scandal.

It was to save the bank from embarrassment that Lincoln and Joe Gillespie once ran away from a session of the legislature. An issue involving the institution's affairs was to be voted upon as soon as a quorum could be brought together. Lincoln and Gillespie, finding themselves in a House packed by the enemy, had to take quick action; they jumped from the window of the church where the meeting was held. Years afterward it was said that Lincoln did not like to be reminded of the episode. But Joe Gillespie recalled it frequently and with gusto. Such happenings belonged in the rugged scenario of early American patriotism in the Middle West. Lincoln, who was not too chary of his personal dignity, must have had his own quiet amusement in remembering the exploits of the gangling young man who was still partly a boy.

So good a friend as Joe Gillespie must have been often in Lincoln's home. He liked what he saw there. The difficult Mary Todd, whom so many biographers have gone out of their way to abuse, presented a different aspect of her character for this visitor to see. Joe thought her an accomplished hostess. He liked her readiness and wit. Her table, he testified, was well supplied with dishes that were artfully prepared. Gillespie's Mary

Todd was far from being the selfish, niggardly shrew of the legends.

There is no question, he wrote, but that Lincoln "thoroughly loved his wife." He may have heard the fastidious housewife scolding because Lincoln would insist on opening the front door in his shirt sleeves or because he persisted in stretching himself at full length on the floor, but Gillespie's ear was sensitive enough to catch the appealing little melody that ran through their life together. Perhaps its orchestration was sometimes tumultuous, but the tune was not obscured. It was a familiar, commonplace one, the humming sound of domesticity.

In the early days of the marriage, Joe Gillespie heard Lincoln call his wife Molly. Later, when there were children, she lost her individual identity to become Mother. Joe saw no barren, psychological distance between husband and wife.

Gillespie saw the confidence, the tenderness, the playfulness that existed between the Lincolns. He did not, of course, know—as present-day exploiters of Mary Todd's story know—that she was finally to lose her mind. If he had, he would have been touched to see that two people, both of whom were maimed on the emotional side of their natures, could, by virtue of intelligence and the willingness always to try again, have given each other so much of comfort, so many of the casual normal values of life.

The mutual trust that Gillespie and Lincoln felt for each other had its final demonstration just as the president-elect was about to set out for Washington. He sent for Joe on one of his last days in Springfield and confided to him that he foresaw war. It could be avoided, Lincoln said, only "upon the consent of the government to the erection of a foreign slave government out of the present states. I see the duty devolving upon me. I have read, upon my knees, the story of Gethsemane where the Son of God prayed in vain that the cup of bitterness might pass from him. I am in the garden of Gethsemane now, and my cup of bitterness is full and overflowing."

But before the interview was over these two old friends had slipped into a mood of comedy that was congenial to both. The artist in spite of himself has left a touching picture of Lincoln facing with humor the burden that he had learned to accept as his own. Speaking of the way in which Buchanan, his predecessor, was trying to destroy any possibility of preventing war, before the new administration could assume control, Lincoln said:

"Joe, I suppose you will never forget that trial down in Montgomery County where the lawyer associated with you gave the whole case away in his opening speech. I saw you signaling to him, but you couldn't stop him. Now that's just the way it is with me and Buchanan. He's giving the whole case away and I have nothing to say and can't stop him."

So they parted. The rest of Lincoln's life was to be conspicuous and short. Gillespie's was to be obscure and long. Yet they were men of the same type, shrewd, large-minded, observant, and wit loving. They were both artists of the kind that will be admired as long as prevalent human values persist. Gillespie himself would have hoped that they might last (as he once quoted John Reynolds's phrase) "till eternity in the afternoon."

CHAPTER SIXTEEN

Lawyer on Horseback

Iɴ the year 1835 there came to the Illinois river town of Pekin a "large, robust, boyish-looking fresh faced young man, a little inclined to corpulency" who immediately announced in the Tazewell *Telegraph* that he was prepared to engage in the practice of law in any of the neighboring counties. His name was David Davis and he was to offer an interesting variation on the theme of the pioneer's progress by becoming, as the years increased, enormously rich and enormously fat. Pioneers did not, as a rule, accomplish either kind of expansion.

Pekin in that day was the landing place for all merchandise coming up the river, and therefore an important community. Peck's gazetteer, with the complete candor which its author never learned to restrain, reported that the "landing was tolerably good at a moderate stage of the river, but too shoal at the low stage." It possessed 12 stores, 3 groceries, 2 taverns, 2 houses for the slaughtering and packing of pork, 2 steam "flouring mills," 2 steam distilleries, an academy, 4 ministers of the gospel, 4 physicians, and 7 lawyers.

Unfortunately, like many another river town, Pekin possessed the kind of condition that favored malaria. Consequently, David Davis did not long remain as one of the lawyers. After a bad illness, he was persuaded to take his ambitions just twenty-five miles east to the town of Bloomington. He arrived, as he reported, with "two bits" in his pocket.

There he lived a long and useful life. From Bloomington he conducted his real estate operations. From it he started out to travel back and forth across the river in his practice of the law. From it he launched the campaign which did so much to make his friend, Lincoln, President of the United States. And to it eventually he returned to die.

Even as a young man, he was rather stout to be a lawyer on horseback. He did not like these tests of endurance and he wrote back to the East from which he had come: "There is some fun and much excitement in practicing law in this prairie state, but not much profit or personal comfort. We have been deluged by rain this spring. The windows of Heaven are certainly open. Bad roads, broken bridges, swimming of horses and constant wettings are the main incidents of Western travel."

In the same letter he mentions Lincoln for the first time, saying that "he is the best stump speaker in the state; shows the want of early education but has great power as a speaker. He worked on a farm at $8 a month to the age of twenty two."

Davis's own early advantages had been usual. He was born to a highly educated father and a wealthy mother on a plantation in Maryland. Even the early death of his parents did not leave him to make his way alone. An uncle saw him through a course of study at Kenyon College in Ohio. Later while studying law he earned his way by serving as clerk to Henry Bishop at Lenox, Massachusetts. There he met Sarah Walker, who was later to become his wife. She started him toward wealth by taking with her to Illinois a comfortable fortune.

The conditions of Illinois's first panic gave Davis his opportunity to grow rich. Merchants receiving goods on credit from dealers in the East had given their real estate as security. But when the crash came their creditors refused to accept the land. Davis and his partner, Wells Colton, specialized in collecting. Much valuable land came into their possession. At the peak of his activity Davis held some 14,000 acres in four different states. He ended his days a millionaire.

But the shrewdness which made him able to capitalize on advantage did not make him any the less a kind and conscientious man. Mortifying the flesh in a literal sense, he rode out year after year in the practice of law because he conceived that to be his duty.

At one moment early in his career he devised another humiliation for his aching bulk by campaigning for the legislature. His opponent was a burly, adaptable fellow who recommended himself to his potential constituents by serving them in an odd variety of ways. Once he even went so far as to construct a coffin for a man whose vote he could no longer woo and by conducting an eloquent funeral service for him. Davis was sure that this feat would mean the election of his rival. But when he was urged by his friends to play the same political game, he answered disconsolately, "I'm willing to do anything in reason. Anything in reason. But I can't pray. I can't pray one damned bit."

Eventually, he did go to the General Assembly. But its ways were not to his liking and he did not seek re-election. He did, however, feel obliged to seek election to the Constitutional Convention because he wished to speak for judicial reform. On the basis of his formal recommendations, the courts were reorganized. The state was divided into nine judicial districts. At a salary of $1,000 a year, Davis became judge of the Eighth Circuit.

To a man who was already wealthy, this additional income must have seemed trifling. Neither the money nor the conditions under which the court sat made the task attractive. Traveling across Illinois in all kinds of weather would have been difficult enough for a man of normal agility. To Judge Davis, who had now achieved his heroic proportions and weighed a full three hundred pounds, it must often have seemed like martyrdom. He could, of course, no longer get astride a horse and had taken to riding in a carriage. Even to descend from his place behind his team was like a minor convulsion of nature. But Judge Davis did not like being laughed at. Groans of sympathy for his horses were greeted with the rebuke of stony silence. The jocular learned to keep their witticisms to themselves. In later days his nickname with the journalistic fraternity became "the Mandarin." Davis hated and distrusted journalists as a result.

There was only one reason why he accepted the post as judge of the Eighth Circuit and that was because he thought it his duty to do so. He wished to make his contribution to the development of the state's tradition. But there proved to be unlooked-for compensations among the hardships. The Eighth Circuit was the one on which Lincoln practiced law. He and Davis became intimate friends.

The moment at which Lincoln first appeared on the circuit was for him a gloomy one. He was just back from a term in Congress where he felt himself to have been a failure. His political career, he thought, was over. His ambition lay on the scrap heap. He could not realize that the quiet days on the circuit were to be the happiest and also the most fruitful of his life. They were his training school for the high office which he coveted and they led at last to the White House.

As the judge and the lawyers of the circuit court moved in a body from town to town, their progress was hailed with as much enthusiasm as though they were members of the circus troupe. Indeed, the court was the poor man's free theater. In it he found the drama, the wit, the homely philosophy that gave his mind exercise. When a lawyer on horseback rode into town and tied up his animal in front of the place where court was to sit, he was greeted by the townsfolk as a friend and a popular entertainer.

Each of the quite extraordinary men who practiced in the Eighth Circuit was able to play this role acceptably. Lincoln played it brilliantly. His hold on the imagination of the people of Illinois dated from the time when he first appeared before them as a man who could interrupt the monotony of their days and spur their nodding imaginations into exciting activity.

Judge Davis, according to his colleagues, "possessed" a large and active mind. He had no brilliancy, but was "the incarnation of common sense." His respect for the law was deep, but his feeling for its abstract philosophy was never reverent. He summed up his own outlook in his comment on the position of a particular pair of defendants:

"If any wanton attack is made on them, they should have a fair defense, nothing more. They are, in common with the rest of mankind, entitled to justice, not to generosity."

His court was a lively place.

One of its lawyers, Ward Hill Lamon, recalled many years after how his jocular colleagues had once made him the butt of a ribald joke. He was a strenuous young man who during a recess discharged his high spirits by wrestling with one of the town boys. In the course of this exercise his trousers were badly torn in the seat. When court reconvened, the other lawyers noticed his plight and began circulating a subscription list the object of which was to purchase more decent trousers for Lamon. Each lawyer set down some frivolous comment. But Lincoln topped them all. "I can," he wrote, "subscribe nothing to the end in view."

Judge Davis once absent-mindedly sentenced a youth to serve seven years "in the state legislature." There was a great deal of ill-suppressed merriment as it was pointed out to him that he had misspoken legislature for penitentiary.

He was a generous friend to beginners. Once a young lawyer unable to prepare his plea correctly was called to the stand by Judge Davis who patiently instructed him in the rudiments of his profession. After a second attempt, it was still not right. Judge Davis took the plea and wrote it out himself.

Sometimes, when Judge Davis wished to be absent from court on personal business, he would ask Lincoln to take his place on the bench. There justice was meted out kindly, honestly—and with a complete, cozy illegality. The law provided for no such substitution. Occasionally a man against whom Lincoln had decided would discover that the judgment had no binding authority and would sue to set it aside. For the most part, however, the impression that Lincoln imparted, of being a just and friendly uncle to the human race, was sufficient to cover the casual irregularity.

The first days during which the court sat in each new town were busy. The lawyers devoted themselves strenuously to the press of affairs. But when the heaviest responsibilities had been discharged, the lawyers would relax. In Judge Davis's room at the tavern they met, night after night, for sessions of high spirit and jocularity such as are associated, in the experience of most men, only with early youth and the college fraternity house.

Judge Davis was the presiding genius over all this vehement fun. He invited whomever he pleased. Sometimes a defendant, up before him for perjury, would be included if the judge had found the fellow amusing. Ruthlessly frozen out was any citizen, however upright, whom the lawyers suspected of being a bore. There was nothing to curb the spontaneity of these occasions. Judge Davis would enter with an air of solemnity into elaborate caricatures of the day in court by fining lawyers who had pleaded too long or charged too little for their services. Lincoln was more than once rebuked for this particular offense.

A high degree of talent and of garrulity prevailed among the men of the Eighth Circuit. They were mighty storytellers, but Lincoln was recognized as the best of them all. His art was that of the actor: fleeting and mysterious, not to be caught in print. The intonation counted greatly. So did the odd gesture and the enveloping atmosphere of goodwill. The best of his wit was reflected in his use of the parable. From the center of its artistry, his verbal exuberance frayed out into all

sorts of puns, distortions, plays on words. But all that he said had the effect of making other men feel, in his presence, that they, too, became witty and large-minded simply by exposure to his compassionate warmth. Many years later Usher Linder sighed, "Ah, what glorious fun we had sometimes."

It was the best moment in Judge Davis's life as it was the best moment in Lincoln's. A curious bond held these two men together through a friendship that was subjected to many trials. The apparent contrast between them could not have been greater. Lincoln was tall, thin, awkward, slow-moving, ill-dressed, given to melancholy. Davis moved his enormous bulk with an air of decisiveness and clothed it in the neatest and most fashionable of garments. Yet the link between them was strong.

Davis helped to create Lincoln as a national figure. He forgot all his complicated personal affairs to go to the first important state convention of the Republican party in Illinois to get its delegates solidly behind Lincoln. A little later, at the national convention in Chicago, he waddled from committee room to committee room bargaining, cunningly if not wisely, for the nomination.

As a result of these maneuvers Lincoln felt badly compromised. Before he left Springfield to be inaugurated, he protested bitterly, "They have gambled on me all around, bought and sold me a hundred times. I cannot begin to fill the pledges made in my name."

But Davis's creative job was done. For the rest of his life he was to walk in the shadow of the man he had helped to make. There were many pleasant moments but they were all anticlimatic to the great scenes of the strenuous life in Illinois.

In 1862 President Lincoln acknowledged his debt to his old friend by appointing him an associate justice of the Supreme Court. Arrived in Washington, Davis was touchingly pleased to discover that one of his colleagues, Judge Clifford, "is a larger man than I am."

Ten years of usefulness culminated in another curious moment of drama. Mr. Justice Davis, the mil-

lionaire landowner, was nominated by labor for the
presidency. In many quarters this act of the National
Labor Reform Convention was treated as a joke. But
not by Davis. Though he cannot have liked the radical
platform adopted at the same time by the convention,
he was pleased to be offered this distinction. From
Bloomington he sent to the convention at Columbus a
message which has become famous:

"The Chief Magistracy of the Republic should
neither be sought nor declined by any American
citizen."

Shrewd politicians have been saying it ever since.

But the impulse toward reform, which in that year
was sweeping the country, only eddied around Davis
and he was presently lost in the stream which later
caught up Horace Greeley as its leader.

When another five years had passed, Davis was
brought to national attention when he resigned from
the Supreme Court to accept his election to the United
States Senate. Ward Lamon thought it a ridiculous de-
scent and warned Davis against consenting to become
once more a "plebe." In his blunt and dramatic way he
pictured Davis in the Senate as being as helpless as a
"stump-tailed bull in fly time."

But Davis longed for an echo of the creative life that
he had lived when he and Lincoln were in their prime.
By an odd irony, this man who had once been so effec-
tual became a national symbol of indecisiveness. In the
Senate he sat among the Republicans but refused to consider himself committed to their party, voting independently on every issue.

So widespread was this ironic view of him that
when a small boy was introduced by his father to the

senator, the child remarked afterward in bewilderment
and protest:

"Why, father, he is a nice man and he wasn't
straddlin' no fence, either."

Others were not permitted to laugh at the aging
Davis because of his weight but he himself might occasionally do it. A year after the death of his first wife he
was suspected by his intimates of having a new emotional interest in his life.

He sighed, "Old as the hills and nearly as big, why
should I marry?"

But he did marry a second time, and soon after
returned to Bloomington to spend his last days in
retirement.

He had lived seventy-one years. The final third of
his life had been devoted to filling conspicuous posts in
national life and filling them creditably. But if he re-
viewed his life as he lay dying his imagination must have
lingered on those rich middle years when, as a man of
thirty and of forty, he did so much to create a new
society and to create also the man who came to per-
sonify its character. He must have thought of the long
drives up and down the Illinois valley; and of the
shrewd manipulations by which he had gathered such
large tracts of its land into his capacious grip; and of
the town he had helped to build; and of the sessions in
his court where law appeared as the unpretentious
brother of common sense; and of the nights in cold,
comfortless taverns where lawyers met and laughed and
in the midst of their laughter conducted a forum of
ideas which proved to be one of the most important that
this country has ever held because it produced Lincoln.

CHAPTER SEVENTEEN

American Sovereign

WHEN Stephen Arnold Douglas made his entrance into the Illinois valley, the beginning of the drama in no way foreshadowed the end. He was little and ill and pathetic. He weighed ninety pounds and stood five feet four inches in height. He was at the end of a boy's odyssey, a journey in which ambition had been desperately at odds with opportunity. No one wanted him; no one gave him any hope. He had passed from town to town putting out a hand in a gesture which suggested both arrogant pride and bitter pleading; but none of the acquaintances whom he approached were able to help him. Each spoke of the barrenness of hope in his own community but allowed his eye to brighten with the suggestion that things would be much better a little farther west or just up the river a little way.

Douglas was born in Brandon, Vermont. Following the early death of the father, the family had moved to Manchester Center. During the lean years young

Stephen managed somehow to pick up an education and
a trade. In his early youth he worked at cabinetmaking
and it was an art that he loved. Later, when his mother
married a second time, he attended a good academy at
Canandaigua, where he studied Greek and Latin, mathematics and logic. But the decision that a legal career was
what he wanted brought a new set of problems. He
could not afford the kind of training which the East
was already beginning to demand. Only in the west
could a career still be improvised.

So he went to Cleveland. There he fell seriously ill.
In a curious fragment of autobiography, written when
he was twenty-five, Douglas said of his prostration:
"I was advised by my physicians that there was no reasonable hope for my recovering and that I ought to be
prepared for my final dissolution which was then expected from day to day."

His "physicians" must have been peculiarly grim
representatives of their profession. But their candor did
not frighten Douglas. During the four months of this
illness he says that he "enjoyed more peace and contentment . . . than during any similar period of my life."
Later this seemed to him to be a cause of "curiosity,
wonder and amazement." To a casual observer it is evident that he was "half in love with easeful death."
Perhaps he made his peace with fear during that bad
time and ever after was able to gamble with career, success, and life itself as though the ordinary rules did not
apply to him.

He himself says that he was reckless when he rose
from that bed. His odyssey carried him on, without
prospects, from Cleveland to Cincinnati, to Louisville,

to St. Louis, and at last into Illinois. He stopped first at Jacksonville.

Besides being little he must have been physically repellent with his great head, his piercing eyes whose stare was uncomfortably persistent, and his truculent-looking mouth. But there was in him the explosive, Napoleonic indomitability of small men. The very comedy of this little fellow's fighting spirit pleased the pioneer sense of drama.

It pleased, first of all, Murray McConnel, of Jacksonville, who gave him lawbooks. Then, as the odyssey took Douglas on to Meredosia on the Illinois River, his temperament pleased a nameless farmer who took him up onto his own horse and carried him to Exeter in the somewhat forlorn hope of finding a school to teach. When that prospect languished in the face of Illinois's early disinterest in education, Douglas's belligerent charm served him still another time, when he walked into a tavern at Winchester announcing in a single breath that he had no money and that he meant nonetheless to have a bed. To what must have been his own intense surprise, the landlord rushed out and rustled up forty pupils for this underfed but assertive little rooster who carried his crest with such fine arrogance.

It amused Illinois for the next quarter of a century to let this chanticleer think that it was his crow that called the sun into the sky. All the rules were set aside to further his sense of importance. His first political speech, made when an older and more distinguished man had set upon Andrew Jackson, was an unreasonable sort of success, profiting more from its unexpectedness than from any devastating point made. It brought Douglas the friendship of tall, rowdy, blasphemous Captain John Wyatt, who took the little man under his patronage because he liked the drollery of the picture they presented as partners in political enterprise.

They did very well in their first job of being fellow conspirators. Wyatt had a bitter grudge against John J. Hardin, state's attorney, and wanted to humiliate him. He did so by the droll device of legislating him out of office. At Wyatt's suggestion Douglas wrote a bill which provided that the office of state's attorney should no longer be filled by the governor's appointment but by election in the legislature. The bill was maneuvered through the General Assembly. Hardin was out and little Douglas was in. Illinois laughed its bellyful over this sly intrigue.

Having learned the formula for getting on, Douglas was able to use it all his life. When he wanted a public office he first remade the rules so that they fitted his pretensions neatly. He may have been "destiny's darling," as Carl Sandburg has called him. But he did not wait for Destiny to smile. He reminded her rather peremptorily of her maternal duty toward him, like a self-confident, spoiled boy. He even went so far as to prod her from behind when her action on his behalf failed to be satisfactorily swift.

Later he got the judicial system all rearranged to suit his convenience. The upshot of his skillful maneuvering was that he became a state supreme court judge at the age of thirty. Even in those days of youthful enterprise, that was a notable achievement.

There had been, of course, a brief apprenticeship in the legislature. Douglas had served during Lincoln's time and, like Lincoln, voted for the disastrous public improvements bill. Unlike Lincoln, he seized the opportunity to repudiate all responsibility for it as soon as he was quite sure that it had been a wrong guess. Douglas, always the perfect prophet after the event, always the possessor of the perfect alibi, said he had known that the bill was ruinous, but he had a mandate from the people whose blind impetuosity would not be warned.

He was to learn, in later years, how to deal more discreetly with such mandates from the people. They could be wrapped up in eloquence and so smuggled out of sight.

For ten years he lived in Springfield and, despite his diminutive size, was one of its conspicuous figures. He even profited by the contrast that he presented to these other giants in the earth who made up the General Assembly. For they amiably decided that with his self-confidence, his leonine head, and his knack of getting on, he must be a giant in his own way. And a "little giant," as Douglas came to be called, is a better object of public adulation than an ordinary giant, especially when six feet of manhood is the routine rule.

During the time Lincoln was becoming engaged to Mary Todd, suffering the torments of doubt, parting from her and coming back again, Stephen was resolutely getting on. He went to all the parties. Three or four times a week the great ones of the community entertained, striving always to maintain the standards set by the aristocratic Ninian Edwards. Douglas danced under the generous glow of candlelight and flattered Mary Todd. Once, when she had been the subject of audacious conversation, Mary responded to the question of whether she would rather marry Lincoln or Douglas by saying that she would much prefer the one who had the better chance of being president.

But there was never any doubt in her strange mind as to which that would be. For Mary Todd had the neurotic's gift of insight. Stephen Douglas had become a fastidious and worldly gallant of the kind she had known in Kentucky. He dressed well. He was good at small talk and possessed all the social graces, but still Mary Todd continued to prefer her restless reluctant lover, Abe Lincoln. Gossip has tried hard to prove that there was romantic rivalry between Lincoln and Douglas before there was political rivalry. But the most industrious efforts display a poor little stock of sentimental melodrama. Mary Todd flirted no more with Douglas than high-spirited girls in worldly societies have always permitted themselves to flirt with eligible, responsive bachelors.

Douglas's interest was quite as lightly engaged. His preoccupations were never with women, though he married twice. He cared first for himself; second, for the lovely abstract idea of power; third, for the Democratic party through which he proposed to become a leader.

He succeeded in almost everything that he attempted. Having been a judge of the supreme court in his own state, the next inevitable step in his progress was to take over the field of national politics as a United States senator. Indulgent Illinois advanced him to that post at an amazingly early age.

She became a legend in the minds of the people who had given him these extraordinary opportunities. He was always audacious, always confident. His speeches before the United States Senate made him a noticeable figure. Not all the attention that he drew was friendly. John Quincy Adams, of Massachusetts, quite inevitably thought him a noisy, bombastic, and rather absurd person. But most of the rest of the world did not agree. Two beautiful women did not.

The first of these was Martha Martin, daughter of a North Carolina planter through whom he came in contact with the art of gracious living. She gave him two children, a set of friends whose attitudes were those dictated by the southern economy, and a superior degree of worldly comfort. When she died he became responsible for her property, which included 150 slaves.

After a period of widowerhood, during which he was distinctly less the fastidious worldling and distinctly more the whisky drinker, Douglas married again. The second match was more brilliant than the first. Adele Cutts was the equivalent of the much-publicized glamour girl of our own day. Indeed, the papers swooned into fatuity with much more abandon than any publication today could master. The Washington *Post*, reporting the wedding, detailed her charms at length, concluding with this verbal sunburst: "On her clear, peachy complexion, there is a perpetual war of the roses—the red and the white—each failing to maintain sole supremacy."

She was hardly more than half Douglas's age. Her distinguished background was revered in Washington society, which had not forgotten her delightful great-aunt, Dolly Madison. She could have married anyone. She chose Stephen Douglas. Illinois was vastly impressed.

It was impressed also by the legends of the splendor in which the Douglases lived. Stephen's flair for being noticed still served him. He cannot have been unaware that the secretary of state was giving a reception on a certain night when he gave one of his own. The official party was a "beggary affair" compared with the one at which Douglas and his beautiful wife were hosts. This fact gave great satisfaction to the homefolk in Illinois. They took vicarious satisfaction in the thought of how "little Douglas" was getting on. He showed the arrogant East that a man from the wilderness knew how to live graciously.

Deeply gratifying also was the way in which this representative of America's rugged simplicity showed Europe just where it stood in the eyes of a democrat. When Queen Victoria declined to see Douglas in ordinary dress, Douglas improved upon the arrogance of the cat by declining to look at a queen. Sitting in the parlor of a fashionable London boardinghouse, he ignored the request of first one servant and then another that he should observe the rule against smoking. When the proprietress herself came to repeat the request, he looked at her with the piercing eyes that had withered many a contestant and said, "Madam, I am an American sovereign." He went on smoking.

He had always believed it. When he was a young man of twenty-five writing about the illness of the penniless boy he had been a few years before, he referred to "my physicians." The humble man awe-stricken by science and by his own unworthy need of its help says, "The doctor told me . . ." Douglas quite spontaneously assumed the royal touch. "My physicians advised me . . ." He was a stricken king, a king in chains, but a king nonetheless and one who would presently claim his heritage with all proper imperiousness.

Everything conspired to give him the point of view of the South. He had been intimately associated with its pleasant way of life and he liked it. In his heart he believed in the right of the strong man to control the destiny of the weak. The policy of expansion was a tenet of his party and the right to introduce slavery into such territories as America might acquire was one which the Democratic South needed to bolster up its own economy. Even Douglas's own state, though it had long since abolished slavery from its territory, was divided in abstract opinion on the subject. He became the mouthpiece of the Democratic party and of its program.

His position was delicate. He had to speak not as an aristocrat, brazenly asserting a divine right, but as a man of the people. And as a man of the people he had to show them the sacredness of their right to hold other people in subjection. Douglas had the adroitness for the job. He was not actually a Southerner, whose attitudes could be accused of prejudice. He occupied a position which could be presented plausibly as that of an impartial observer. Through him the southern philosophy was lifted out of the arena of sullen, selfish contentiousness. It took on the look of an abstract consideration.

But an equally adroit and much stronger opponent had been set up against him.

It has always seemed strikingly dramatic that the two men who became the voices of America's two selves, divided in a desperate clash of ideas, should have been fellow strugglers for a foothold in the same world, fellow townsmen, sharers of the same village culture.

We attribute such brilliant climaxes to the deft hand of fate. But there is a simpler and more realistic explanation. Illinois became the forum in which the issue of freedom was thrashed out for definite reasons.

If Douglas was conveniently removed from too-close identification with the solidifying culture and philosophy of the South, Lincoln was just as conveniently removed from too-close identification with the solidifying culture and philosophy of the East. Unconsciously, America had ordered a change of venue for the trial of the case and two men, equally well trained in law, were assigned the task of arguing out the issue. Both were wary and keen. They knew each other's ways and each other's power.

The advantages seemed all to be with Douglas. He was a national figure. Lincoln was obscure. Douglas was a man of the world; Lincoln was a backwoodsman.

Actually the subtle weight of influence was all the other way about. Douglas had not grown in spiritual authority with the years; Lincoln had. Douglas had enjoyed too many easy successes to have earned great distinction. Lincoln had known enough of failure to have unburdened himself of purely selfish objectives. He was still ambitious; he still wished to be great. But now before self-interest came a principle, one that he was ready to champion with the profound, undistracted, unwavering authority of a great love.

CHAPTER EIGHTEEN

Advance Agent for Civilization

JESSE FELL arrived in Bloomington in 1832. He came, as he said, "carrying a knapsack and feeling as big as Solomon in all his glory." That buoyant spirit did not desert him until the moment of his death more than a half century later. In the intervening years he had been continuously a builder and creator. His imagination made towns spring up all over the prairie. He nourished their infancy through times of hardship and of panic. He supplied them with schools; fostered the means of communication between them; beautified them with trees.

His name does not appear in the volumes of American biography. He sought no conspicuous offices and he held no glittering distinctions. Yet he represents the best and most touching kind of resolute idealism. Jesse Fell was a man who really believed in the future—not in the immediate future which, if it is tactfully wooed, has gifts to offer of money and reputation, but in a distant day when grandchildren and great-grandchildren might live in the security of the institutions he had worked tirelessly to create and under the shade of the trees he had planted in the prairie soil.

He came out of Pennsylvania, where he had been born to Quaker parents. His mother was so ardent a follower of Hicks, in his schism from the main body of Friends, that she became a preacher of the cult.

Because of his frail health, young Jesse was not considered to be capable of a strenuous way of life and his father thought of apprenticing him to a tailor. With gentle determination, Jesse rebelled, saying that he wanted to "learn a better business."

Ignoring the delicacy of his physique, he crowded the teens with many activities. He earned his way through one school by working in the kitchen garden. He kept store and took a post as a teacher. At twenty he was a practiced debater on public issues like the tariff and was ready to create a life for himself in the West.

He was a long time in reaching his goal, but they were not wasted years. The lack of money made it necessary for him to edge his way from one milestone to another: working for a printer, here; selling books along the highway; stopping, there, to study law.

After being admitted to the bar at Springfield, Fell set out for Bloomington. The field of the law was open to him there, as were all the other professions. The community was just six years old and in its casual, haphazard councils the voice of no clergyman, lawyer, or journalist was heard. There were none.

Very soon Fell began to put the affairs of Bloomington's hundred inhabitants in better order. To support himself through the first winter on the prairie, he tutored the children of William Brown in a near-by community. Clearly he tutored them to his entire satisfaction, for later he married the daughter Hester. It was a family group to which so stanch a man would naturally gravitate. William Brown was the sort of idealist who, in a year of crop failure, sold his excellent corn for the usual price of $1 a bushel. His house was a place of meeting for the entire community, a gay and gracious social center. Hester completely justified Jesse's faith by supporting him in all his ventures, through good times and bad, with unwavering energy.

The law was not really to Fell's taste. He found its duties confining and irksome. From Pekin he imported the plump young David Davis to take over his books and his practice so that his imagination could range as wide as the prairie itself.

Land fascinated him. He wanted to see it peopled with the right kind of sober democrats, living under the dictates of passion like his own—for education, for social service, for freedom.

He understood soil and knew how to evaluate its potentialities. All the techniques by which land could be acquired in the midst of the wilderness were familiar to him and he did not hesitate to use them. It was part of his lifework to interest eastern capitalists in this corner of the world and to buy and sell land with their resources. But he was not like the ordinary land speculator from whom Illinois suffered much. He lived on the land; he served it, prospering only when it prospered and suffering when it suffered.

Twice panic stabbed through the orderly pattern of his plan for building a new world. In 1837, with the collapse of the disastrous internal improvements program, Jesse Fell's affairs were seriously hit. But he did nothing to find a special shelter for himself in this storm. He surrendered all his lands and, though he had to avail himself of the bankruptcy laws, he eventually paid every cent of his private indebtedness.

When certain leaders talked recklessly of repudiating the state debt, Fell campaigned against any such plan. He dared to suggest to frightened, angry people that they must submit to increased taxation in order to preserve their credit before the world.

He himself returned to the unsympathetic practice of law in order to support his family, but the attraction of the land was too great and presently he was once more deeply involved in real estate operations. He was not a grandiose empire builder like La Salle. Rather, he disciplined his hopes to bring them within a scope that his talents could control. Central Illinois was his field and out of its soil he called into being one town after another. Pontiac, Lexington, Towanda, Clinton, Le Roy, El Paso—his imagination created them all.

And having established them, he continued to give them uninterrupted thought and care. He rode long and far in all weathers, swimming the swollen river, defying the dangers to his still precarious health. He tied his towns together with a system of roads. He bought timberland and built sawmills. He himself lived in many places, moving his family with him as the scene of his extensive operations shifted. But always he returned eventually to Bloomington.

It was in 1859 that the second panic interrupted his design for building a solid civilization in the West. This time he was more firmly rooted in the soil and was less seriously shaken. But while other men forgot obligations that they had assumed toward the building of schools, Fell shouldered a double or triple load, signing notes and assuming personal responsibility for the continuance of the work he was unwilling to see dropped.

He was a leader in the movement to introduce railroads into the West. Like a faithful townsman he campaigned and maneuvered to make sure that their way should pass through the communities in which he himself was interested. While Stephen Douglas fought for the grant of great tracts of public land to the Illinois Central Railroad and while Jesse Fell undertook to justify the ways of politicians to the citizens at home, both leaders became shining marks for attacks from the enemies of the railroad. But Fell's honest purpose was simply to conquer distance; to provide a link between the Illinois River and the Ohio River so that the frontier world might be drawn close to that of the East.

Every route that led deep into the mind of man irresistibly attracted him. In the course of his life he owned and edited several newspapers. The impulse to direct public opinion would seize him in the midst of his multiple activities; then he would buy a printing press or take over an established paper. Writing with the earnestness and conviction that had made him, even as a boy, a public debater, he would fight the issue of the moment. When the community had somehow met its crisis, his interest would flag. The paper would be sold or passed on to a son-in-law, but the impulse to persuade and guide would simply lie dormant until another issue flamed across the Illinois sky.

He was deeply concerned with the need to improve the quality of teaching in his corner of the world. As advance agent for civilization, he knew that only by elevating standards of instruction could the level of general intelligence be raised. So he fought a valiant battle for the building of a normal school and, as a loyal citizen, fought to get it located in one of his own towns. He approved of the kind of citizen who would be attracted to a community where school life dominated the scene. A piece of Bloomington was isolated for the purpose. Fell donated land; he played an elaborate game of strategy with Peoria, which also wanted the school; he superintended the inspection tour of the committee. At last he won, but it was a victory that was to cut deep into his own resources of both money and imagination. For before the building could be built, the panic had swept over Illinois and the other backers went into hiding. Jesse Fell, his brother Kersey, and two other men of conscience and audacity saw the project through.

The new town, cut off from Bloomington to be the site of the school, was called Normal. Before a single structure had been built on the land, Jesse Fell had planted 12,000 trees, mostly from his own nursery. His example stimulated the imaginations of all who later came to settle in the town, and they vied with one another in the beautification of their grounds.

A child once asked an elder whether or not there were trees in heaven. "I really don't know," the man replied: "but if Jesse Fell gets there and finds none, he will hunt around and find some and plant them."

In politics, as well as in all his other activities, Jesse Fell was the quiet unobtrusive collaborator with principle rather than its exhibitionistic champion. He wanted nothing for himself in the way of conspicuous attention. He used the machinery of government to achieve ends which he considered good and preferred to influence the course of events from behind the scenes. He was the innovator of ideas, the framer of resolutions, seldom the "speaker of the occasion" or the recipient of applause.

While the Whig party continued to offer him an outlet for his gifts of organization, he was completely loyal to its discipline. He was ever present when a rally was being planned and executed, though he declined all nominations for public office. When the Whigs, their community of interest blasted by sectional differences over slavery, began to quarrel bitterly among themselves, Jesse Fell thought he had finished with all the heart-stirring excitements of campaigns and slogans, stump speeches and elections. His interest in politics, he said with more of sentimental fervor than he was accustomed to use, lay buried in the grave of the great Whig, Henry Clay.

But Fell was mistaken. The wildly diverse political elements which wished to make common cause of their opposition to the spread of slavery began to set up housekeeping together in the new Republican party. Jesse Fell recalled his heart from the grave and set to work as one of the organizers in Illinois.

He had crossed and recrossed Lincoln's path many times in the course of his life. When he first set out to find the town of Bloomington, he had stopped en route at New Salem and heard great stories of Abe, the wrestler and the storyteller, then at the Black Hawk War. Later the two men had met at Springfield in the office of Stuart, Lincoln's first law partner, who was also Fell's friend and benefactor. For many years they had worked together in the struggles of the Whig party.

It was inevitable that a man like Fell, whose genius

was to help shape the destiny of other men rather than to claim attention for himself, should have understood the potential importance of Lincoln's career many years before Lincoln understood it. His urgings were among the many which prodded the reluctant, slow-moving man into greatness. It was Fell who originated the idea of a series of joint debates between Lincoln and Douglas. He first suggested it in 1854, long before the actual occasions added their striking drama to American history. And it was Fell who first spoke aloud the hope that Lincoln might one day be president.

Fell was one of the speakers at the first important convention of the new Republican party in Illinois. It met in his own town of Bloomington on May 29, 1856. Lincoln was the man of the hour. After years of caution and uncertainty, years in which his philosophy was slowly taking shape out of the painful doubts of many sleepless night, Lincoln was there as a leader, ready to receive from the people their authority to organize and to direct the spiritual force that wished to destroy slavery. He was ready to give eloquence to the convictions which had grown in him, and in the men who thought like him, in terms of the profound simplicities of moral conduct.

So Jesse Fell heard the man whom he had helped to tutor in ambition declare with passionate and uncompromising fervor the great code of freedom which the rest of his life (and his life itself) would be given to defend. Looking as though he stood seven feet tall, his face illumined with the reverence for truth that made him seem to one observer "the handsomest man I ever saw," Lincoln delivered the famous "lost speech." In it he warned that any interpretation and limitation of the scope of liberty which made "things" of Negroes might soon make "things, of poor white men." With a firmness of resolution deeply impressive to those who heard him, he insisted, "The battle of freedom is to be fought out on principle." And at the end, he declared:

"We will say to the Southern disunionists: 'We won't go out of the Union and you shan't.'"

These words lighted fires in men's minds. Jesse Fell, hearing them spoken at last, knew that his intuition had guided him well, that Lincoln was the man.

It was Fell who in 1858 presented Lincoln's name as Republican nominee for the post of United States senator from Illinois. His resolution stated:

"Lincoln is our first, last and only choice for the vacancy . . . despite all influences at home or abroad, domestic or foreign, the Republicans of Illinois as with the voice of one man are unalterably resolved to the end that we may have a big man with a big mind and a big heart to represent our big state."

Thus began the series of debates on the question of slavery which Jesse Fell's adventurous mind had been demanding. Douglas was the candidate of the Democratic party for the Senate. As the two men moved from one Illinois town to another campaigning for office, the significance of the discussion which they conducted gradually became apparent to the country as a whole. The Illinois valley had become a forum of freedom in which an issue which was of enormous importance to the nation was being put to a great preliminary test. Lincoln and Douglas, debating in the little towns of Ottawa, Freeport, Jonesboro, Charleston, Galesburg, Quincy, and Alton, demonstrated to men far beyond the limits of Illinois the strength of two contrasting philosophies. When they had finished, many a man knew much more clearly than before just where his own sympathies lay.

Jesse Fell, who collaborated so admirably with destiny, was part author of one of the great dramas of our history. He had helped to bring together the lanky boy

who had been a grocery clerk in New Salem and the frail boy who had been a schoolteacher in Winchester. They were moving once more against the background of the Illinois valley. Neither was any longer young. Lincoln had to put on his spectacles to read a passage from his notes. Douglas sometimes had to fortify himself with a drink or two before he felt quite adequate to the mane-tossing and the ferocious air of authority that his audience expected of him. But each had become, within his state, the strong man of his party. Lincoln and Douglas were the defenders of important, opposing political philosophies. The two boys who had come to Illinois river towns to make good were starting out again to do battle for all that they had learned of truth.

Fell's faith in Lincoln survived the defeat of his candidate for the Senate. Even in the moment of defeat, when the buoyancy of a less vital man might have been at least temporarily snuffed out, he began urging presidential ambition on his favorite candidate. It was at Fell's urging that Lincoln wrote out the autobiographical sketch that was to become so famous. Armed with it, the quiet, unassertive campaigner began using his very considerable influence in the East to get favorable attention for Lincoln's name. Fell was the first of American press agents to operate on the grand scale.

When the presidency had been won, he still wanted nothing for himself. His role was, as always, that of the unobtrusive counselor. Since Illinois had the office of chief magistrate, he urged, it would be unwise to antagonize the rest of the country by giving Illinois any other conspicuous office. Faithful to this principle, he accepted no public post but went back to his own round of duties in Bloomington.

The coming of the Civil War found him still there struggling hard, in the early black days, to restrain his fears. To Owen Lovejoy, he wrote:

"Can it be possible that the Almighty (who will pardon my presumption) is so poor a general as to suffer this war to come to a close without sweeping as with a besom of destruction that damning sin that has thus culminated in Civil War?"

In 1862 he liquidated his private affairs and entered

the army as paymaster, with the rank of major. He served for eighteen months before retiring from service.

He returned to Bloomington. There he lived to the end of his life, devoting his energies to the development of a gracious and generous way of life. Busily he shook, out of his capacious sleeve, a manufacturing plant, a foundry, a hotel. He was one of the first to urge the need for a state university. His vision of what it should be was far more in sympathy with the advanced thought of our own times than with the undemanding standard of his own. He said:

". . . we must have not a university in name— another pretentious high school—but what has not yet been realized—a university in fact, a grand and comprehensive school . . . in harmony with the advancing civilization of the age."

He wanted the university for Bloomington, and did not get it. But he went on building for the future. And every form of human distress found comfort in his imaginative understanding. At Normal he built a home for the orphans of soldiers. There, too, his theories showed an extraordinary degree of foresight. He wanted his orphans to have vocational training; when his wishes were disregarded, he disclaimed responsibility for what he regarded as the bungling inadequacy of an old-fashioned program. "Don't call it my school," he protested. "It is not what I wanted it to be."

In no incident of his life did Jesse Fell more touchingly reveal the dignity and decency of his faith than in his farewell to Lincoln. On Sunday, April 23, 1865, the president lay dead but was not yet buried. The Reverend Charles Ellis rose in his pulpit in a Congregational church in Bloomington to preach on the perplexities of the hour. He had been an ardent abolitionist and his heart was not yet unpacked of all its bitterness. The blame for Lincoln's murder, he said, might better be assigned to Adams, Jefferson, and Washington than to Booth. For the founding fathers had been indulgent toward the principles of slavery. Lincoln himself was shamefully at fault:

". . . he had not the moral courage to step forth like a strong man in his might to do what his better nature told him was his highest duty. He sacrificed the demands of God that he might not offend a political party."

Bloomington was hysterical and indignant. Mob violence was threatened. Jesse Fell might have been forgiven for being among those who nursed their righteous rage. He had known Lincoln intimately; he had helped to create him; he had nursed his ambitions. In all the world there were few men who had ever been permitted to call Lincoln by his Christian name, and Jesse Fell was one of them. The shock of personal loss was fresh and overwhelming.

Yet it was Jesse Fell who rose before his fellow citizens and, in Lincoln's own name, urged tolerance and understanding. The issue of freedom of speech was more significant to him even in that moment than personal feeling. "As we have free pews," he urged, "let us have a free pulpit." And the mob, which had intended to punish the Reverend Mr. Ellis violently, went home subdued.

So Fell went on to the end, generous, creative, vigorous. Great men came to see him often as he grew older. He was not easy to find on his large grounds. Usually he was in some far corner, turning over the soil to plant a tree. One of his children would be sent to "chase after Father" and bring him back. He was not always quite tidy when he was found. Patiently and humorously he would submit to a great deal of brushing and smoothing and patting to make him presentable. Too much of his energy was required to put society in order; there was not quite enough left to keep his person immaculate.

As the years increased, his untroubled heart seemed to grow lighter. The warmth of his sympathies bloomed, toward the close, in a special kind of gaiety. Surrounded by grandchildren and the friends of grandchildren, he was a favorite of their circle. Once a young woman invited him to a dancing party and he wrote some engaging doggerel by way of acceptance:

> But I must warn you in advance
> My Quaker foot it will not dance.
> A thousand times I have lamented
> That Fox and Penn were so demented
> As to proscribe what all can see
> With half an eye is poetry;
> If not in words in what is better
> In motion, life, spirit, letter.
> Yes, if I could, I'd skip and prance
> In all the ecstasy of dance
> For I am young and supple, too
> I'm not quite three score ten and two.

Useful men are not always charming. Charming men are, perhaps, seldom useful. The quiet genius of Jesse Fell permitted him to be both.

CHAPTER NINETEEN

Illinois Cavalier

W ARD HILL LAMON reached Illinois in the
year 1847. He had been born in the worldly atmosphere
of Virginia and, at the age of nineteen, possessed all the
traditional traits of gallantry. He loved to foregather
with the boisterous boys in a tavern to sing comic songs,
exchange lively stories, and drink in deep, long draughts.
He was natty in his dress. The exuberance of his vitality
bloomed in luxuriant growth of mustache, which he
wore long and glossy. Surcharged with energy, he was
forever flinging his six feet two inches of hard bone and
healthy muscle into any fight that he could find.

These physical encounters were, for the most part,
friendly. The social life of men without women, in
early Illinois, was much like that of any schoolyard. In
moments of relaxation the boys fell to wrestling and
roughing with a hearty delight in mere activity.

But Lamon was not always circumspect in the display of his prowess. Once, when he was quite new to

Danville, the town where he took up residence in Illinois, he and a boon companion felt irresistibly impelled to beat a grocer, Jacob Schatz, because he refused to sell them an unlimited amount of whisky on credit. Legal recourse seems not to have been available to the victim of this adventure, but, nursing his bruises, Mr. Schatz thought of an appropriate revenge. He stopped selling whisky.

Among the women of Danville, Ward Hill Lamon was regarded as an Adonis. It was of considerable assistance to his reputation as a man of charm that he spoke with a southern drawl. Better still was the affecting tone of his singing voice when he dipped into his large repertory and brought out such items as "I Wandered to the Village, Tom" and "The Lament of the Irish Immigrant."

Wherever Lamon was to be found there was a pleasant stir of activity. In one of the early years of his residence in Danville he promoted a fair, which gained a kind of immortality in the anecdotes of the community. From Virginia, Lamon had brought high standards of what a fair must be. Clearly, no such event could be complete without horse races. Since his own trotting horse was the only one entered, Lamon ran it against its own record and solemnly awarded himself a $5 purse as owner of the winning animal.

As he began to thrive in the new world, Lamon found that plenty of whisky was available to him without exercising undue pressure on the successors of Jacob Schatz. Liquor, which he found completely potable, could be purchased at the old McCormick House at 18¾ cents a quart. Lamon spent a great deal of time there in Homeric drinking bouts. But to any who ever challenged him about his habits he protested, with the sportsman's bravado, that he had never yet drunk so much that he could not speak, with perfect lucidity, the line:

"She stood at the gate welcoming him in."

Between periods of impressing the boys with his fists and the girls with his fine black mustache and his songs, Lamon devoted himself to more solidly profitable enterprises. He engaged in the sale of real estate and studied law in his private hours. He was presently admitted to practice in the Eighth Circuit.

Three years after his arrival in Danville he married Angeline, daughter of Elud Turner, his partner in real estate transactions.

On the circuit he became an intimate of that circle over which Judge Davis presided and of which Lincoln was the animating spirit. From the moment of their first meeting, Lincoln and Lamon became close friends. The shadow of the giant lay protectively over a long period of Lamon's life. He moved at the heels of his great benefactor through perils, triumphs, and tragedies. Always Lamon was the more noticeable figure of the two as he went about bristling and bustling with importance. He seems sometimes to have mistaken himself for the show instead of realizing that he was merely the prologue. Lincoln was ever indulgent. He drew from the vitality of Lamon something that he needed.

The contemporaries of the two men were often puzzled by this friendship. Temperamentally the contrast could not have been greater. Lamon was noisy and full of gusto. Lincoln was subdued and, even in his role as entertainer, unassertive. Lamon was so convivial that, when he entered a new community, he made with unerring sense of direction for the nearest bar and stayed there until all its habitués were his intimates. Lincoln was lonely and aloof. His far deeper gifts of friendship and of understanding, while they roused confidence in nearly everyone he met, roused also a kind of awe which kept him from being jostled too familiarly. Lamon's most conspicuous talent was for drinking. Lincoln did not drink at all.

Yet it was clear that Lincoln delighted in the company of Lamon. Had he been self-conscious about his destiny he might have said, after Caesar, "Let me have men about me that are fat: Sleek-headed men and such as sleep o' nights." Except for the matter of sleeping at night, Lamon would admirably have fitted the requirements.

But there was a still stronger link between the two men. Lamon represented for Lincoln the youth that he had never had, the exuberant, careless freedom in which circumstance had never permitted him to indulge. Lincoln, who was born old, felt some secret need of fulfillment which was vicariously satisfied when Lamon drank deep, grew merry, and brayed comic songs at the top of his lungs. As an artist in the expression of human emotion, Lincoln was moved by a desire to contain within himself the impulses of all men. He was never close to the impulse after profligacy; but, through Lamon, he at least touched it.

Lincoln liked to have Lamon present at the sessions in Judge Davis's rooms. He enjoyed the moment when wit gave way to song and Lamon began exploring his repertory of ballads. It was under such circumstances that Lincoln first heard "Dixie" sung, and the tune was ever after associated in his memory with pleasant, friendly communication between men.

The two were also professional partners. In the old Barnum building of Danville they shared an office which had their names on the door, though their joint efforts had to do only with cases arising in Vermilion County. They agreed very well on the whole, though Lincoln was sometimes disturbed by what he considered to be Lamon's excessive charges. On one occasion he forced his partner to return part of a fee already collected.

In 1857, when he was not yet thirty years old, Lamon was appointed prosecuting attorney of the Eighth Circuit. He moved to Bloomington to be closer to Judge Davis and the center of the circuit's activities. His partnership with Lincoln automatically ended and he formed a new one. But the intimacy of their friendship continued. When Lamon's first wife died, Lincoln was present at the funeral.

Like Fell and Davis, Lamon was an indefatigable press agent for Lincoln as a figure in politics. His services were much more distinguished for the exuberance of the loyalty they displayed than for their discretion. Typical of his boyish desire to be useful was the incident of the Republican convention which nominated Lincoln.

It was assumed by the politically wise that the Republican nomination in 1860 would go to the party's best known and most distinguished member, William Henry Seward. But, from the standpoint of tactics in the game of pursuing office, it was the misfortune of Seward that his views were too well known. His enemies would not permit him to gather strength enough to win the nomination, preferring to let the dark horse, Lincoln, get the lead and finally win the race. A contemporary observer commented on the outcome that it "continues to be a mystery to the layman and a perplexity to the learned."

But the boys of the old Eighth Circuit had had their share in bringing about the unexpected result. Judge Davis's unwearying efforts in committee rooms had been supported in a characteristically dramatic way by Ward Hill Lamon.

The night before the balloting was to take place in the convention hall at Chicago, Lamon had had an extremely busy time. From the barrooms and other centers where strong young men with lusty lungs were likely to be found, he gathered together a small army of followers. For many hours, which they seem to have found refreshing rather than exhausting, Lamon instructed them in the art of shouting. Enthusiasm for Lincoln was their theme without words.

Next day each was supplied with a completely unauthorized card of admission, bearing a forged name. Lamon's claque was rushed to the convention hall, and each time Lincoln's name was mentioned it went mad with well-rehearsed and highly infectious zeal. The lungs of the men from Illinois made a finer clamor than those of all the other states combined.

Lincoln was far away in Springfield, stretched out despondently on a couch in the office of a fellow lawyer. He did not know how Judge Davis was bargaining on his behalf. He did not know how Lamon was, according to the dictates of his temperament, turning the whole convention into a noisy vaudeville, but he could not have stopped them even if he would. For they had picked their friend as a man of destiny, and destiny was supporting their shrewd guess.

When the shouting of triumph had died away, Lamon went romping home to campaign for his former partner. In Bloomington his private affairs had simplified themselves. Joseph Gurney Cannon, later to be famous in Congress as "Uncle Joe," had succeeded him as prosecuting attorney in the Eighth Circuit. Lamon devoted his time to collecting back fees and did so well at it that he amassed a small fortune. With this security he went to Springfield, became a member of Governor Yates's staff, and married Sally Logan, daughter of Judge Stephen T. Logan.

This last step was wisely taken. Sally became the perfect embodiment of feminine loyalty wistfully pictured in Lamon's little verbal test for sobriety. No matter how far he migh wander and how late he might return, she always "stood at the gate welcoming him in." Only once did her loyalty waver, and that time Lincoln intervened to assure Sally that her husband was the stanchest of men in the discharge of his duty. The small rift was quickly closed.

When Lincoln left Springfield to be inaugurated, he took Lamon with him as personal bodyguard. Picturesquely prepared for any emergency, the young man wore upon his person "a brace of fine pistols, a huge bowie knife, a blackjack and a pair of brass knuckles." But he did not change his habits. In the course of the journey Lincoln became worried about a satchel which contained his inaugural address. Lamon, searching for it, found instead a bag which contained a bottle of liquor and a soiled shirt. He commented on the incident: "The whisky was of good quality. I returned the shirt."

The rest of Lamon's personal history belongs to the footnotes on the Civil War. Lincoln appointed him marshal of the District of Columbia and honored him with a variety of duties. Swaggering about in a resplendent uniform was much to Lamon's taste. He lived superbly in a Washington mansion. His extravagances, in the conduct of both his public and his private life, roused great resentment in Congress. He became the target of endless criticism, part of which was intended for himself and part of which was directed over his head at President Lincoln.

His delusions of grandeur impelled him to one reckless gesture after another. He tried to raise a regiment and then expanded his ambition until he saw himself at the head of a brigade. But the whole plan fell through and much of his private fortune went to settle the bills which his vanity had run up.

In Lincoln's second campaign Lamon went back to the old stamping ground in Illinois, traveling over the old Eighth Circuit making speeches. His name was rhymed with that of Damon in a bit of doggerel which identified Lincoln as his Pythias.

And when the president lay dead, Lamon led the procession, in all its solemn splendor, back to Springfield.

He had twenty-eight years still to live. They were spent in a variety of activities, but to none of them could he give vitality of the old kind. It seemed to have gone from him with the death of Lincoln. He practiced law but without enthusiasm. He wrote of his relations with Lincoln, but the memories were sketchy and inadequate. He got into wrangles over his attempts as biographer, and finally surrendered all other interests to wander from place to place in an effort to restore his broken health.

The last scene of any importance shows him at Denver enacting an epilogue to his life of conviviality with another bon vivant as his companion. Eugene Field once entered a room where Lamon lay sleeping stretched out on the floor. The versemaker retired, leaving behind a characteristic example of his talent for sentimental comradery. In four tinkling stanzas he saluted Lamon for the music of his snore and for the innocence of conscience which thus left him free of "vain ado." He called upon God to guard Lamon's "last sweet sleep of all" as tenderly "as I do now." Lamon was pleased.

Into the dominantly melancholy tone of Lincoln's life, the friendship with Lamon introduced the notes of deep-throated, uninhibited laughter. The glossy cavalier's impulse to overdo with reckless extravagance everything that he attempted relieved momentarily the tension of Lincoln's cautious, quiet ways. Something essential to the pioneer world was embodied in Ward Hill Lamon. His impulses were seldom ill-natured even when they were most violent. He dramatized the effort of a crude, lusty, young society to snatch fun out of its meager way of life.

This perhaps might be his epitaph: He made the worried giant smile.

CHAPTER TWENTY

Conquering Hero

O N a day in April, 1860, the steamboat *Itasca* landed at the wharf in Galena, Illinois, and down its gangplank walked a man carrying a kitchen chair in each hand. These clumsy objects may have made him a little conspicuous as he trudged toward land, with wife and children trailing behind him. The garment that he wore about his stooped and rounded shoulders may also have helped to make him a little noticeable. It was an old army overcoat of sky blue, faded and worn, no longer beautiful even in the martial glory of its cape.

People who noticed this arrival of a surly-looking man, burdened with the symbols of his bondage to a frowsy domesticity, probably shrugged their shoulders and guessed that there was another of the casuals of the frontier, a failure washed up by the Mississippi River. He was a failure, looking, not very confidently or even resolutely, for a new chance.

Anyone who may have made that shrewd deduction was completely right, but no Galena poet or seer could have had the audacity to foresee that, within five years, this dreary newcomer would be not merely the most important man in Galena but one of the most petted and sought-after men in the entire world.

His name was Grant. The world was presently to know him as Ulysses Simpson Grant, though the names

given him in baptism were Hiram Ulysses. The careless and imperious habits of the senator who recommended Grant for West Point were responsible for the change.

The arrival in Galena was, for Grant, another downward step in a personal history that had led from disaster to disaster. He had never been happy. From infancy his life had been shadowed by the figure of the strange, gaunt woman who was his mother. The victim of a disastrous negativism, she must have chilled the exuberance of her child at his first expectant glance. She seems never to have been aware of him. When he visited her after becoming the national hero, she turned toward him unsmilingly from the stove where she was cooking and said, "Well, Ulysses, you've been a great man, haven't you?" and then went on preparing supper. She accepted none of her son's frequent invitations to visit him in the White House.

Young "Ulyss" loved animals and was more comfortable with them than in human society. He loathed his father's tannery where he was supposed to cut flesh from hides and endure the sickening odors of the curing process. His boyhood contemporaries found him a baffling creature. He was a prude who would not listen to dirty stories or show his nakedness at the swimming hole. His strength and bravery saved him from the abuse reserved for the delicate minded and antisocial. He was never called sissy, but some rebuke had to be meted out to him. So his young associates punned on his name, calling him "Useless."

He went to West Point to escape the tannery and was not happy there. His whole physique remained essentially unsoldierly. No self-esteem awoke in him to make him stand erect or to try to wear his uniform with dash. He received many demerits for missing buttons. Scholastically he did reasonably well, especially in mathematics. He dreamed of devoting his life to teaching this subject in which he excelled. He asked only for a small sheltered corner in a menacing world.

But no one offered such a haven. He went on in the service of the army, an outsider in the midst of its bluff, masculine conviviality. A taste for whisky was the only one which he shared with the comrades of this too-small world. Whisky unburdened Grant momentarily of his sense of inferiority, warmed him out of the chill that had been put so early upon his spontaneity, loosened his tongue and gave him moments of fine audacity. He probably did not indulge his appetite much more than the other young officers, all of whom were used to drinking deep. But the change that whisky wrought in Grant's temperament caused his participation in debauches to attract attention. Men of few vices are often blamed more sharply for their failings than men whose repertory of mischief is so wide as to make their friends never think of virtue in connection with their names. Grant was scolded by drunkards for drinking just as a Baptist minister might be.

He went through the Mexican War, following the flag with complete loyalty but hating the war itself. He was given the routine honors of faithful service and, with this much support to his self-esteem, he assumed the responsibilities of marriage. The first gesture of the young man who had turned over a new leaf was to sign the temperance pledge. Total abstinence, he piously declared, was the only cure for the liquor habit.

Grant loved his Julia Dent quite reasonably well, though he seems not to have been restless when he was separated from her two years at a time. The service took Grant to California and Julia found it best to stay with her father in St. Louis. The worst feature of the separation was that the pledge was forgotten. Grant's colonel grew impatient. After a first warning, the young captain signed his resignation and handed it over to his superior officer to be sent to Washington if he could not behave better. He did not behave better for long and, presently, he was out of the army.

He returned to his family in disgrace, like the disapproved-of little boy he had always felt himself to be.

His exuberant father-in-law didn't like him. Having consented grudgingly to the marriage he was even more grudging now that the scrubby-looking fellow had lost his foothold in the world. For his daughter's sake he supplied a patch of land and a thousand dollars with which the ex-soldier was to outfit himself as a farmer. Grant, with doleful, prophetic humor, called the place "Hardscrabble" and was defeated even before he began. Later he tried the real estate business with an optimistic friend named Boggs. But the bland cajolery necessary for success in this endeavor was a role to which Grant was quite unsuited. Nothing more ridiculous had ever happened to him except when he was assigned to the role of Desdemona in an all-soldier amateur production of *Othello*.

Another bleak failure was soon chalked up against his record.

The elder Grant was now out of the tannery business. Two of his more tough-minded sons, Orvil and Simpson, had been established in the leather goods trade at Galena. It was decided that the best thing to be done with poor, blundering, irritating Ulyss was to give him a clerkship, under his younger brothers, in the store, and there he dutifully went.

After landing that April morning at the Galena wharf, Grant and his family made their way on foot over miserable roads, first to the leather goods store on Main Street and then to the nondescript two-story brick house where they were to live. The badness of the stretch of road leading away from his house was to make history in Galena. After he had first begun to distinguish himself in the war, it was hinted to him that civil honors in his town might await him at the close of the struggle.

"I'd like to be mayor of Galena," Grant admitted. "Then I might get a sidewalk built from my home to the depot." When he did return to Galena, at last, a banner greeted him which read: "General, the sidewalk has been built."

No one knew him in Galena except as the pitifully inadequate new clerk who never could tell the price of a saddle without asking one of his brothers. He was hardly worth the $800 a year they paid him, and they did not fail to let him understand how much he owed to their indulgence, The women of Galena called on Mrs. Grant. For after all, her father was a man of property and Mrs. Grant herself owned slaves. But the unprepossessing man who was her husband had no intimates and scarcely any acquaintances. When it later became important to dig up reminiscences of Grant's year in Galena before the outbreak of the war, there were not enough stories to fill more than a page or two.

The war brought him notice in Galena long before it chose him for real distinction. The first flurried meeting in the courthouse failed to develop a philosophy or even a stable point of view. Many of the townsmen were proslavery in their sympathies. The chairman himself wavered, and worried, and felt that there was much to be said on both sides.

It was Grant's moment of decision. He was a West Pointer; he had served in the regular army; he was a man to whose opinions the laity must defer. There were neighbors who did not trust this curious man who was known to be a Democrat, the son-in-law of a man whose commitments were all to the philosophy of slavery, the husband of a slaveholder, but John Rawlins trusted Grant. He was the young lawyer who represented the bustling Orvil and the hardheaded Simpson Grant. He knew their brother too, and had come to feel respect for his ideas on soldiering.

Together, Rawlins and Grant traveled about the vicinity of Galena, calling for volunteers. Sentiment in favor of Lincoln and the North quickly solidified, and on the lawn of the wealthy Washburnes Grant began to drill raw recruits.

When it came time to elect a captain, Grant would seem to have been the logical choice. But he refused to be nominated for the post, perhaps because he feared that local prejudice might refuse him the honor, but more probably because he was holding out for bigger game. He had been a captain in the regular army and felt himself competent to command a regiment.

When the newly organized company set out for Springfield to be properly enrolled in the army, Grant went along. He had packed a little satchel, and then made his way on foot to the railroad station. There was a tremendous to-do as the Jo Daviess Guards, so named for their county, entrained. Patriotic ladies kissed patriotic boys. Bands played. There was a pervasive atmosphere of benignity and mutual congratulation.

From it was excluded only one untidy little man who sat with a pipe clenched between his teeth, in his eyes the habitual expression of the outsider looking in. Yet he was the only one among them who was of the slightest real importance. For destiny had her capricious eye on Grant.

He went to Springfield, but no one was interested in him. He could not break through the cordon of good fellows looking for jobs who surrounded Governor Yates. He had made up his mind to go back to Galena, when the governor got his eye on him quite by chance and feeling some vague little nudge from the elbow of destiny, said, "Come to my office tomorrow, Captain Grant, and maybe I can find something for you to do."

If Grant had not already become well acquainted with despair, his assignment might have broken his spirit. He was put to ruling forms in the adjutant general's office. But at least he had not been completely beached by the surging tide of incompetence. When a drillmaster was needed at Camp Yates, Grant was sent there. He wore a cavalry sword over his civilian clothes because he had no money with which to buy a uniform. The unsoldierly look of this improvised army was not improved by the appearance of its drillmaster.

But no post of permanence or dignity was found for him. Grant sighed, "It is strange that a man of my experience and education cannot secure a command."

The reason, oddly enough, was the same that had made him fail at selling real estate and leather goods. He was the sort of man who permits himself to become deep-sunk in the sin of poverty. Society always finds it best to ignore such a man as long as it possibly can.

At last when that jolly fellow, Colonel Goode, drove his fellow officers into rebellion and they demanded his removal, Grant was pushed into his place because Governor Yates could think of no one else.

The 21st Illinois Infantry was made up of the immediate descendants of the wild boys with whom Lincoln had wrestled. They had not changed their habits. The spirit of independence was still so strong in them that they thought saluting officers a silly indication of subservience. Into the barracks they proposed to introduce the brawling jollity of the barroom.

Grant had a different idea. He wanted discipline and he got it by outdoing the wild boys in resolution. One ruffian, nicknamed "Mexico," got drunk and challenged the whole regiment to try to arrest him. Grant ordered him tied to a post. "For every minute I stand here I'll have an ounce of your blood," Mexico yelled. "Put a gag in that man's mouth," Grant commanded. Later he untied Mexico himself. "Now salute me and go to your quarters," he said. Mexico saluted.

So the most fantastic of success stories began to be written. This man, who had never managed to look like a soldier, produced a whole regiment of model soldiers. This man, who always seemed to feel that he was defeated before he began his experiments in a peaceful society, never knew when he was defeated in war. This man, who had improvised the career of a private citizen so badly, planned a campaign for an army which led to an unbroken series of victories and finally to triumph for his cause.

The same inadequacies which had led him into so many blunders in his early years were to cast their shadow over his years of splendor in the White House and in the world of affairs. Grant's history was to be rounded out, as it began, in loneliness and submissive despair, but he had a long-protracted moment when the world (and what was more important, Galena!) was at his feet.

It is plain that the capitulation of Galena mattered more than all his other triumphs. In that little town he had reached the lowest point to which humiliation can drag a man's self-esteem. Patronized by the few who knew him, utterly neglected by most, he sat biting moodily on the iron of despair. Then suddenly Galena was his. He was given a fine house in which to live. His slightest gesture was regarded as significant. Once when he absent-mindedly tossed an unsmoked cigar into the street, an observer leapt at it and preserved it as a valuable souvenir.

Grant demonstrated his gratitude by surrounding himself with men from Galena. There was John A. Rawlins, the young lawyer, into whose stern, overbearing care Grant gave his conscience and the whisky bottle. Rawlins had "flashing black eyes" and "quivering muscles"; when he advised, Grant listened like a dutiful child. There were merchants, jewelers, clerks of court, doctors, and engineers all of whom had jogged up and down Main Street with Grant and who now followed him into the field.

This was the contribution that Illinois made to the Civil War. It was to have no battlefields, but it offered its men: two significant leaders and the wild boys whom Grant had made over into soldiers.

And along with the men there went women. There was Clarissa Emely Geer Hobbs, for example. She, too, had lived in Galena and there had married her husband. James Hobbs thought his health delicate and turned from the exactions of medical practice to the law. But when the Civil War broke out he volunteered, not as a medical officer but in any post that could be given him. He was detailed as a hospital steward.

Clarissa decided to go along. She provided herself with a "stout new dress, a pair of calf skin shoes, and some necessities" that could be thrown away in any emergency. She packed them all into a satchel and went over to Dubuque to offer her services.

At first they did not know quite what to do with

this resolute lady. The colonel in charge of enlistment said, "Mrs. Hobbs, there is no provision made for women nurses." Mrs. Hobbs said, "Well, I'm going, colonel."

The colonel evidently knew a decisive woman when he saw one, for he went dutifully to see what break in military red tape might be made. He returned to report:

"If you are willing to be enrolled on the roster as a soldier . . . you can draw your rations and have two blankets issued you."

During the war Mrs. Hobbs drew her rations and her blankets but no pay at all. She went to war, suffered privation, fought smallpox, risked death—all with the casual sense of doing the day's necessary job, just as she had previously cared for the house and reared the children. She was the perfect example of the heroine in homespun, all unconscious of her virtue but unconscious of nothing else that went on about her. She lived to be a very old and magnificently dignified woman in whose lovely face humor and insight high-lighted serenity and righteousness.

And Mary Bickerdyke of Illinois stomped resolutely off to war, determined to take no nonsense from officers as she went about nursing their men. One fidgety medical man got seriously on her nerves with his everlasting questions about where she had come by this and that thing which she needed to give comfort to men in hospital beds. For the most part she ignored this slave to correctness of procedure, but once he prodded her beyond her strength by asking on whose authority she had taken certain supplies. She turned on him abruptly:

"I took them on the authority of the Lord God Almighty," she said. "If you know of a higher, I should be pleased to hear of him."

And Mrs. Bickerdyke got on with her job. She did it better, on the whole, than did most of the generals whose names are much more widely known.

In the shadow of Lincoln, Grant, his soldiers and his nurses, moved out of Illinois onto the larger stage upon which the eyes of the nation were turned.

CHAPTER TWENTY-ONE

A Wonderful Lady

O N May 4, 1865, there appeared in the Springfield *Journal* the advertising card of an energetic citizen
of the republic. With no show of false modesty she announced herself as

A WONDERFUL LADY

and went on to explain that she was the "Greatest
Astrologist, Clairvoyant and Female Physician now living." She had arrived "for a short time only." Those
"wishing to know their past, present and future events
of life" as well as "those wishing information of absent
friends" might consult with her. Terms: "Gentlemen,
$2; Ladies, $1."

From the rooms which she had taken for the day,
the female physician looked out on the streets of Springfield. They were crowded with people who moved end-
lessly back and forth in quiet, expectant mood. Occasionally two small boys would dart out of the throng,

chasing each other, trying to trip each other up in an effort to restore the normal mood of daily life. But these brief excursions served only to emphasize the subdued and tense atmosphere of the streets.

People came to consult the wonderful lady at gratifyingly short intervals all day. Their mood was exactly right for conveying the kind of wisdom she had to offer. Their minds were already dwelling on the great mysteries of human experience, and she had little difficulty in establishing communication with their bases of belief.

Some of the men came in shuffling and red-faced and apologetic. They seemed anxious to deny, with a shrug or an intonation of irony, the very faith that had brought them. But these were troubled times. No one knew what lay ahead in this moment of national calamity. A man could not have too much advice. He must pass up no bets that might guide the future conduct of his affairs. After a short interval devoted to perfunctory skepticism, the male client would begin asking eager questions. Would he be successful in the undertaking he had just launched? or that he was planning to launch? Was this the time to risk all? or should he wait?

With soothing authority, the wonderful lady told each client what she knew he wanted to hear.

Occasionally one of the red-faced visitors would make a small gesture of gallantry, but the effort was halfhearted and the wonderful lady knew how to discourage such impulses. This was no time for indulgence in any distracting interest.

The members of her own sex were much more interested in that department of wisdom which had to do with "information of absent friends." They spoke in phrases which the wonderful lady recognized as being

borrowed from the headlines in the paper. They remarked upon the wisdom of providence which had removed this or that relative before he had had "to see
this fateful day." The wonderful lady gave each client
messages from her dead. They were happy in heaven,
the dead repeated again and again. Heaven was a place
of light. The dead awaited, with patience, reunion with
their dear ones.

In moments of inactivity the wonderful lady stood,
with the lace curtains drawn discreetly back from the
high windows, studying those who might come to consult her next. Her eye was caught by a sign in the
window of Mackenzie, the bookseller just across the way.
He was attempting—rather ineptly, the wonderful lady
thought—to capitalize upon the fact that there were
many visitors to Springfield. He was having a sale of
"superb pictures" in "old walnut frames." His advertisement screamed for attention:

BEAUTIFUL THINGS! WHAT BLISS TO GAZE AT!

The wonderful lady felt a contemptuous pity for
Mackenzie. This was not at all the sort of day on which
people would stop to look at pictures. They went past
his store without even a passing glance at his windows.

When eleven o'clock came people who had traveled
far to reach Springfield that day began to be hungry.
They pulled packages out of their pockets and, sitting
down along the highway, began to munch at sandwiches.
Soon the yard in front of the house where the wonderful
lady had taken a room was littered with bits of paper.
The landlady bustled out to protest, but a passive crowd
turned its back on her scoldings. A few moments after

she had strenuously tidied her premises they were strewn with refuse again.

The midday mood of relaxation threw the visitor to Springfield off guard. The wonderful lady's grip on the lace curtain tightened as she saw a pickpocket slipping his hand into the coat of a man who lounged against the wall of Mackenzie's store. But three other loungers saw him at the same moment. He was caught and kicked a distance of ten feet into the street. The would-be thief lay for a moment in the dust as though he were hopeless about the possibility of escape. But presently he scrambled to his feet and disappeared in the crowd. No one seemed now to feel any responsibility toward him. The man lounging against Mackenzie's store showed his wallet, shrugged his shoulders, and went on eating.

So the day wore on. In the early afternoon the crowd disappeared from the streets. The wonderful lady, knowing that she would be free for a few hours, consulted her occult books in the interest of brighter séances. At four visitors began to straggle in once more. She was busy until late evening.

When it was over at last, she counted her takings with satisfaction. It was the best day she had ever had, much better than any circus day she could remember. Funerals were superior to fairs, because people were feeling serious. Of course, it wasn't every day in the week that you could have a funeral of a President of the United States—and a martyred president, to boot. But she was glad she had had the sense to make the most of it. She shook the heavy purse in her hand. This would see her through the pretty thin times that were likely to come.

The wonderful lady sighed, experiencing the pleasant letdown of accomplishment.

It was too bad about poor Abe Lincoln, getting shot like that just when he had won his war. But, after all, life must go on. And it had been a good day.

BOOK III

Experiments in Living

CHAPTER TWENTY-TWO

It Has Happened Here

THE unending quest for the good life has led men down many strange bypaths of experiment. The passion for leadership has disturbed many curious, confused minds. During the nineteenth century the American soil became the scene of many such adventures directed by many such leaders. A basic uniformity runs through these variously embellished designs for living. They began with an eager abstract concern for the Good and ended with dictatorship. They began with prophecy and ended with profligacy.

The state of Illinois had its share of these dramas. Typical of them was the adventure at Bishop Hill, where the Swedes wrestled with the angel and did not, in the end, have his blessing. There were weird overtones of passion, hysteria, and madness to the story, for the Swedes of Uppsala achieved a strange degree of fervor when the prophet of righteousness, Eric Jansen, stood up in his pulpit and urged them to repent.

He was a creature of formidable ugliness and fascination. Two prominent front teeth gave him a monstrous look. But that did not prevent him from attracting large numbers of Lutherans away from the state church against the decadence of which he thundered out reckless denunciations. Inevitably he was persecuted and inevitably America suggested itself as the proper refuge for a prophet who had not found honor in his own country. Jansen had to escape from his tormentors, ignominiously disguised as a woman. His too-easily identified front teeth were knocked out to lend plausibility to the masquerade. He went on skis across the Norwegian frontier. The voyage across the Atlantic was a tragic nightmare. But it ended at last, and Jansen arrived finally at the tract of land in Henry County, Illinois, to which he gave the name of Bishop Hill, a translation of Biskopskulla, the Swedish parish in which he was born.

Many of the things that happened at Bishop Hill in the first months of the colony were so tragic that one marvels at the ability of men to keep the sparks of dignity and faith alight in so dreadful a storm. The Bishop Hill colonists lived in dugouts and were cold and hungry; they fell ill of cholera; they watched their children die; they died themselves, and their poor wasted bodies were thrown into shallow trenches and covered with a few spadefuls of dirt. Even when they faced no immediate threat of death, they worked long hours on insufficient food and had no graces or comforts in their lives.

For none of these disasters, which legalistic minds with unconscious irreverence define as acts of God, was Eric Jansen responsible. His reputation suffered unduly perhaps from the fact that he chose not to share the sufferings of his people. While they were cold, he was warm; while they starved, his house was filled with food; while they cared for the sick among them as well as their lack of knowledge enabled them to do, he had his own physician whose services were denied to the rest; while they died trapped by a set of dangers which they did not understand, he ran away to safety.

Nor did it serve Jansen's reputation with the outside world that he imitated the self-indulgent habits of his fellow prophet, Joseph Smith the Mormon. When Eric Jansen's wife charged him with infidelity, he merely shook his head sadly and said that she could not bring such accusations against him except for the fact that she was deficient in faith. He did not deny the accusations; indeed, it would have been little use to do so. Too many people had reason to know that he nourished his spirit on fleshly comforts.

This was a recurring feature of the prophet's way of life, one which should be examined without leering cynicism. It takes imagination, vitality, and a love of domination to be a prophet. Those also are the assets of a lover. It would be well if a lover could discipline himself and direct his imagination so that it might not injure others. But when a prophet is also a dictator, he seems always to feel a great compulsion to demonstrate that he alone is superior to the discipline he imposes upon others. So the dictator-prophet can hardly fail in his private life to be a bold and exacting lover.

There are exceptions, of course. Some dictators canalize their passions entirely in the direction of hatred, leaving love quite out of their lives. They are, on the whole, rather more unpleasant than the reckless lovers.

It is certainly true that Jansen antagonized many men by the demands he made of their wives and daughters. There was a moment when Bishop Jansen, as he came to call himself, had a revelation forbidding marriage to his followers. That proved to be a serious mistake and he had to have a hasty counterrevelation. But he came by his death through interference between man and wife. An adventurer, John Root, had come to the colony and married the prophet's cousin. Later, when Root wished to leave the movement, his wife was not permitted to go with him. There were mighty excursions and alarums for a long time afterward, with Root stealing his own wife away from Bishop Hill and with Jansen persuading her to return. It ended, as such episodes were likely to end among men in Illinois, violently. The Bishop Hill experiment ended in a squalid flurry of melodrama when Root thrust his gun through the window of the courthouse at Cambridge and shot. The prophet died, cursing with quite unabated vigor.

It is easy to make a sexual monster of Jansen. A vigorous young novelist, remembering Freud, recently has done so. But it is, perhaps, too easy. The effort puts a mask on the face of Jansen and leaves the most interesting aspects of his personality unexplored. He had great power and the fact that it was, in part, hypnotic does not explain it away. Many sensible people believed in him to the end. They praised the resolution which had enabled him to break what was for them intolerable bondage.

In the later phases of the experiment, Jansen proved to be an admirable executive. The farms at Bishop Hill were prosperous. Machinery was introduced early. The plants in which the women worked were well operated and triumphantly productive. The Bishop Hill standard of living was high, the conditions of life comfortable.

The economy was completely communistic. Private fortunes had been turned over to Jansen in the beginning of the venture. In theory, all property was held in common, though actually title to land and buildings

was vested in Jansen's name. Yet with the death of the leader this whole sturdy-seeming domain crumbled. By lashing frequently at their lack of faith, the leader had created a faith stronger than he knew. It could withstand anything except the evidence that it had been ill-founded.

When Jansen lay dead, his followers did not mourn. They waited confidently for the third day, when it was assumed that he would rise from the dead. It was the beginning of the end for Jansen's movement when he failed to justify the fanatical belief that he had exacted of his followers. It ended in lawsuits, countersuits, and courtroom oratory.

There must be a meaning in the fact that such experiments always trace out the same rising and falling line. Perhaps this significance may be discerned: the strait jacket of dictatorship does not lie comfortably on the shoulders of vigorous men. It irks those who wear it and those who see it worn. When he is given a free choice, even the man who has seemed patient under dictatorship prefers the easy comfortable garment of democracy.

And there is this also to be noticed: dictators, though they may begin with the highest zeal for reform as Jansen did, come to love power more than all the values for the defense of which they have seized power. When that has happened to them, they are no longer good leaders.

So, in the social experiments of Jansen, Illinois offered itself to the nation as a forum for the discussion of the comparative values of democracy and other ways of life. Not without violence, not without cruelty, not without injustice, democracy won.

CHAPTER TWENTY-THREE

The Cold, Unconscious River

THE "cold, unconscious river" is the phrase with which Mark Van Doren tries sensibly and yet imaginatively to offset all the unctuous love of the pathetic fallacy which has represented rivers as the "shining," "playful" friends of man.

During the thirties and forties, the people who lived along the banks of the Illinois River tried to think that it was their ally against hunger and need. They flattered the river and coaxed and caressed it as desperate men and women try to placate spoiled bullies. And a great part of the time the cold, unconscious river was quite indifferent to their needs and hopes.

In Peoria, for example, the newspapers wooed the river by giving it much publicity. The most prominent column of page one was devoted to its caprices of rising and falling. Sometimes the editor's comments were hopeful, as when he said in apologizing for the shrunken aspect of his paper:

". . . the Illinois River rising, we look for a heavy supply of printing paper by one of the first arrivals. Our subscribers cannot more regret our cramped and awkward sheet than we do, but if the elements continue to favor us, our former size will soon be resumed . . ."

Sometimes the fatalistic note of despair appears:

"Whether the January thaw will occur in the beginning of the next week and raise the rivers so as to afford us a supply of groceries, time only can determine."

When the groceries did come they were joyfully listed as a matter for public rejoicing: "10 bags of St. Jago coffee; 6 bbls. N.O. sugar; 10 kegs Dupont's powder." The last item was as important as the groceries because it helped to supply food.

But the most frequently recurring tone is that of resignation:

"We have not until this week been without some hope that the river would rise so as to admit the arrival of steamboats. The worst fears are now realized. The river is probably frozen over throughout its length and must remain so until spring."

Even when they were cut off from convenient access to the outside world by this inconsiderate behavior of the river, the people of Peoria tried to maintain a gracious and civilized way of life. It was not always easy. As one editor records with a candor that baffles the newspaperman of today:

"The first meeting of the lyceum was held on Tuesday evening. We are informed that very few persons were present and that from the absence of regularly appointed debaters the exercises were dull and altogether devoid of interest."

There were more successful evenings when the population got together for vocal and flute music. The editor tried to elevate the taste of the community by reprinting verses headed by such notations as this:

There is fine poetry in the following . . .

These lines occur in one of his selections:

. . . And they did feed upon each other's lips
So pure did seem their mutual confidence.
Perhaps their love was also pure. Who knows?

(It seems rather an odd question to raise unless the poet intended to answer it. Oddly enough, he did not.)

A curious effect of contemporaneousness is given the Peoria papers of the 1830's by such headlines as this:

"Prospect of a General War in Europe."

Other trials being many, the local booster could console himself with this fact:

"No portion of our entire state embracing an equal amount of population has been as healthy as Peoria. In the past year, there have been but six deaths, including two in a neighborhood, one to three miles distant."

When it was able to get through, the Illinois River Express Line in one period ran daily packets between St. Louis and La Salle. Among its boats were the *Ocean Wave*, the *Gladiator*, the *Avalanche*, the *Prairie State*, the *Prairie Bird*. In a gazetteer of the time, one of these advertised:

"From its superior accommodations, the well-known urbanity and unwearied attentions of its officers to the comfort of her passengers, heretofore, the traveling public may rest assured that the *Avalanche* will be the passenger packet of the season."

The captains needed other qualifications besides urbanity. Along the river were hangouts of thieves who murdered crews outright and carried their cargoes on to New Orleans. In more amiable moods these racketeers merely scraped the boat's calking, assured the owner that it was sinking, and then, while pretending to help with the rescue work, made off with most of the boat's merchandise.

The river early entered into the folklore of the people living on its banks. They told and retold the story of one Hugh Barr who in 1828 at Pekin saw the first steamboat coming up the Illinois and thought it "some infernal contrivance of the Indians to frighten or harm him." Like a hardy pioneer, he seized his gun and set out, his madly excited dog beside him, in pursuit of "the offending mystery." The pilot was unfamiliar with the channel and ran by mistake into one of the lakes. Finding no outlet he was backing out when Barr, ready for battle, began hurling defiance and abuse at him. It was with some difficulty that the crew succeeded in placating him without damage being done.

The people loved jokes about the river. A Peoria paper printed a long fish story of which the hero was a cook on the steamship *Peoria*. He used as bait a hog that had died on board, attaching the whole carcass to the stern cable by means of a meat hook. This unusual line was inadvertently left all night in the water. The passengers woke next day to find the boat being carried, stern foremost, downstream in spite of the engine. The cause was, of course, that an enormous catfish had swallowed the bait and was now hurrying home, towing the steamship behind him. Captain Keese, being used to such emergencies, got out his rifle and shot the catfish.

The editor seemed to feel it necessary to add at the end of this account the parenthetical notation "(a hoax)."

Evidence of the precariousness and meagerness of the life runs through all columns of the papers but is particularly evident in those devoted to advertising.

The Reverend David Page, with his lady and Miss Mary Boardman, announces that he will accept one hundred pupils at a fee of $4 for twelve weeks. He adds a little sternly that "no pupil will be continued more than twelve weeks unless his tuition shall have been paid."

Joseph Slough "respectfully informs his friends and public generally that he has returned to his old stand on Water Street near the steamboat landing where he will be happy to accommodate all who may favor him with their custom at reduced prices corresponding to the hardness of the times."

Miss Nancy P. Aiken finds it necessary to dispose of, at auction, six beds and bedding, one brass fire set, two bureaus, and other items too humorous to mention, including one bass viol.

There are constantly recurring variations on the theme of tragedy. The bursting of steamboat boilers is a weekly occurrence on one or another of the chain of rivers in which the people of Peoria were interested.

"We learn from Captain Barrett of the steamboat arrived on Tuesday from St. Louis that the steamboat *Corsican*, while on her way from New Orleans, was accidentally sunk near Memphis having on board 300,000 dollars belonging to a colony of Germans bound to Peoria. No lives were lost. The steamboat *Alton* had succeeded in drawing the sunken boat near shore so it is probable that the money may be recovered."

If it brought sorrow, the river quite as unconsciously brought joy. In celebration of the Fourth of July, the citizens of Peoria went on a moonlight excursion to La Salle aboard the splendid steamer *Altoona*. There was a fine brass and string band on board for dancing.

The steamboats also brought such famous people as Miss H. Irving and Mr. Neafie to play *Don Caesar*

de Bazan at the Peoria theater. The doors opened at a quarter past seven and the curtain rose at a quarter to eight o'clock. Miss H. Irving, the reporter thought, was "indeed a dream of radiance."

Journalistic candor did not abate during these years when Peoria was growing up. An obituary article on Benjamin Mitchell points out bluntly that, though he had early "acquired strong influence here," it had been "greatly impaired of late and his death hastened by his indulgence in the intoxicating bowl. Another warning to the 'temperate drinker,'" the editor severely concluded.

The Fair was one of Peoria's great assets. The Chicago press praised its enterprise in putting on so excellent a spectacle and added that its "citizens exhibited noble hospitality in throwing open their houses to entertain those for whom there was no hotel accommodation." Peoria, it further observed, "is about the second city in Illinois, largely engaged in the manufacture of high wines and can boast some of the finest distilleries in the West."

But during the Fair, the editor was "not aware that there was much more drunkenness than common."

He was pretty severe, however, with the farce of electing, as policeman, one Hays "who has since been so deeply intoxicated as not only to be unable to attend to his duty, but so as to need assistance of the calaboose himself. We dislike to mention these things too publicly, but it is time these evils were exposed."

Culture was already overtaking the West in the middle years of the century. The *Daily Transcript* contains an item about Mr. M. Fay, who came by steamboat from the East. The story, one suspects, was written by Mr. Fay himself. It noted the fact that, at the Fair, Mr. Fay had manfully competed and obtained two first-class premiums for engravings and lithographs.

"Such a man, with such goods," the paragraph goes on, "we must cheerfully hail to our city with pleasure and confidence. Not like those itinerant Jews who impose on the credulity of the public by importing worthless impressions from worn-out steel plates and bogus oil paintings. A good picture is mute but pleasing to contemplate and admire. A good steel impression will last twenty years, but a worn-out or forced one becomes imperceptible in less than two and of the latter quality there are tens of thousands lately imported for the American market. Therefore, if you wish to be gulled, pitch in."

People began gradually to lose any impulse even to try to flatter the river into good conduct. A Peoria editor in a mood of dull despondency admits:

"The River at this point is now about at a stage with sufficient water for the boats of the size usually employed here. Yet there is very little doing on the river now. We heard a river man remark yesterday that there is much less business to do than there is water to do it. There is usually a dull time at this season, and it has been made much more so than common by the money crisis. Dull times are these."

In 1857 there was revival of talk about improving the river. Everyone had his theories and wrote them to the papers. Peoria and Chicago had a mighty battle about such matters as dredging and introducing dams and locks. But they could not agree on what was best to be done. Chicago blamed the whisky trade at Peoria, calling it selfish and reactionary.

But the truth was that the river was no longer needed so desperately. The railroads had come.

CHAPTER TWENTY-FOUR

The Anonymous Great

MODERN man lives in the midst of the deafening roar of events. At the moment the clamor is particularly loud and reverberates through an unusually wide arena. None of us permits himself to get far from the sound of a radio. That is not difficult to manage, since our houses, our cars, our barbershops, our restaurants are equipped with the means of bringing oracular voices to our ears. We hear cities being bombarded halfway around the world as we dine. The defiances of governments are hurled past our heads from morning to night and only sheer willpower could enable us to be ignorant of what is going on in London, Paris, Warsaw, and Moscow. The cults which counsel serenity will soon have to begin teaching us the technique of preserving our inward peace within some fine iridescent shell of indifference.

But ours is the first generation that has been able to hear the capitals of Europe in the very process of inventing contemporary history and that has had the privilege of observing destruction on the screen only a few hours after it has been so righteously wrought. A hundred years ago in Illinois people could live on their farms in the river valley and be almost totally ignorant of what the movers and shakers of the earth were up to.

If you ask for the privilege, a library in Chicago will let you go through a shallow pasteboard box containing a dozen little diaries. Each of these tiny volumes is six inches long and two and a half inches wide and contains perhaps fifty pages. They are written mostly in pencil, and the spidery lines must be painstakingly and painfully examined under a magnifying glass. And in that box is contained all that a hard-working man of varied talents learned with the aid of a first wife and, after her death, a second wife, during fifty-five years of pioneering. There lies the sum of their energies, their hopes, their thinking, and their wishing. Your fingers can enclose the whole of the meaning that they found in the adventure of human existence.

It is immediately evident that John Montgomery Roberts was a superior sort of man. Though farming was to be his lifework and though he worked at it with an unwavering industry which finally gave him success, still he had the decorative interests of a man of imagination. He was an amateur artist who filled his diaries with notes on the technique of drawing and on the craft of making "crayens." What was better still, he filled pages with charming sketches of the country near where he settled. The passion for drawing did not desert him even when his hands grew stiff with labor and family responsibility narrowed his margin of leisure.

In late middle life he was still stopping, on his infrequent journeys, to make a roadside drawing of Kickapoo, or Knoxville, or Jubilee College.

He loved learning for its own sweet sake, and the pages of his diary contain such notations as that the deepest soundings were in the Pacific Ocean and that "the Dead Sea is the lowest body of water on the Globe."

Obviously, he was a reader. He had the habit of copying down the improving sentiments which he encountered in his literary adventures, especially the ones which squared with his own convictions. With Queen Caroline he shared this item of a credo about feminine virtue:

"I consider that woman to be most estimable who while she brings to the world all the charms of society, that is to say: taste, grace and genius, knows at the same time her reason and her heart against that insipid vanity, that false sensibility, that violent self-love . . ."

With great patience John Roberts copied the whole of a rambling sermon into his diary. Perhaps he set it there as a tribute to the excellence of the two women whom he married and both of whom he loved with a sensitive man's adaptability.

And yet this man, who was clearly responsive to the stimuli that a love of literature and of life could give him, went through a striking period of contemporary history and remained almost wholly unaware of it. The slave question . . . Lincoln . . . the Civil War . . . none of these critical problems impinges directly upon him or takes his mind from the immediate problems of planting and harvesting; marrying and burying; trying to preserve one's health and putting money in the bank.

These are the concerns of a daily life that was honorable and attractive.

Mary Wood Burhaus Roberts, the first wife, opens this brief family saga in the year 1831. She was not, poor child! the right wife for a pioneer. She makes her first appearance in the diary suffering from ague, and suffering variously she goes on from page to page. She has just married John when her diary begins. He is looking for a place to establish himself and his young wife. They settle at last upon a location near Bloomington. But Mary, whose vitality is low, cannot claim to be wholly happy. She misses her family and she touchingly confesses:

"I wished for them in vain but the tender attention of a dear husband in some means consoled me for the loss of those dear companions and reconciled me to my situation."

It was not a sentiment to elevate the self-esteem of a young lover. One hopes that Mary kept such lukewarm commendation to herself and let her busy John get on with his job, unhampered by knowledge of her neurotic longings.

Literature usually presents the pioneer woman as a creature of inextinguishable vitality. In our fanciful pictures of her she never stops defending her little brood against wolves and Indians. It is a poor day for her when she has not given witness to her possession of each of the rugged virtues at least twice over. It shames us for our softness and makes us wonder how soon the frontier would have had us whipped to our knees.

But neurotics existed in the prairie cabins. And Mary was one of them. She found her only pleasure in the display of her sensibilities. Her diaries tell almost nothing about the routine of farm life. Instead, she devotes herself to ladylike apostrophes, of an eminently literary nature, to the changing seasons.

On March 1st, she writes: "Welcome, welcome, delightful season when all nature seems to live anew, the trees which have been stripped of their foliage put forth new buds and are covered with verdure."

The coming of spring, she observes, may be compared to the spring time of life. And this thought pleases her so much that, just over the page, she repeats all her slightly Biblical phrases. Repetitiously the trees once more put forth buds, become covered with verdure.

When she was not occupied with writing innocent little prose poems to nature, Mary Roberts gave herself to the demure consideration of sin. One is sure that she had no model in John. Her eyes are on vague, unidentified miscreants who have heard "the syren song of vice and tasted her unhallowed pleasures."

While Mary thus occupies herself, John is busy with a round of duties in which he has the assistance of his father and his brothers Darius and Ambrose.

John's entries, all guiltless of punctuation, read like this:

"Darius killed an eagle measuring six feet eleven inches from tip to tip.

". . . raised Father's and Ambrose's house very dry great want of rain."

Here and there throughout the diary one catches most pathetic glimpses of the heroism with which these people faced the problem of trying to keep alive. The preoccupation with health, even in the mind of healthy John, runs like a motif through the book. More entries are devoted to it than to any other topic. Though all the people of the story have been dead these fifty years and more, it is still appalling to realize that they had to trust in such remedies as these:

"For vomiting blood take two spoonfuls of nettle juice . . ."

"For cramps tie a garter smooth and tight around your knee on going to bed."

In June, of 1838, Mary began to succumb slowly to whatever disease she had tried so touchingly to cure. With his usual laconic honesty, John writes:

". . . very warm fine growing weather ploughing out corn the first time Mary not expected to live long . . ."

Toward the end of July the struggle was over. John records simply:

"Mary W. Roberts died my Dear Beloved Wife with whom I have lived better than seven short years."

Then he remembers all the excellent sentiments with which Mary herself was so well supplied. He is ashamed of his bluntness. Like an echo of Mary's own voice come exclamations added not with any hypocrisy, yet with a forced accent:

"Oh, what vacancy! How doleful?"

In an access of earnestness, wishing to please Mary, he even remembers to put in marks of punctuation.

The pioneers never expected to live long alone and John Roberts followed the tradition of the time. A little more than a year after Mary's death, he makes the characteristically blunt entry in his journal: "Married Miss Ann Waters."

Between this entry on the sixth of the month and the next made on the eighth, the honeymoon has taken place. John's emotional nature has been quickened, and when he writes in his journal again he dares for a moment to express the wild hopes that can shatter even his reticence:

"Again commenced house keeping. . . ."

"Oh may my enjoyment be as happy as I anticipate. May our lives be wholly devoted to God."

The shadow of Mary, one suspects, still hovers over John's thought. Contentment in his first marriage was marred by his wife's combination of low spirits and high sentiments. He is wistfully afraid that something of that kind may happen again. And it is the memory of Mary speaking also when, having dared to hope for the compensations that earth can give, John apologizes for them by pretending to think only of heaven.

He need not have worried. Ann proves to be the best and most sensible of companions. The house is filled with children now. The sound of their running footsteps echoes through a record of family life that is multiplied in vitality many times over.

Ann's sentiments, unlike those of Mary, are simple, direct, and final. They do not fray out into vague generalization. She says what she means: no more, no less. She goes on a visit to Peoria with her husband and comments bluntly on the experience of the day:

"Sabbath evening came to Mrs. Cook's—went to church with her to a Universalis [*sic*]—most miserable discourse—contradictory."

Her resolution had to see her through many bad times. In December, 1861, she records:

"About a quarter to nine in the morning, my Ellen breathed her last." She goes on bravely to record the details of a losing struggle against diphtheria.

A few days later she writes with heartbreaking simplicity:

"The first Sabbath without my Ellen. It is so lonely. But she is in Heaven."

Despite the interruptions of tragedy, John and Ann made a good life for themselves. John worked hard and prospered. It must have been the boom in agricultural prices toward the end of the Civil War that gave him so comfortable a margin of security. He says nothing of reasons but merely records:

". . . went to Peoria . . . transfered 40 shares stock in Second National Bank to my wife Ann . . . deposited $750 in Bank . . . very hot . . ."

He need not have taken such scrupulous thought for Ann's protection. Her best security was John's energy. He survived her. Indeed, he lived long into the period of his children's maturity; saw them leave home in hope; saw some of them return in trouble; saw the drama of family life acted out in all its rich complication of detail.

On October 22, 1886, he made the last entry in his diary: "Frost and clear." It might have been a comment on the climate of his own old age. The hand which traced out those words wavered, but it could, nonetheless, bear down with resolution on the lines and make them stand out with a kind of aggressive legibility. Frosty his mind, too, may have been but it was still luminously clear.

On the next day he was dead.

He lived and died an unknown man, one of the millions of unknown men who have really made our world. His great asset was the unobtrusive courage which enabled him to live a long time and transform a part of the wilderness into a neat, well-managed, prosperous farm. Complementing courage, there was in him a creative vitality that seems to have been almost inexhaustible. He could work eighteen hours, deal strenuously with the problems of family life, and still have energy left for making little drawings of the world as he saw it. He loved "first nature and after nature, art."

Though he did not distinguish clearly, there were several elements in his love of nature. They included a spontaneous affection for a wife, devotion to God, and a tender sense of responsibility toward children. It is impossible to do more than guess at his politics; it is impossible not to recognize that he was a good man with a creative type of mind.

And in such good men we must still repose the hope of our civilization.

BOOK IV

And Even Now

CHAPTER TWENTY-FIVE

Barge-Line Sailors

Two and a half centuries have passed since La Salle first dreamed of making the Illinois River a highway of trade. The hopes of men who came after him into the valley flickered fitfully; flared up; then all but died out. It was in 1848 that the work of "little Cook" finally saw fulfillment in the opening of the Illinois and Michigan Canal, which linked the river to Chicago and the Great Lakes. For a time this waterway served the interests of northern Illinois admirably. But as Jesse Fell helped the railroads to ray out in every direction, commerce on the canal gradually dwindled and then stopped. Finis seemed to have been written to the story which La Salle started with such a dramatic flourish.

Then, suddenly, the tenacity with which a good idea clings to the collective mind of man was revealed once more. During the first World War a new necessity—that of moving troops quickly and efficiently—

suggested that the waterways might still be useful. Army engineers set resolutely about the task of making America's system of streams navigable. To the passive unruliness of nature they opposed new mechanized forces. Rocks that stood in the way of future traffic were blasted out; the caprices of the Illinois's "mighty crooked water" were sternly corrected.

Plans inspired by war survived for the uses of peace. It was not until 1933 that the Illinois Deep Waterway was completed and opened. For the first time the Illinois was thoroughly disciplined. A chain of locks and dams at strategic points declared man to be in control of the future destiny of the river. Chicago's diversion of water from Lake Michigan into the Illinois, by way of the Sanitary and Ship Canal, ensured navigability at all times of year.

Traffic on the river immediately revived, increasing from year to year in tonnage and multiplying even faster in value. The United States government, itself operating the Inland Waterways Corporation, opened the new facilities of the river to private companies. Today, a lively procession of boats moves up and down the Illinois. They carry machinery and manufactured goods out of Chicago; corn from the rich agricultural districts of Illinois; coal from the rich bituminous district. At St. Louis the boats exchange the cargoes going south for ones which have been brought up the Mississippi from New Orleans. Back up the Illinois the traffic turns, carrying sugar, sulphur, binding twine, lumber.

The vision of La Salle has at last been justified by the army engineers. Seen from the bank or from a bridge, the towboats which propel the cargo-laden barges before them look a little like determined sheep dogs nosing their charges firmly toward home. But, actually, mechanized efficiency leaves nothing to chance in the management of the traffic. Steam-driven capstans wind on their spools, first, "nigger lines" and, later, heavy cables which lash the barges into absolute rigidity. Four, six, or even more of these, strung out in double line before the towboat, must be maneuvered by skillful captains and pilots through all the difficulties that "slack-water navigation" makes numerous. Even on the blackest night the traffic continues and the navigator must know his stream as well as he knows his own living room.

The towboats are of several kinds. Some belong to the oldest and most honorable tradition of river traffic. These old-fashioned steamboats are, however, in the minority. Modern efficiency has generally succumbed to the attraction of the Diesel engine. Gleaming stretches of brass in the big boats mask the tremendous, but thoroughly disciplined power which gives them amazing agility. In a narrow lock the towboat with Diesel power moves back and forth, maneuvering its complicated string of barges into place and snorting all the while with what sounds like a gleeful assertion of control.

Making the best of two worlds, some of the boats combine the picturesqueness of stern-wheel paddles with the efficiency of the Diesel engine.

Traffic conditions also control the size and appearance of the towboats. Those, for example, which go into Chicago must be small and adaptable. The bridges there do not open because, for reasons of economy, the Army has preferred not to install the machinery to open them. The towboat must, therefore, somehow lower itself to get under these barriers. When a bridge is near, the pilot-house descends like an elevator.

"Subbasement," a frivolous member of the crew sings out as it touches bottom; "bargains in children's toys, hardware, and crockery."

At the same moment, the smokestacks dutifully fold over on the deck, making obeisance to the city.

The bigger boats which cover the lower stretches of the Illinois, taking the cargo to St. Louis, meet the smaller boats halfway down the stream. Usually near Marseilles they meet and there—it may be under the somber picturesqueness of an overcast night—they exchange cargoes. Then each goes back the way it has come.

Since the small boats must handle the same cargoes as the large ones, the former are of necessity less fast. But speed is no part of the contract with either. For the small boats the maximum rate for downstream travel is five miles an hour; for the larger boats, seven, or at most, eight miles an hour.

The traveler on a towboat must manage to reduce his tempo deliberately, for time seems to stand still. A string of barges, each 300 feet long and each capable of carrying a load of 3,000 tons, requires a tremendous amount of pushing, and impatience must be excluded from the temperament of anyone who rides behind them.

But the traveler on a towboat is not bored. He finds himself in a curiously engrossing world of men. It is a microcosm of human society with, of course, the important difference that women are excluded from it. But present in essence is every hope, every fear, every prejudice, generosity, shade of opinion that the human mind and heart have ever entertained. All this is dramatically evident in a crew of twenty-one men, divided by the traditional, hierarchical rules of shipboard, yet held tightly together by the smallness of their world. The captain has his place at table, where only he may sit. Yet all the men down to the newest deck hand come to the common table, where the democratic rule of equality subtly triumphs over the rules of rank and station. In the ribald exchanges of the dinner table, one barge-line sailor's dignity is quite as likely to be sacrificed as another's. It would be a foolish captain who would claim immunity from this leveling verbal sport.

All the strange and lively contrasts essential to the temperament of a barge-line sailor are embodied in a certain Captain Peterson of a certain towboat on the Illinois River. He is not large, as a traveler expects a ship's captain to be. Indeed, he is of less than average height—alertly, humorously simian in appearance. His deeply tanned face wrinkles up into a complex pattern of shrewd lines as he hides his pride of calling under a testy pretense to hatred of all capricious rivers on the face of the earth. He realizes that he is honoring an old convention of the sea in thus denouncing the inconveniences of the sailor's life. It is as though he wished self-consciously to claim for steamboating on the Illinois all the old and honorable traditions. He likes to think that he springs out of a history of uninterrupted brilliancy instead of being the recently adopted foster child of commerce.

A vein of wild, Rabelaisian poetry runs through his copious talk. None of his wit is borrowed from the stock of radio and comic strip. Each sentence contains a figure of speech which violently jolts the mind of a listener out of sluggish inattention. Until the imagination learns to accept these similes, borrowed largely from the field of physiology, it receives from Captain Peterson's talk one shock with every sentence.

Captain Peterson is ambitious, untiring, authoritative. Yet each of his qualities masquerades as something else and something less dignified than itself. He ridicules his ambition, making it seem to be fatuity; his energy is daubed with irony until it is made to look like drooling idiocy; authority walks his ship with an air of shrewish irascibility. But no one is deceived.

The captain represents the great American comedy of getting on without seeming to leave others behind. His pilot carries behind the austere mask of his fine face the less happy memories of a story that also is typical. Miller, a casual observer is able to see, has had no ordinary sort of history. He has the withdrawn manner of a man who is willing to ask no one to share his private tragedy. He speaks quietly and makes no effort to imitate the bluff comradery of the captain. Yet he is friendly and, toward a stranger on the towboat, he displays a tact which lends welcome support to hospitality. As one of the deck hands says, "You can't beat Miller for a gentleman."

He himself is on the towboat because the depression has knocked him unceremoniously from the comfortable position to which his ambition had carried him.

He was born in Kentucky and, at an early age, had worked on the boats. But he had not been content with the small and uneventful world of rivermen. A series of well-earned promotions in business had made him, at last, superintendent of a large district for an important coal company. His employer, the owner of a many-million-dollar concern, was a personal friend. The future seemed assured.

Then the costs of coal production and of distribution increased. Other fuels offered their rivalry. Industry contracted. At forty-three, Miller found himself suddenly, and through no fault of his own, without a job. Presently he was without a wife, as well, for crises in business and divorces seem often to go together. He had to begin again at the bottom of his world where he had been as a boy of fifteen handling ropes as deck hand on the boats.

But already ambition is stirring in him once more. He has worked his way back to the post of pilot and he looks forward to the moment when he may become a captain.

He is stubborn in his loyalty to what he believes. No mere personal misadventure can turn him from the principles upon which his career has been based.

"I have a better right than most men to hate capitalism," he tells the stranger on the towboat. "It bounced me up and it bounced me down. But I don't hate it. I believe in it."

The cub pilot also is a victim of the depression. He had once intended to study medicine. But the goal seemed dizzily high. Too much money was required to see that kind of program through and his indulgent parents were no longer able to help him. He became a wanderer. In New Orleans he had worked for a Mexican sculptor. From there, he drifted onto the boats.

F. D. Harmon must be unique among Americans because he has no Christian names. His casual parents thought initials quite enough. But the owner of the towboats has a different opinion. The cub pilot must, if

TRAFFIC ON THE RIVER HAS REVIVED.

Bohrod

ON OF LA SALLE HAS BEEN JUSTIFIED.

he wishes to be on the payroll, put a proper kind of signature to it. A great deal of time on the towboat is spent in thinking up droll names for F.D.

In New Orleans a movie scout had once urged the cub pilot to have a screen test. That news surprises no one on the towboat because the crew has already decided that he looks a great deal like Dick Powell. But F.D. was not interested in a screen test. Hollywood seemed to him an insane sort of place.

And at the far end of the hierarchical order of the towboat is the second cook. He is a delightfully confused creature. He allows the stranger on the boat to sit with him while he recklessly and wastefully peels vegetables for dinner. With equal recklessness he peels his young mind down to its naked prejudices.

Henderson has his name, in an exact copy of his own signature, tattooed on his forearm. That, he explains, is because he has been embarrassed in the past by the fact that in his native city he has a double who is "plenty tough." Sometimes the police have picked up Henderson, wanting the other fellow. It is convenient to have this easy means of identification.

Henderson's great love is the barge-line sailor's union. It has lately succeeded in raising his rank from that of "mess boy" to "second cook." The change has made Henderson feel enormously important.

But there are strange confusions in Henderson's mind. The union is good because it gives him increased self-esteem. The meek, he feels, have inherited the earth. But there are still social differences which must, in his opinion, be bravely recognized and firmly retained in the American scheme of things.

"What I can't tolerate about Chicago," he says,

allowing his southern accent to become broad enough to cover a multitude of racial prejudices, "is the way— when you go to a show—a big buck nigger can come in and sit right alongside of you. I like a nigger, but I want him in his place."

According to Henderson, Calhoun County in Illinois has the right idea. In that wedgelike bit of land which lies between the Mississippi and Illinois rivers, just before they flow together, a Negro may not set foot for fear of legal penalty.

The union which has made Henderson a second cook and won his enduring devotion thereby does not have the love of Miller, who must belong to it against his will, nor of Captain Peterson, who finds that it sometimes threatens to interfere with his prestige as captain of his ship.

Once his ship had been forced by an emergency of the moment to leave Chicago without a mate. Arlington, an earnest deck hand, had appeared before the captain to protest that this was counter to union rules. Captain Peterson had patiently pointed out that Blackie, the mate, had been obliged to remain in Chicago to get his name replaced on the payroll. If he did not he would lose a week's wages. Arlington was torn between loyalty to a fellow sailor and loyalty to the union. "I wouldn't want Blackie to lose no pay," he kept murmuring thoughtfully.

So in the end mutiny was averted. But Captain Peterson, if he ever has to face such a crisis again, hopes its leader will be Long John Silver armed with a dirk, rather than a deck hand armed with a copy of his union rules. The traditions must never again be made so ridiculous.

When the traveler among the barge-line sailors changes towboats at Marseilles he finds himself in the midst of another drama. A special set of circumstances have created a holiday mood on this second boat. An Illinois River boat has broken down and a substitute has been borrowed from the Missouri River. With it comes its captain, pilot, and crew. But since the Missouri captain and pilot are not licensed to navigate the Illinois River, an Illinois captain and pilot have been added to the boat's personnel.

Straightway the pilothouse becomes an arena with a local team and a visiting team matched in the display of their prowess as wits. The two captains vie with each other in abuse, morning, noon and night. In the brassy clamor of their struggle all claims on heart and mind die, except those of comedy.

Honors, the traveler feels, go easily to the Illinois captain. He stands six feet four, the great sturdy pillar of his body surmounted by a boy's head. The pleasant juvenility of his face seems unmarked by any expression except that of a vague drollery. The Missouri captain proves to be a dull fellow who can match witticisms only with woeful clichés.

He tries to restore his self-esteem by shooting (illegally) at the birds along the shore. They all escape as though they were the witty words he could not quite catch.

Coming on deck after he has slept, or tried to sleep, the Illinois captain complains bitterly of the fly that has ruined his nap. "That ole fly," he says, looking like a gigantic boy, "sure tickles when he crawls around your nose. Makes you so mad you wish he's big enough so's you could hear him holler when you stomp on him."

The feud between the two captains has chiefly to do with the supposed inefficiency of the Missouri crew. A hundred miles from St. Louis the Illinois captain endearingly observes:

"Those ole boys of yours they so slow, if one of them started to fall down right now, we'd be in St. Louis before he hit the deck."

These are the sons of river tradition. Their ways, their language belong to Denton Offut or to Lincoln. Though they are the products of the river's old age, after a long period of unproductiveness, they could not be more perfectly its creatures if they belonged to an unbroken succession of rivermen.

CHAPTER TWENTY-SIX

Local as a Turtle

A FEW miles south of the point at which the Illinois empties its waters into the Mississippi lies the town of Alton. As it is the end of a journey on the river, it may very well be the beginning of another trip of rediscovery through the river towns.

Alton has intimate memories of significant moments in our past. There Lovejoy lived and died and is buried. On the square near the river where the mob pushed the crusader's press into the water, Lincoln and Douglas spoke from the same platform in the last of their series of joint debates. A small patch of ground in the older section of the city is crowded with souvenirs of bitter conflicts.

Today Alton values these memories. It has raised a monument to Lovejoy in the cemetery. A bit of his press, rescued from the river, is on display in the office of a newspaper. If there are still those who wish that restless, demanding men like Lovejoy need never disturb the peace of community life, they do not say so in public addresses.

Like many another American community, Alton is a place of dramatic contrasts. Its physical look is varied, charming, and disturbing. Part of it lies close to the shore and the rest climbs up the terraces of the valley wall, reaching at last magnificent heights from which many beautiful, modern houses look down on the river. On the low-lying ground close to the water's edge are the communities called "Mexico," "Dogtown," and "Hollywood." Here men, women, and children live in dwellings slapped together of ragged, gray pieces of driftwood. When the river floods out the residents of Hollywood, they are received as temporary guests of people of their own kind living on the higher ground. When the waters fall, they go back home.

In Dogtown the houses of the Negro population crowd together with the air of cheerful fraternity which members of the race manage to achieve under even the least promising of circumstances. Here also is evidence of a nostalgia for other days and other traditions. In spaces between the rambling street and their own sagging porches the Negroes have gardens, the more ambitious of which are as large as the surface of family dining tables. In them they grow cotton plants, carefully tending the pink and yellow blossoms, priding themselves exuberantly on their success if they manage to make them live so far north.

Alton prides itself upon its Piasau bird. This is the painted monster of the rock with which the Indians used hopefully to try to frighten away white invaders of their land. Father Marquette saw the creature with its dragonlike body, its terrible claws ready to snatch and its jaws to bite. He dismissed indulgently the stories told by his fanciful Indian children of the pains that the Piasau bird might inflict.

To the antiquarian it would be impressive to see it still there on the cliff above the railroad tracks, if one did not know that the original was long since chipped away by a material company, much in need of lime and innocently unaware of its vandalism. Within the memory of the oldest living inhabitant, a bit of the claw still remained. But before anyone became conscious of a need to preserve the past, even that souvenir was gone. Now a public-spirited citizen periodically raises money to have it painted back, in gleaming colors, on the cliff somewhere near the location of the original bird.

The irreverent observer is likely to find it less an object of antiquarian interest than an odd bit of testimony to our native fondness for substitutes. In its aggressively gleaming colors, the Piasau bird looks like an advertisement for something. One feels inclined to look for a motto under the bird's claw: "Wear Piasau garters. They never lose their grip."

The citizens of Alton like to philosophize about the history of their community. A traveler's casual symposium may bring together the opinions of a genial editor, whose mind when it is nudged with a question gives forth remembered passages of many public addresses; of a contemplative radical, who reads Marcus Aurelius and Karl Marx while he waits for the loaves of bread to turn brown in the oven in the early morning hours at his restaurant; of an alert and intense spinster, who proves to be much the most realistic of the group. The editor points to the thriving industries. The radical thinks of differences between the way of life of the city's thirty millionaires and the way of life of so many of its 30,000 inhabitants. The woman goes briskly about the job of equalizing those differences by giving away her inherited wealth to many needy agencies of social welfare.

Together, these intelligent observers assemble the portrait of a community that has been curiously affected by its most memorable moment. The murder of Lovejoy postponed, for half a century, the industrial development of the city's resources. Many of those who had been unsympathetic with the abolitionist's views, as well as many more who had agreed with them, felt the shadow of Lovejoy's figure over their lives. They moved away to escape it. The citizens who stayed behind continued to resent him. Only now have they begun to make their peace with his memory.

It was not until the seventies that the interrupted industrial development of Alton began once more and then proceeded to boom tremendously. Because of the break in the normal routine of a city's progress, contrasts in its ways of life have been made peculiarly vivid. American enterprise, proceeding with uneven speed, has traced out a pattern of movement which leaves the successes and the errors of expansion unusually clear.

The stretch of country from southern to central Illinois which Joe Gillespie used to cover in three days of intense martyrdom is spanned now in three hours. And there on the prairie lies Springfield, "Our Town" for the entire nation.

Springfield has always been at peace with its past. The tendency of many of its citizens is to live still in the great days. They treasure the souvenirs of the

Lincoln period and feel more at home with their ancestors than many Americans feel with their living
cousins and brothers. "Springfield," as a shrewd observer
has said, "is local as a turtle."

It is not that the city has failed to show an interest
in both the conveniences and the oddities of our civilization. A five-and-ten-cent store now occupies most of
the block where Joshua Speed had his modest place of
business and where Lincoln had his law office. A movie
palace has replaced the show house where Lincoln once
saw Joe Jefferson act. Buses, instead of carriages,
"flourish" along its highways. And yet the town looks
as though it would not be in the least startled to see its
great man stroll abstractedly through the streets. Nor
would he be puzzled by changes in its appearance.

The same trees crowd into a shade over its highways. The house where Ninian Edwards once entertained his guests so magnificently looks still as though it
might at any moment become again the scene of a gay
party. (Unfortunately, progress speaks authoritatively
even in tradition-loving Springfield and the Ninian
Edwards house is doomed to disappear soon.) The frame
dwelling where Lincoln and his family lived fits cozily
into the landscape. It looks today as though descendants
of the Lincoln boys might come darting out the front
door to swing on the gate of the high picket fence.
There is no smell of the museum to the Lincoln house.

Because Springfield loves the past it has treasured
it gracefully. Modernity has learned the tact which
allows to the old its dignified place and does not permit
it to seem quaint and pathetic. The garish and blatant
vulgarity which makes the great metropolis—as well as
all the imitative, neon-lighted little towns—look like a

bargain basement on a one-cent sale day, Springfield has spared itself.

There are no violent contrasts in Springfield. Nearly all its inhabitants are connected with the state government and all of them lead the same sort of life. In street after street of tidy, modest houses, small cars stand before the doors, gardens flourish about front porches. Combined with these traditional evidences of middle-class energy, respectability and prosperity are evidences of a simplification of existence that suggests the Old World village. The whistle of the baker's boy sounds through the residential district; his motorcycle stops in the brick-paved street; he alights and goes from front door to front door, taking orders and making deliveries. Springfield has made the best of two worlds, helping itself to the convenience of the new and the attractive simplicity of the old.

Through its streets flows an unhurried way of life with which Lincoln and Ward Hill Lamon would have felt at home. Lincoln talked to just such crowds as assemble at the exposition grounds during Fair Week. The girls wear breeches and helmets in imitation of the motorcycle racers who are the pets of the celebration. They do their hair in the style popularized by the latest Hollywood favorite. Children munch at the mountainous pink confections which have become the symbol of dissipation throughout America. Small boys crowd about a racer showing the universal impulse of hero worship as the cyclist runs on, in maudlin, exhibitionistic fashion, about the sacred ecstasies of speed. Yet girls and boys together make up a crowd as different as possible from any that you would find in Chicago or New York. This is a midwestern crowd with nothing

surly in its jostling eagerness and nothing brazen in its
jocularity.

Ward Hill Lamon, who once ran a fair of his own,
would be comfortable among the exuberant corn-fed
youths, with muscles bulging under their short-sleeved
shirts and laughter bursting from their throats. They
crowd around the barker of a side show who is crying
up the lurid attractions of an entertainment inside.

"Revealing secrets too intimate to print," he chants
over and over again. "Too hot to handle and too cold
to keep."

Shouting jokes and making gestures at one another,
the experimental adolescents let the incantation work
upon them. They are hilariously skeptical. Indeed, they
know they are about to be cheated. But this is the time
and the place in which to be cheated, and they submit.

Even the throngs of travelers who visit Springfield
from every state in the Union do not alter its look of
being the perfect village. The place puts the spell of its
neighborliness upon them and they visit the memorial
parks, the Lincoln house, the Lincoln tomb, in a mood
neither too self-consciously reverent nor brassily indifferent to tradition.

Springfield is in itself an appropriate monument
to the unpretentiousness and goodwill for which Lincoln
is remembered.

Through green tunnels of high-standing corn one
travels, in August, from Springfield to Jacksonville. The
look of the soil is rich and all along the way there is
evidence of its generosity toward human effort. In many
an agricultural district, even in those which give signs
of prosperity, the spaciousness of farm buildings tends
to dwindle in the corner where the family dwelling

stands. But not here. The houses are large, well cared for. Clearly the fertility of the soil about which the early explorers of this land wrote home so ecstatically has not been exhausted.

Jacksonville woos the imagination with its look of serene antiquity. Few American communities, with actually only a hundred years of history, have managed to age so gracefully. The elms which spread their branches wide and high over the streets are partly responsible for the effect of dignity and of aloofness from the dusty struggle of existence.

But there is a psychological factor too. Jacksonville was, almost from its beginning, called "the schoolhouse of Illinois." It had a female seminary long before most of the world had been persuaded to accept the idea that females were susceptible to the refining influences of education. And here Edward Beecher presided over the destiny of Illinois College. Several generations ago Jacksonville settled into the measured stride, the contemplative habit of the academic spirit.

On the campus the original building still stands, looking in its substantial, red-brick squareness neither quaint nor out of place. It is now the headquarters for all the literary societies of Illinois College. Under its roof the boys and girls meet to read each other their essays, their sonnets, their blank-verse tragedies; under its roof also they have a certain kind of special benediction which helps them to keep their town completely charming.

It was in Jacksonville that Stephen Douglas, after his year of schoolteaching in Winchester, settled down to the practice of law. There he exercised his magnetic qualities on his neighbors and so won the first of the many offices that he was to hold and the title of Little Giant, which was to last him a lifetime. In the bleak little public square which deceptively masks Jacksonville's charms as one first approaches it, local pride points to an old structure said to have been in early days the boardinghouse where Douglas lived. It gives one nothing but sympathetic twinges of indigestion.

All the other structures associated with the past have become shrines of a more interesting sort. Jacksonville has been the home of many governors. The house of Thomas Duncan has been taken over by the Daughters of the American Revolution. Set back from a street where there are now many fine houses, it is half lost in the shrubbery. The trees help to obliterate its firmness of line. Its whiteness is no longer assertive. The building seems to be retreating quietly into time. It should not surprise the Daughters overmuch if they wake one morning to find that their home has without warning quietly disappeared.

The residences of Richard Yates, the father, and Richard Yates, the son, both governors, have been incorporated into one hospital; the estate of Colonel John J. Hardin, who lost his life at Buena Vista as a hero of the Mexican War, has become the setting of another.

And even now Jacksonville continues to be the schoolhouse of Illinois. Because of its very special tradition it has attracted to itself such state institutions as the School for the Blind and the School for the Deaf and Dumb.

Though some of Jacksonville's citizens are strenuously employed in the manufacture of such goods of use and enjoyment as creamery products, flour, paper, and cigars, they have inherited the academic tradition.

Most of them pass through Illinois College en route to their business occupations. They leave with its spell upon them. In the houses that they build and the grounds that they landscape its serene spirit is re-created, so that Jacksonville has the look of being one large, uninterrupted, and very beautiful campus.

CHAPTER TWENTY-SEVEN

◆ Further Pilgrimage

PEORIA looks down genially from her terraced heights upon one of the most charming stretches of the river. At its feet the Illinois widens out into Lake Peoria. Under a summer sun the surface of the water gleams with the metal of every kind of craft. From the lumbering towboats to the nattiest yachts, everything that is propelled by wind, steam, or the stout arm of man is represented at the docks of clubhouses along the shore.

When it despaired at last of winning the river to its use, Peoria did not turn away from it as a means of entertainment. Even on a weekday there is a jaunty, holiday look to the place as it is approached along the shore.

But this pleasant front only momentarily conceals the city's look of enterprise and resolution. Situated in the midst of fertile farm land, near important coal fields, Peoria could not manage to be idle. It is strenuously concerned in the manufacture of farm implements, hardware, boots, drugs, paper, and china. That list omits the product which has been in the past, and is once more, the chief source of its business—the manufacture of rye whisky.

The reputation of Peoria has suffered at the hands of comedians who achieve their effects through the familiar formulas for drollery. Its very name has been used to suggest all that is parochial in American society. Nothing could more clealy betray the parochial attitude in the mind of the satirist. For Peoria's history is peculiarly free from the usual evidence in small-city life of prejudice, bigotry, and narrowness.

Among its fine traditions it cherishes the memory of the great agnostic, Colonel Bob Ingersoll. Peoria was his home during the period when his striking gifts were reaching maturity. With his brother Clark he established a law firm that immediately became prosperous. Associating himself with leading democrats of the period, he was immediately accepted as an equal among them though he was then only twenty-seven years old. Peoria found his vigorous, masculine attractiveness irresistible from the first. He was considered "the hondsomest man in the West." His broad shoulders, auburn hair, keenly intelligent blue eyes recommended him to large audiences the moment he stepped onto a platform, even before he had uttered a word. When he began to speak, his earnestness and shining goodwill completed the conquest.

Peoria and the other river towns, where his oratory quickly made him popular, admired him also for his audacity. He was in his early career a democrat and, during Lincoln's campaign for the presidency, he took to the stump for Douglas. Once he was pitted against a leading Republican, Judge William Kellogg, who in his opening speech appeared to have demolished in advance any plea that the upstart politician might offer on behalf of Douglas. With a complacent impression of having won the day without a struggle, Judge Kellogg sat down.

But Bob Ingersoll was not the man to be so easily eliminated. He got to his feet and nonchalantly tossed a verbal bomb full into his opponent's face.

"The Fugitive Slave Law," he said, "is the most infamous enactment that ever disgraced a statute book. The man who approves of or apologizes for it is a brute."

He proceeded to describe the horrors of slavery and to fix upon Republican policy all the odium of strengthening its hold on American economy. Only Douglas's doctrine of Popular Sovereignty, he said, could keep slavery out of Kansas and Nebraska.

He had stolen the Republican's whole show—and a brazen steal it was, with very little of sound logic in it. But the West liked such impudent raids, such wild dashes for liberty when in a tight place.

It was at Pekin, Illinois, that Ingersoll made the first of the startling antitheological lectures upon which his reputation was to be based. It was ever his way to catch up the theme of idealism and make it his own before anyone to whom his unorthodox views were distasteful could accuse him of cynicism. In that first adventure into heterodoxy he declared:

"We are standing on the shore of an infinite ocean whose countless waves, freighted with blessings are welcoming our adventurous feet. Progress has been written in the very soul. The human race is advancing."

From that moment on, he allowed nothing to deter him from speaking out the ideas which were to make his name a synonym for some, of blasphemy and corruption. But Peoria, knowing Bob Ingersoll himself to be good, never permitted his abstract ideas to injure him. He prospered greatly and was loved for his generosity and goodwill.

When he became attorney general of Illinois his circle of admirers widened. He won an overwhelming percentage of his cases and his eloquence never failed to have precisely the effect that he intended to create.

When his unorthodox views threatened to limit his political career, he said:

"My beliefs are my own and I wouldn't sacrifice one of them to be President of the whole rolling earth."

Peoria never ceased to think Bob Ingersoll the smartest as well as the best man in the world. Understanding him proved to be an excellent training school in tolerance. When Carry Nation was flinging her hatchet about in every saloon that she could invade, Peoria had a humorous thought. Its leading newspaper invited her to become its editor for a day and to print whatever she liked about the city's favorite occupation, the manufacture of rye whisky. She accepted, and Peoria was amused when Mrs. Nation professed to see a sinister significance in the fact that workmen were not permitted to drink their product on the premises.

"What would you think," she asked, "of a dry goods concern that would not allow its employees to use what they make?"

After her evening meeting in the Opera House, Mrs. Nation was invited by reporters to go to Pete Wiese's saloon. She spoke at length to those gathered at the bar about "poor, drugged and depraved men and women." She saw, as she reports in her autobiography, "a large picture or rather statuary of naked women among some trees." She said it must be smashed. Mr. Wiese treated her "very kindly" and said, "it will be boarded up." Mrs. Nation firmly believed that he did so. When she went back to Topeka, Mrs. Nation was pleased to receive $50 from the saloonkeeper.

It is easy to believe that Mr. Wiese had profited by the tolerant and understanding spirit of Bob Ingersoll.

Peoria today is a place where liberal ideas and standards of thought prevail. It numbers among its citizens a newspaper editor, a librarian, and a bishop who regard their local history with a humorous insight and a fastidious concern for truth that is quite worthy of their fine, local tradition. It is a source of discomfort to such people that tourists who visit the beautiful little memorial park just across the lake from Peoria, believing it to be the site of La Salle's Fort Crèvecœur, should be so deceived. The view of the lake is handsome. The landscaping of the grounds has been done simply and with taste. The monument has dignity. There is absolutely nothing wrong with it except that it is not the true site of La Salle's fortress, and everyone knows it. The actual one is somewhere down among the railroad tracks. The commission appointed to place the monument reported vaguely that the attractive piece of ground chosen by them would be prettier and really more satisfactory until such time as the public came to know better.

Our native passion for substitutes still keeps tourists well content with the present arrangement.

A trip along the Illinois River, north and east of Peoria, is full of variety and of surprises. Traveling by water, one has often the startled impression of having penetrated into a deserted world. Only the lacy handi-work of bridges and of steel towers supporting power lines suggests the busy ubiquitousness of man. The greenery that crowds down to the water's edge seems to know no other form of life than that of the long-legged cranes wading near by. But in a car a traveler is never, for long, out of sight of the beginning or end of a village. A familiar pattern, of which hot-dog stands, tourist courts, and filling stations are recurring features of the composition, gives the landscape a cozy sort of monotony.

It is the jocose informality of American life that would seem most striking to a traveler unused to its tone. Even the highway signs find opportunities for puns and pleasantries. The leading citizens of Henry have not forgotten that their community once rejoiced in the possession of a lock and dam. Though they have lost those treasures now, they still proclaim to strangers, in the conspicuous lettering of a sign at the outskirts of the village, that theirs is "the best town in Illinois by a dam site."

The same cheerful readiness to make the best of all present limitations put upon prestige or upon am-bition runs through all groups of Americans. The deeply bronzed, pleasantly impudent boys who have helped to make a magnificent park at Starved Rock feel at no disadvantage before the world. They do not look or act like "the underprivileged." Each is, like Stephen Douglas, an American sovereign who presides over his realm with confidence. Exuberantly, they address gray-haired men as "Bud."

Rustic stairways, constructed by the CCC boys,

climb the heights where Tonty had his fortress and where the Illini tried to save themselves from the Potawatomi. Bridges and well-cut trails join the cliffs overlooking the river. A lock and dam by the foot of the rock has greatly changed Starved Rock's look of isolation. The army engineers have brought the atmosphere of busyness into a scene that even recently looked inviolably aloof. A steamer for tourists scurries in and out of the ravines exploring, in hourly trips, the settings of legendary dramas three centuries old. And onto the grounds that lie flat about the rock, motorcars pour by the hundreds on evenings when they become the scene of political rallies. Illinois has made itself at home on this historic spot.

Sinclair Lewis has said that Main Street is a highway that stretches through every state of the Union. It might be said that Tobacco Road is another such national highway.

Looking for the site of Father Marquette's mission to the Indians, for the actual land where he baptized them under the Virgin's banners, one comes upon the Illinois section of Tobacco Road. Near Utica a narrow path, so overgrown with bushes that it is difficult for a car to push through, leads along the river. Here Marquette landed and saw a pleasanter place than he would see today.

One passes the dismal huts of squatters. Heaps of garbage decay in the sun. A rusty bedspring completes a bit of sagging fence.

An all but unintelligible inhabitant of Tobacco Road points out across the fields and tells you in broken English, "All over! Much Indians! Much fighting."

He leads you to the spot where, as you learn afterward, Bishop Schlarmann of Peoria lately celebrated the mass in memory of Father Marquette's mission to the Indians.

But it would require Father Marquette's own high incorruptibility of imagination to "live pleasantly" on those fields today.

Leaving the river, pursuit of Illinois tradition takes one north through Freeport, where Lincoln and Douglas had their most important debate, and on to Rock River, where Black Hawk lived. To its charming scene he returned, in Lincoln's youth, to make a last hopeless stand for his race.

In a private camp on the river the late Lorado Taft created a monumental statue of Black Hawk in cement. Idealized as "the noble savage," Black Hawk looks down on the theatrically beautiful valley. Just at the point where his image stands the scene has all the sweet, subtle variety brought to a landscape by the little twists and turns of a stream, lying at the bottom of a deep-cut valley with wooded hills and open, sunny fields above.

Margaret Fuller once visited here. She had by that time "accepted the universe" and she found this corner of it worth pages of eulogy in her diary, and a poem besides. She spoke of a gnarled fur tree which still stands at Black Hawk's feet. She gave to the path through the woods the name it still bears, "Deer Walk." Nothing—she said, with that air of surprise which Americans then felt when they praised their own country—nothing in all Europe was more beautiful.

At Galena, in the northwestern corner of the state, a sentimental journey must end. The memory of Grant broods over the town. The humble house from which he strode through muddy streets, en route to the Civil

War, is still there and so is the more pretentious one presented to him by admiring neighbors when he returned a hero. It is well supplied with official flags, family Bibles, and such samples of Mrs. Grant's housewifeliness as a dish of fruit preserved according to a forgotten Indian formula.

More exciting to the imagination is the town itself, with its rare charm of unexpectedness. The streets obviously were never planned at all; they just happened long ago. Rambling curiously over the narrow ledges of a steep hill, they lead a traveler into many an impasse. One must travel the whole length of the crooked main street to find the opening which leads to the tier above. Then one must travel all the way back to find the museum.

The museum is worth finding. In Illinois there are many of these modest monuments to historical enthusiasm. Without any subsidy—in fact, with no money at all—this one has been created out of local pride. All its treasures have been donated. It has some valuable oddities, like the very bad painting by the very good cartoonist, Thomas Nast. It shows the surrender of Lee at Appomattox with all the figures life size.

But the most valuable thing it possesses is the spirit of its founder and superintendent. He is Richard Gear Hobbs, a native of Galena who, after a long career as a Methodist minister, has returned in his late eighties to embark upon a new career—that of preserving an important part of the American story.

He tells a visitor his family history and it seems to epitomize all the enduring courage and endearing buoyancy of the American temperament at its best.

His grandparents left New England, with a group

of hopeful young married couples, to settle in the West. They lived first at Alton. But things did not go well there and, when rumors floated down the river about mines in the north, they dispatched a delegation to investigate.

Encouraging news was brought to Alton at the moment when this particular pioneer grandfather had reached the end of his resources. He had accumulated nothing but debts and his household goods were about to be sold to satisfy his creditors. When they were gone he would have nothing. Ruefully regarding the pathetic pile of his possessions, a thought came to him.

"Someone will have to take them to town to be auctioned off," he observed to the sheriff.

The law nodded in agreement.

"You'll have to pay someone to do it, won't you?"

Again the law agreed.

"Then why not pay me?"

He bundled his goods into a wheelbarrow. The job brought him seventy-five cents. With that capital he went north to start life all over again.

Within a month he had "struck it rich" in the lead mines at Galena. Within a year he was authentically a millionaire.

He lived long enough to lose the whole of his fortune. But not before he had educated a daughter and seen her married to a doctor. It was this woman, mentioned before in these pages, who insisted upon being enrolled as a soldier, to go along with her husband to the Civil War.

Through that courageous woman's son one seems to reach back far into the history of Illinois. It is like touching the firm hand of America.

CHAPTER TWENTY-EIGHT

Shrine on a Hilltop

THE way to visit New Salem is in the company
of two young and very active boys, preferably boys just
ready to embark on their teens. They will scuttle and
explore and disappear and be recovered only after long,
exhausting searches. They will drive their guardians
close to madness or infanticide by laying unrighteous,
slightly soiled hands on everything that is sacrosanct and
untouchable. They will cast covetous eyes on public
monuments, obviously entertaining the pious hope that,
by the removal of a fairly fundamental bolt, they may
see the whole thing collapse into an interesting ruin.
Indeed, the door of the cell reserved for those who violate shrines would seem constantly to be swinging wide
before the guardians of such explorers of history.

But, in retrospect, the effort will seem worthy beyond almost any other resolved upon in a long parental
career. For the custodians of such unquiet, searching
boys will see that they are really seeking something, after

all. An extraordinary and a beautiful thing happens. Wonder breaks like a sunrise over minds that have long lain fallow. Ideas take root in unworked, but receptive soil. Souls that have been given over to a kind of surly, desperate contemplation of such dramas as those of the comic strips suddenly quicken to the strange excitement that an awareness of the continuity of history can offer.

I know that there is some sad process in childhood which dispels the clouds of glory that we are said to bring trailing after us into this world; there is something that chills infant wit and precocious creativity. There is also, thank heaven! something that thaws the mind at the first touch of belief in the richness and variety of our world. I saw it happen at New Salem.

For a long time the ghost of a town lingered on its hilltop overlooking the Sangamon River. Even after its inhabitants had drifted away, like Lincoln himself, to the greater comfort and convenience of other communities, the houses stood—empty, shaken by the winds that blew over the prairie.

In 1847 a traveler en route to Petersburg stopped at New Salem and found it desolate. "Once it was a busy, thriving place," he recalled. "What rollicking times there were some ten years ago! It is said that a horse race came off regularly every Saturday afternoon—a drinking spree followed, perhaps a fight or so, and at night those disposed took a turn at old sledge, or poker. But the glories of Salem have departed."

If he had returned in 1866 he would have found "one lone and solitary hut"; a year or two later, not even that. New Salem had completely "winked out."

But the memory of Lincoln made it live in many minds. He had walked out of obscurity onto the world's great highway of thought long before the last building had crumbled before the winds and the hands of vandals. People began to wonder about New Salem. It was there, they began to be aware, that Lincoln had learned all that was fundamental to his genius: belief in the wisdom of the common man; ability to speak that man's language and to make poetry out of his casual phrases; congeniality with that neighbor in all his ways, both the rough and the tender.

The artists came to understand that, if there could be a shrine to Lincoln's spirit, it must be on that hilltop where he had wrestled for fun, and bested bullies, and played with children, and tended store, and wakened to ideas, and nursed his ambitions in secret.

Excitement over Illinois's centennial celebration in 1918 greatly stimulated interest in the village. That concern had become self-conscious as long before as 1897 when the Old Salem Chautauqua was organized. In 1906 William Randolph Hearst purchased a 62-acre tract, containing the site of the village, and gave it to the Chautauqua Association. In 1917 the people of Petersburg, making gracious amends for having elbowed the town out of existence, organized the Old Salem Lincoln League. They brought old settlers together on the hilltop for the purpose of identifying landmarks. As part of a Centennial pageant, several of the old houses were restored. But these first efforts were regarded as unsatisfactory. Log cabins built on the sites of the Rutledge tavern, the Lincoln-Berry store, the Hill-McNamar store, and Dr. Allen's residence were torn down to be replaced later by authentic reproductions.

In April, 1918, the Illinois legislature agreed to take over the site and to maintain it as a state park.

In 1932 the work of restoration was begun in earnest. The result is New Salem as a visitor sees it today, a completed village, dreaming in the sun. It is as though an eddy in the flow of time had whirled the visitor back into the 1830's to show him a corner of the world that has not been subject to the effects of change and decay.

All the houses are there just as they were in Lincoln's time. You may step onto the covered porch between the homes of Joshua Miller and Jack Kelso and

all but see the two families of sisters and their husbands eating their meal together. Over the mantel of Jack Kelso's cabin are books by Burns and Shakespeare, the like of which the pioneer student lent to Lincoln. You may see in the houses of Peter Lukins and Henry Onstot the trundle beds for children which were pulled from beneath the great beds of their parents. You may see lying on the table in Dr. Allen's residence a pair of spectacles curiously equipped with adjustable temples so that every member of the family might use them.

In the Rutledge tavern a rough ladder with well-worn rungs leads to the loft where Lincoln slept along with all the other male guests. The large room downstairs has among its pieces of furniture the actual chair which is known to have been Lincoln's favorite. In the Hill-McNamar store in a desk with pigeonholes, an exact copy of the one which Lincoln used when he was postmaster of the village. The reproduction of the Lincoln-Berry store has a comfortably long counter like the one on which the young Abe used to stretch his great length to read of an evening, his ears resolutely shut against the boisterous clamor of the village life that went on about him. In a back room is a short and narrow bed like the one on which he used to fold himself at night. Stout ladies among the 1940 tourists climb onto a bench to look through a window into the intimacies of this chamber. They cluck their tongues over Lincoln's discomfort in that bed exactly as though they felt, in a sudden access of motherliness, that something should be done about it.

Though only ghosts live in these houses, the most scrupulous care has been taken to make the incorporeal inhabitants feel at home. In the various homes there are spinning wheels, and rows of bottles containing drugs with which to guard against cholera and smallpox, and kegs of whisky, and surveying equipment, and churns, and iron kettles, and pewter pitchers. Strolling up and down the rustic streets, the visitor passes the blacksmith's forge; the mounting block from which Ann Rutledge, who was always a lady, mounted her horse to ride sidesaddle; the well in front of the Lincoln-Berry store.

Experts have guarded jealously against the appearance of anything spurious in the village. The houses are for the most part built on the rediscovered original foundations. Deeds and legal documents have been studied to discover the size of individual cabins and, whenever possible, the arrangement of the rooms. The cabins, with their puncheon floors and walls, are of the more solid kind of construction which pioneers in Illinois had learned to produce by previous experience in other places. One is even able to follow New Salem's progress in the art of living. While the early cabins, like that of Clary's grocery, are completely primitive, the ones built later show the refinements made possible by the arrival of the blacksmith and other mechanics.

Every object placed in the cabins has been passed on for authenticity by a committee of austere and sober judges. If it is not obviously a hundred years old, its genealogy must be traced into the 1830's before it can be accepted. Among the articles actually in use during Lincoln's day are wooden benches on which Dr. Regnier's patients used to sit and wish, no doubt, that they were elsewhere; a sewing basket owned by Mrs. Samuel Hill, the aristocrat of New Salem; a whisky flask purchased at the Offut store, trunks, a chest of drawers, a footstool, two hickory chairs, and a hammer—all owned by the Hills.

It is not a mystical sense of the past that a man or a boy takes away from such an admirable, conscientious, expert staging of a great drama. It is a renewed and deepened belief in its actuality. Out of all the swinging of axes, plying of needles, and cooking of meals that went on in New Salem sprang the vitality that produced a fine spirit, one which contained within itself the genius of all simple, steadfast living.

Even the young WPA guide who shows visitors through New Salem seems to feel that he must speak for the realistic view of Lincoln and his life. He tells once more the familiar story of how Lincoln walked miles into the country to return the few cents that he had inadvertently overcharged a customer.

"But what I never knew till recently," the young man goes on, "is that when he got there he was invited to stay to dinner. He didn't do so badly by himself, after all."

Of course, he was invited to dinner! one sighs with a sense of relief. Always before, that famous anecdote left in the mind of the hearer a kind of rebellion. It has been told so often as though Lincoln had trudged all those weary miles just as an object lesson to posterity.

But, as told by the WPA guide, the story at last made sense.

Why couldn't they have told us in school that he stayed for supper, to share in the decent neighborliness of the time? Would it really have marred the moral of his delicate ethical sense?

My sons and I thought not.

CHAPTER TWENTY-NINE

Steamboat Elsie Preserves a Tradition

IN the old days there was a lock and dam in the neat, gingham-aproned town of Henry on the Illinois River. It made life pleasant for those who like to have a little stir of activity, now and then, to mark the progress of the day. People always gather to see a boat go through a lock, and there is much amiable banter between the men on the barge and the men on land. It is as good as going down to see the train come in. Indeed, the tradition is much more genial. It is obligatory upon the sailor, far more than upon the engineer, to express himself with charm and originality. Engineers on locomotives merely wave like superior beings; they are aloof and just a shade condescending. Sailors are wags and everyone expects them to make a good, conscientious effort at comedy.

So, when it was decided that there was a better place for a dam than at Henry, a social center was destroyed along with the lock itself. The dynamite that blew the cement structure to pieces crumpled something in the population living near by. One imagines them going about their daily tasks wearing the haunted look of people who cannot keep themselves from the expectant attitude even though they know that what they wish for will never happen again. Subconsciously they waited for the whistle of the steamboats, for that deep-throated, confident, yet gentle sound of command —the sort that a humorous, well-loved father knows how to make.

But one member of the community at Henry did not take her privation with the humility of her neighbors. Elsie did not like what was happening to her world and she proposed to do something about it.

To those who have the destiny of the river in their charge Elsie wrote a letter describing what the charm of life had been in Henry while the lock was still there and to what meagerness it had shrunk and shriveled now that the lock was gone. It must have been an eloquent letter, for back from St. Louis came the official order that all boats, as they passed the house of Steamboat Elsie, were to whistle in salute to a gallant spirit. Perhaps the officials did not say, but they must have felt, that she belonged to the Barbara Frietchie school. She would not let a fine thing die.

When I went down the Illinois River I watched eagerly for the small white cottage of Steamboat Elsie, half fearing that the romantic story I had heard might prove to be a legend. The spot was easily identified. In her yard, this land-bound lover of water has built a miniature lighthouse. Beside it stands a great wheel from one of the old-fashioned steamboats.

I felt a kind of tension as we approached. Traditions, I have always secretly suspected, wither at my appearance. There were great days just before I was born; great doings in a neighborhood just before I came to live in it; giants in the earth just before I arrived to occupy it. It would be my sort of luck to pass Steamboat Elsie's house just after the whistling order had been rescinded.

But for once I was on the scene at the right moment. The pilot whistled and there, in an instant, was Elsie herself, rushing as though to the shock of war. She waved across the railing of the porch, her black crown of hair bobbing excitedly up and down. Then she caught up a megaphone and began calling.

"Hello!" she said.

From above in the pilothouse someone answered, "Hello!"

"How are you all?" Elsie shouted.

"We're swell. How are you?"

"Swell! When will you be coming back?"

"In a few days."

"That's good."

I felt as excited as though I had been present at a great event. For somehow these banal pleasantries, shouted through a megaphone, had a greater significance than when spoken between two men on a street corner. They expressed, because they were intended to express, the mutual goodwill of people who are devoted to the same tradition.

When I was motoring back up the Illinois valley, I went to see Steamboat Elsie. She wasn't there when I first arrived. But her husband greeted me with the casual acceptance that people of the barge-line tradition extend to one another.

Steamboat Elsie's husband is a barber and she is a beauty operator. Elsie is licensed as a barber too. But nowadays she leaves that duty to her husband. They used to live in town and went to their river cottage only for weekends, holidays, and vacations. Now they live in it the year round. Elsie has her beauty shop in one corner of the cottage. Her husband still does his barbering in the town.

They paid $20 for the privilege of building on what was once a dump. All the labor of carrying away the rubbish and reclaiming the land beneath it they have done themselves. They have planted fast-growing trees and developed a fine lawn. They did all this because they love the river and want to be near it.

The house shows the nautical motif in its whole decorative scheme. The table lamps are ships in full sail. The pictures all bear witness to Steamboat Elsie's dominating passion. There is among them a fine photograph, taken from the air, showing Elsie's house and before it on the bosom of the river a steamboat with a fine big cargo.

High on the bank the cottage stands, gleaming in its white and red paint, as trim as a steamboat and as gay.

While we waited for Steamboat Elsie to return from town, her husband showed me all the treasures of her collection. These items are gifts from the barge-line men who know how to appreciate her enthusiasm. I saw the wheel with the marks on its handles where, in difficult weather, the old captains and pilots had put their weight to control the movement of the boat. They actually walked from handle to handle.

I told the husband of a Chicago newspaperman

whom I had met. He professed to feel betrayed because the boats on the Illinois River no longer have such wheels. A system of levers works more efficiently if less picturesquely. We agreed that the true lover of the river does not need to have his imagination nourished by such trifles. Nor does he demand that every pilot look like Mark Twain. The river and its tradition have vitality enough to produce new forms of greatness.

As we talked, Steamboat Elsie appeared. She is small and dark and quiet. About her love of the river she feels a decent reticence. She cannot dramatize it or exploit it. At first I tried to employ an interviewer's tricks to nudge her into expressiveness. My questions were intended to make her confess how she had come to feel so great a need to hear whistles. I wanted a romantic declaration about man's immemorial yearning for the sea; but I would have settled for a bit of personal gossip—some little anecdote, perhaps, about a seafaring great-grandfather who had visited all the romantic ports of the world.

But Steamboat Elsie was incorruptibly honest. Loving the river was just an idea of her own.

And finally I saw that she was right to be so honest. It was more dramatic and more touching that way. There she sits in her shop among the shining instruments of beautification, thinking of the barge line. Her patrons know that even the task of installing a permanent wave must be interrupted if there is a boat to salute.

She has become useful to the barge lines. If a steamboat's radio fails to work, Chicago may call Steamboat Elsie and ask her to give a captain a message. He is to stop at Naples, perhaps, and pick up a cargo of corn.

Wives of barge-line sailors go to Steamboat Elsie's house to meet their men or simply to talk to them through the megaphone. Everyone associated with the river traffic goes to see her, adds to her collection, picnics on her lawn. They feel for her, I think, that special respect which the craftsman feels for the good amateur; that the artist reserves for the collector who really understands the subtleties of technique; that the actor gives to the loyal first-nighter who can be counted upon to laugh and to cry at the right times.

Now, there is talk of making her lighthouse really function. It may be put in the official Light List. Then Steamboat Elsie will belong.

She deserves to, for she has labored with good sense and resolution to preserve a tradition.

CHAPTER THIRTY

The Poets Explore

WHEN the century was in its teens a group of young men began to change the habits of poetry. Its climate had been that of enervating warmth. In the drawing rooms of the well-bred, writers of verse had learned to satisfy the demand for elegance, choosing to forget that daintiness and anemia often go together. They rolled their tongues over peppermint phrases and ignored the world.

The new writers led poetry, not out of doors precisely, but behind doors from which it had fastidiously averted its gaze: those of factory and farmhouse; slaughterhouse too, and even the morgue. A chilling, stimulating dash of realism was flung full in its face and poetry, renouncing limp aestheticism, found that it could still stand up.

The men whose names leap to mind as leaders of this rebellion against the taffeta-cushion school of thought are Edgar Lee Masters, Carl Sandburg, Robert

Frost, and the late Nicholas Vachel Lindsay. The realism of Frost, though it was wholly honest and deeply moving, spoke with a New England reticence which distinguished it from the realism of his fellow rebels. He stood alone. The others were all "wild boys" from Illinois.

They were not actually young, if the youth of a Chatterton or a Shelley is to be set up as the standard of precocity in poets. These were full-grown men who had been out in the world and had had a variety of illuminating experiences. Masters was the eldest. At forty-five, after a career as a lawyer in Chicago, he began publishing volumes of verse. Lindsay had been a social worker, an Anti-Saloon League lecturer, a wandering minstrel peddling "Rhymes to Be Traded for Bread." Sandburg had been a soldier in the Spanish-American War. He had worked in a brickyard and a barbershop. He had delivered milk and harvested wheat, and washed dishes in hotels in Denver and Omaha and Kansas City. Finally, at thirty-five, he had become a newspaperman in Chicago.

Some deep-rooted impulse had prompted each of these men to seek out the people; to learn the pattern and the color of their thought; to hear them speak and capture the intonation of their voices. It was to the great mass of mankind that they addressed themselves, exactly as Lincoln himself had done before them.

Their identification with Illinois was very close, indeed. Masters was born in Kansas, but as a boy he went back to Petersburg to live where two generations of ancestors had lived before him. Mentor Graham, grown old, quarrelsome, and litigatious, still lived there in the

1870's and the memory of Lincoln hung close to the houses, the streets, the country roads.

Sandburg was born in Galesburg and as he walked across the campus of Knox College, carrying his pails of milk, he stopped sometimes to look at the tablet commemorating the fact that one of the Lincoln-Douglas debates had taken place on a platform reared against the side of the school building. Sandburg himself has somewhere written:

"I was born on the prairie and the milk of its wheat, the red of its clover, the eyes of its women gave me a song and a slogan."

Lindsay was born in Springfield and, though he wandered far, only his death separated him for long from its deeply shaded streets. He told me once: "I consider myself a citizen of Springfield and a guest of whatever place I may live in for a time."

Filled with this sense of belonging to the prairie, all three poets began to write about it copiously, ardently. They searched their tradition for its meaning and wished to canalize, in the fullness of its exultant tide, their own deep sense of its importance.

Masters was ever the most thoughtful of the three. Even in his early poems he intellectualized the theme of the past and its meaning. The bitterness of what he has called "this poor world's hopeless hope" crept into such poems as "Starved Rock." Masters told the story of the siege of the Illinois Indians and of their desperate effort to get water by letting down buckets which the Potawatomi destroyed. He concludes with a despairing application of the story's significance.

This is the land where every generation
Lets down its bucket for the water of Life.

We are the children and the epigone
Of the Illini, the vanished nation.
And this starved scarp of stone
Is now the emblem of our tribulation,
The inverted cup of our insatiable thirst.
The Illini by fate accursed,
This land lost to the Pottawatomies,
They lost the land to us,
Who baffled and idolatrous,
And thirsting, spurred by hope
Kneel upon our aching knees,
And with our eager hands draw up the bucketless rope.

This was not his invariable tone in remembering
the Illinois valley. Even in the *Spoon River Anthology*,
which contains his bitterest and most scornful indict-
ment of the influences which debase human life, his
voice rings out sometimes in sudden challenge to his
own despondent fatalism. In his epitaph for Lucinda
Matlock, he makes her remember with quiet contentment:

I spun, I wove, I kept the house, I nursed the sick,
I made the garden, and for holiday
Rambled far the fields where sang the larks,
And by Spoon River gathering many a shell,
And many a flower and medicinal weed—
Shouting to the wooded hills, singing to the green valleys.
At ninety-six I had lived long enough, that is all,
And passed a sweet repose.
What is this I hear of sorrow and weariness,
Anger, discontent and drooping hopes?
Degenerate sons and daughters,
Life is too strong for you—
It takes life to love Life.

Masters's restless, questing, speculative mind has made him many things in the course of a long career. He has been the savage realist, writing with scornful fury about the shocking experiences of life. He has been also the poet of nature, interested for long periods at a time in the most intricate of philosophic abstractions. The very breadth of his intellect, encompassing as it does so many interests, has made him seem less the child of his time than Sandburg and Lindsay. Perhaps for that reason the anthologists, looking for typical work, tend to pass him by.

But it is probably the note of personal anger in his work that robs it of some part of its claims to dignity and permanence. A broken private hope is betrayed in his recurring intonation of scorn. It appeared most inopportunely in his biography of Lincoln. Masters, as the son and grandson of Douglas Democrats, may have allowed to sprout, in some dark corner of his mind, a curious spite against Douglas's triumphant rival. But even that loyalty to Douglas cannot justify the belittling and ill-founded insinuations that appear against Lincoln in the book which he has made bold to call *Lincoln, The Man*.

Such traces of spite are particularly surprising in a writer who could bring such magnificent qualities of insight, compassion, and generosity to the problem of biography as Masters revealed in his account of his brother poet, Vachel Lindsay.

Though Masters has made so many confused, troubling, and contradictory interpretations of his Illinois inheritance, he possesses a thoughtful and subtle intelligence. His cerebrations are alight sometimes with anger, sometimes with tenderness, not infrequently with both. The uncertain light of his mind reveals in him that gift of chaos which George Russell (AE) thought good for poets.

Lindsay wrote always out of the warm faith in the democratic tradition which he was still hugging close even when personal disappointment drove him into retreat from life and finally to suicide. His life was one of violent shocks. The beginning of the World War, for example, disturbed his sense of close identification with all mankind. He imagined how this bitter disappointment in the progress of human hope would rouse Lincoln's spirit.

> He cannot sleep upon his hillside now.
> He is among us:—as in times before!
> And we who toss and lie awake for long
> Breathe deep, and start, to see him pass the door.
>
> His head is bowed. He thinks on men and kings.
> Yea, when the sick world cries, how can he sleep?
> Too many peasants fight, they know not why,
> Too many homesteads in black terror weep.
>
> The sins of all the war-lords burn his heart.
> He sees the dreadnaughts scouring every main.
> He carries on his shawl-wrapped shoulders now
> The bitterness, the folly and the pain.

Something of the fervor of the religious fanatic got into Lindsay's poetry. He beat the drum for faith in man's destiny like an earnest lieutenant of the Salvation Army. He invented ballads to be sung to the old hymn tunes which were an important part of his own cultural heritage.

But his wanderings had opened his eyes to the hard actualities of American life as well as to what remained for him its radiant hope. He protested:

Let not the young souls be smothered out before
They do quaint deeds and fully flaunt their pride.
It is the world's one crime its babes grow dull,
Its poor are ox-like, limp and leaden-eyed.
Not that they starve, but starve so dreamlessly,
Not that they sow, but that they seldom reap,
Not that they serve, but have no gods to serve,
Not that they die, but that they die like sheep.

He was a troubled troubadour going about the world reciting his rhymes with unwavering enthusiasm but getting little bread in return. It was important to him that he should get his photograph in the papers because that meant the possibility of extending the audience for his gospel of beauty. He faced the camera with a strange mixture of arrogance and placative slyness. He talked to interviewers about his distaste for women's clubs, because he depended on women's clubs for bounty. And in the end this snarl of contradictions—love of beauty, fear of indifference to beauty; faith in destiny, dread of tomorrow; eagerness for the welfare of mankind, panic about his personal responsibilities—closed about him, taking his mind and spirit captive.

Society will justify his faith, in its roundabout way, by valuing his ballads for a long time and by listening often to the curious ingenuity with which he gave a booming orchestration to his themes.

Both Lindsay and Sandburg acknowledged their debt to the Lincoln tradition by becoming, like Lincoln, entertainers. Sandburg is a familiar figure everywhere in America today. He has traveled back and forth across the country, letting his friends know of his prospective arrival in the sly message:

"Pretty boy coming with guitar . . ."

His is surely one of the most memorable faces of our time. Sandburg looks as though he had been carved out of granite. As he sits on a platform strumming his instrument, singing the songs of the South and the West, of the plantation and the mountain and the harvest field, he seems the fine rugged embodiment of all those profound simplicities of life which give themes to ballads.

Of all the Illinois poets, Sandburg has most effectively paid tribute to his inheritance. Sandburg's volumes tracing the Lincoln history from beginning to close represent one of the finest achievements of our contemporary literature. These big books are put together not out of great solid blocks of theorizing and generalization. Though the portrait is of heroic size, the artist's touch is fine. Delicate strokes high-light the color of the personality.

One marvels at the patience with which such a mass of detail has been brought together. The work is always that of a poet who can make a great truth shine out of a casual phrase.

The characteristic intonation of Masters's work is that of bitterness which sometimes becomes strident with scorn. The characteristic quality of Lindsay's voice was that of breathless expectancy. An almost unbearable excitement pounded through all his work.

The intonation of Sandburg is neither scorn nor expectancy. It is less eccentric than either and perhaps less personal. He has done what Lincoln did: made his artist's mind the repository of the wit of the people. Sandburg receives the rich ore of the thought and speech of everyday life, refines it into gold, turns it into poetry.

Perhaps it is no coincidence that three of the strongest voices heard in the early years of America's poetic renascence came out of Illinois. These men were the inheritors of a tradition of freedom and they have used their skill to give the people's thought clear utterance. They have drawn attention to the needs and the hopes of the worker. Their own hope has been to keep the new generation from multiplying many times over the tragedy, recorded by Masters in *Spoon River Anthology*. It is Abel Melveny to whom Masters gives the reflection:

> I saw myself as a good machine
> That life had never used.

STEAMBOAT ELSIE CAUGHT U

PHONE AND BEGAN CALLING.

CHAPTER THIRTY-ONE

Miss Fleming Remembers

O NE of the pleasantest things about being in search of the past is that everyone wishes to help you find your way. Any other service to what must hopefully be called literature is a lonely business. A writer ordinarily goes about looking dazed and preoccupied. His neighbors are sure that he is vaguely insane and wish that he could manage to be less conspicuous about it.

But it is different with the task of tracing out the pattern of the old days. Everyone is eager to guide the hand that gropes for this design.

There is a generous woman living in Marseilles, on the banks of the Illinois River. She and I have had long conversations on paper, all about orchards and preachers and family life in early Illinois. Her memory, through that of her father and mother, reaches deep into the past century. Many of those memories have directly to do with the river.

Laura Fleming has seen the river give of serenity

and beauty and prosperity. She has seen it take away in its moments of caprice. But still it is her river by virtue of the love she has felt for it, and she wishes to have its charms correctly understood.

She remembers how her maternal grandfather, Thomas Harrington, came to Illinois from England. He had stopped in New York State long enough to build a house for his parents and to acquire a wife for himself. Then his youthful impetuosity prompted him to bundle young wife, infant daughter, and a chest of books from England into a covered wagon and to strike out for the West.

With a bookman's reckless enthusiasm, he lent his library to the men in Marseilles who were working on the Illinois and Michigan Canal. There was just one honest man among his friends. This nameless gentleman returned a bound copy of the twelve issues of the *Westminster Magazine* for the year 1781. The rest of the library went into that limbo to which unreturned books are assigned.

Thomas Harrington did not live long to brood over his loss. Within a year of his arrival in Illinois the river had taken him. As he was crossing to his tannery on the south bank, his boat capsized in the swollen water of spring and he was drowned.

His young widow, left with a child to rear, went from house to house spinning, weaving, and even making shoes. There was no money with which to pay for such services, and Mary Harrington took whatever she was offered in exchange for her labor. When she married a second time, her courage, industry, and thrift had brought together a fine dowry of cows, heifers, sheep, chickens, ducks. Solyman Bell, her new husband, received with proper gratitude herself, her six-year-old child, and all her entourage of livestock.

Miss Fleming remembers how her paternal grandfather, John Fleming, took his family hopefully to Illinois and how he saw his hope collapse almost on the instant of arrival. Exposure and overexertion killed him, and his wife was left on the banks of the Illinois River to make her way alone. Neighborliness runs through the symphony of pioneering like a gracious melody. It was Solyman Bell who assumed responsibility for the bewildered Flemings.

Nathan, the eldest son, had stayed behind in Pennsylvania. He was getting on well as manager of a potash factory. The job paid $6 a month, and no enterprising young man could afford to give up such an opportunity. Yet when he heard of his mother's plight, Nathan forgot everything else. He put a month's wages in his pocket and, with all of his possessions on his back, set out to find his family. He had covered five hundred miles before he reached them, five hundred miles of dazzling snow and bitter weather. The whole distance had been trudged on foot. He was snow blind when he reached the river, and his eyes troubled him long after.

Still through the family records, Miss Fleming remembers how Nathan, at eighteen, and his brother Isaac, at sixteen, worked for Mr. Bell to earn a living for his mother and the younger children. When he had an opportunity Nathan bought land of his own in the first "canal sale." He worked his farm for five years and then the gold fever seized him. But he made no fortune in the Far West and finally, at the age of thirty, he felt himself drawn back to his land on the banks of the river.

He married young Mary Harrington in the year

after his return. Thereafter he was never far from the river. He did allow himself to be lured off to a job as a bookkeeper at Ottawa. But presently he was back at farming again within sight of the water, first on his own bit of land and later on the large tract belonging to Solyman Bell. He lived to be ninety and it seemed to be his sympathy with river ways that kept him strong to

the end. His wife drew the same sort of vitality from her love of the land by the river. At eighty-four she, like Lucinda Matlock, had "lived long enough, that was all."

Miss Fleming remembers many charming things about those river ways. She remembers how the whole family would go to fish on its banks. The mother and the younger children would sit with poles in their hands through a whole Saturday afternoon. The father and the older boys would join them when the farm work was done and dusk was falling and the whippoorwills were beginning to call.

She does not forget the river in its moments of imperious grandeur. When the ice broke up in the spring, cakes almost as big as a house would come crashing out of the creek. They plunged and lunged through the willows, carrying everything before them.

Once in the fall some horses were marooned on a bit of land that was cut off by the caprice of the river, and the Flemings had to wait until the water had frozen before the animals could be led safely across. Even then straw had to be thrown on the ice, and the frightened horses complained and tossed their heads and threw out clouds of protest from their steaming nostrils.

The image is still clear to Miss Fleming of her father standing at the kitchen window tirelessly studying the beauty of the river as it rounded the point, glad that he had returned to it from far wanderings.

And the whole life of a child there by the river seemed good. Even the schoolhouse was within sight of the water. Miss Fleming's mother was a director of the school (long before the day of women's rights!). She boarded the teacher, feeling that one more mouth to feed, along with the five of her sons and the two of her daughters made no further trouble worth considering. The neighbors had the same feeling about the Fleming household. There were already so many people under the roof that there might as well be more. So it was in Nathan Fleming's house that cards were played and square dances danced on many a Saturday night.

Miss Fleming remembers about the work of the farm by the river. There were no fences, in that time, except those made of boards and of hedges. These were easy to break through and the Fleming boys used to laugh and say that they had to be live fences for the stock.

Nathan Fleming sent a hundred head of cattle to Chicago each fall, and a carload of hogs too. Before husking, he butchered a "porker" and sometimes a sheep. In December, the family appetite called for beef. One would be strung up in the crib, and Miss Fleming's mother would take a son's hand and guide it in the sawing off of a large piece for the roast. The family democracy gave each member a job to do. The boys were put to work as soon as they were able to reach the handles of a corn plow. The initiation of the girls began in their mother's vegetable garden. Miss Fleming remembers that often there were six kinds of vegetables on her mother's dinner table and not a morsel left of any dish when the meal was over.

And she remembers Solyman Bell's orchard of five hundred trees. The Fleming young could scarcely be persuaded to wander far from it in the times of its yielding. The apples had fine names: the *Maiden Blush*, the *Northern Spy*, the *Bellflower*, the *Winesap*. Miss Fleming remembers a time when the cellar was so full of apples that there was no room for a load of *Russets*. They were buried in the ground with a covering of straw, and in the spring they were delicious.

She remembers how the provident lived in a small river town fifty years ago. Her father was vice-president of the bank and assessor for the township. He had business interests of a dozen kinds that kept him often away from home. So it was his wife who ran the farm and in odd moments raised, each season, six hundred chickens as well as ducks and geese and turkeys. Yet the burden of these duties did not dissuade her from indulging in the luxury of a flower garden where there were tulips and bleeding hearts and lilacs and syringa. She stood in it at evening and forgot the turbulence of domesticity—all the managing and mending and weeding and feeding. Life for a moment was concentrated in a scent from a garden and a glimpse of a river.

People with long memories like catalogues. Miss Fleming remembers the horses: Old Dock, Baffel, Kate, and Kit. Queen was a sorrel and Clipper a chestnut. They were fine racing horses. Miss Fleming remembers triumphantly: "When we got them to racing, we were in it."

There was a great parade of preachers along the Illinois River. The important ones, like Edward Beecher, had a mighty chorus of competition in the towns. Men like the "Reverend Martin" held revival meetings for the sheer love of the work, riding on horseback from his farm to any near-by community that seemed to be in need of exhorting. Miss Fleming remembers the "Reverend Agard" who "doubtless had his place in the world" but who "wore a plug hat and kid gloves which was too much for homespun people." In her ears still rings the echo of the Reverend Daniel Young's mighty voice. About his sincerity there could be no doubt, but "he was chiefly noted for the strength of his lungs."

And now as she sits remembering all that she has seen, Miss Fleming wonders if the men who have wished to improve the river have really served its interests. Her doubts escape into verse. She recalls the days of her childhood when:

Deep and dark thru the valley scene
The river rolls mid shimmering green . . .

Then man saw the possibility of the river as a deep waterway. So they treated it to all kinds of indignities. "Huge blasts shook her bosom . . . they took her dear rocks away . . ." Now the big boats do "pass up and down on her waters." But those who loved the river in the time of man's innocency, before it was possible to change the whole look and character of land and water, listen in vain "for the whippoorwill's low pleading in the marshy place."

With the new greatness, something of the old world's charm has been lost.

CHAPTER THIRTY-TWO

The Struggle for Water

HUMAN life, in the simple and idyllic dream which almost everyone secretly treasures, is reduced to a pattern of fundamental needs. A man must have land on which to live, to build a dwelling, to raise his food. He must have a companion to share his little stronghold against the world. He must have water with which to quench his thirst and cultivate his garden.

As the design of a society becomes more and more complicated, the satisfaction of those needs becomes more complicated too. Conflicts arise out of the struggle to achieve satisfaction. But still the things that man must have, whether his interests are identified with a unit as small as the family or one as big as a nation, are simply food, security, love, and water.

Ever since the turn of the century the Middle West has been involved in a great family fight over water. The struggle began with a problem which may have seemed, in the beginning, private and personal to the city of Chicago. The rapid growth of that community suddenly made it necessary for the citizens to safeguard health by finding a new method of disposing of sewage. Determined to achieve their objective as inexpensively as possible, the city fathers were pleased with a plan devised by engineers. It was to reverse the course of the Chicago River, which once flowed into Lake Michigan but could be made to flow the other way, flushing sewage through its waters out of the city and into a sanitary canal. The canal, linked to the Des Plaines River, would dispose of waste at last in the Illinois River.

Those who conceived the plan were doubly pleased with it. Two purposes were served simultaneously. The second of these was the creation of a waterway link between Chicago and the Mississippi River. In the days of the explorers there had been tedious portages between Chicago and the headwaters of the Illinois. But according to the scheme of the engineers—with the Chicago River told peremptorily to about-face, with a canal dug, with the navigability of the Upper Illinois artificially improved—Chicago could make its way, comfortably and swiftly, to the Mississippi.

The success of the whole plan, of course, depended upon the diversion of water from Lake Michigan. Chicago applied to the secretary of war for permission to take what she needed; a permission was granted with this limitation: no more than 4,167 cubic feet per second were to be diverted.

Chicago appears to have thought blithely that no one could really care if she helped herself to twice that much. Withdrawal amounted to 8,500 feet or more when, at last, the states bordering on the Great Lakes became alarmed for their own interests. Fear that the level of all the lakes might be lowered, to the serious disadvantage of navigation, prompted a formal complaint to the federal government.

Fights of this kind inspire eloquent men to the utterance of many proud, angry, and urgent words. But they are slow and majestic affairs, despite all this show of eagerness. As early as 1903 many observers were buckling on their verbal armor and preparing for a struggle. In 1908 litigation first began in the courts. It remained there continuously for twenty years before any definite decision could be reached. In 1913 the government's case was simplified in the hope of hastening a solution. But still another ten years were to elapse before the federal government won a victory. During part of that time, Judge Kenesaw Mountain Landis, then on the Federal District bench, held the matter firmly "under advisement." In the end, when baseball beckoned him beguilingly away from such troublesome problems, he passed the case on undecided to his successor who, very promptly, gave a decision in favor of the federal government.

There was still an appeal to the Supreme Court, and that maneuver consumed another six years. Charles Evans Hughes, at that time not on the bench, was appointed by the Supreme Court as special master in chancery to review the case. In January, 1929, Chief Justice Taft read the decision, which held that Chicago had been lawfully authorized by the secretary of war to make the diversion of water from Lake Michigan but that "in increasing the diversion from 4,167 cubic feet per second to 8,500 . . . the drainage district defied the authority of the National government. . . ."

The court announced its duty "by an appropriate

decree to compel the reduction of the diversion to the point where it rests on a legal basis and thus to restore the navigable capacity of Lake Michigan to proper level."

Once more the problem was referred to the special master to determine the form of the decree, and the final decision was that Chicago must gradually reduce its diversion to 5,000 cubic feet per second by the year 1935 and to 1,500 cubic feet per second by the end of 1938.

But the Middle West could not be expected to renounce so pleasant and invigorating a family quarrel just because the Supreme Court had, at long last, reached a decision. The sounds of battle and dispute have gone on ever since.

In every phase of the struggle the sly and not-unattractive ingeniousness of the human mind has been evident. The Sanitary District of Chicago, in a bill of exceptions and objections to the Hughes report, warned the Great Lakes states—"more in sorrow than in anger" —that they faced a serious problem if Chicago were to divert less water than she had been taking. Lake levels, Chicago said, were steadily rising, not falling. If the protection offered by the diversion from Lake Michigan were withdrawn, riparian rights, docks, wharves, piers, and similar structures would inevitably be damaged.

Power interests on the Great Lakes were unimpressed by this argument. Canada rushed into the dispute, bringing the excitement of international conflict to what had been merely a family fight. In America the view prevailed that this was in no wise a matter of controversy between friendly countries. In the treaty with Canada governing boundary waters, acquiescence in the diversion at Chicago had been bought at a definite price, that of permitting Canada to take, for power purposes at Niagara Falls, a great deal more water than America took. Still, excitable patriots in Canada cried out that, if Chicago would not give redress, there was no place to go but "to the foot of the throne." Loving the sound of his own voice, one such orator screamed lustily: "Surely, the prayers of ten million people will be heard. We should apply to his Majesty and we will . . . get the balance of our right."

America answered, without the aid of a tremolo, that the midwestern states, which alone had a population greater than that of all Canada, were under the imperative necessity of opening up water routes to the ocean. If eastern Canada persisted in holding up the possibility of a waterway, via the St. Lawrence River, the Middle West must turn, with redoubled energy, to the project of completing a Mississippi system.

As is quite permissible in such struggles, the Great Lakes states fought now on Chicago's side, now as her opponent. When Chicago seemed to "secede" from the Middle West by joining with New York in its opposition to the St. Lawrence waterway, the voices of many neighbors were raised in protest. Yet, whenever the suggestion has been made that Chicago should not be allowed to divert enough water to maintain the navigability of the Illinois River, the neighbors have executed a prompt volte-face. The tone of the discussion has become sweetly reasonable as Chicago is asked to admit that the army engineers are right in saying that the amount of water allowed by the court is sufficient to maintain Illinois River navigation.

And the fight still goes on.

Congressmen from Illinois have even now as one of their favorite projects that of increasing the amount of water that may be legally diverted from Lake Michigan. Sadly, they say over and over again that 1,500 cubic feet per second is far from being enough; that 5,000 feet would not be too much. The Great Lakes states still dissent. Their attorney generals come together at the first indication of difficulty, shouting with unabated vigor. Canada, too, is ready to be righteously indignant on the slightest provocation. The tremulous harmonies and vigorous dissonances of the dispute may be expected once more to sound loud and clear on the American air.

If the amount of attention that the Illinois River receives is to be taken as a measure of its security, the future is bright. For it is certainly not neglected. The barge line of the Inland Waterways Corporation, operated by the federal government, has been profitable. It is to be sold to private enterprise in the belief that it may be made more active still. The whole of the Middle West, no matter what may be its quarrel with Chicago, wants and expects to use this access to the sea, just as La Salle dreamed, so long ago, that his midland empire might use it.

In its somnolent persistence, the Illinois flows on. Man has created a strenuous and varied drama on its shores. There have been shouts of battle and moans of desperation. In the midst of this flurry of excitement and egotism, the dweller on the banks of the Illinois has often been inclined to dramatize his relationship to the river. He has tried to woo it, to placate it. When such attentions have failed, he has cursed it.

Man, the stubborn sentimentalist, has to teach himself over and over again that there are no moral virtues in nature. Rivers have only beauty and usefulness. The Illinois has its share of both. Quite recently its usefulness has been made greater than ever.

Those who are interested in its future should be comforted to remember that the Illinois survived the glacial melodrama and held to its course. On the present level of its usefulness it can probably be counted upon to outlast the time of man.

Acknowledgments

A study of the Illinois country must begin with the comprehensive *Centennial History,* published by the Centennial Commission in 1922 to celebrate one hundred years of statehood.

That proves to be a surprisingly pleasant way of embarking upon a project, for the whole work has been done not only with scholarly thoroughness but with literary distinction. With one's appetite thus whetted it is delightful to find that other Illinois records are lively and stimulating.

The admirably edited *Illinois Historical Collections* take one back to sources in the form of explorers' journals, governors' letter books, distinguished citizens' diaries. The *Journal* of the Illinois Historical Society, the Fergus Historical Series, the *Transactions* of the Illinois Historical Society—all bring to life the great figures and the lesser figures in a casual, not too reverent, way that makes one aware of the good, familiar humanity of these people.

Anyone whose historical studies are concerned with the figure of Lincoln must come to feel how fortunate our biographical literature is to have interpreters like Sandburg and Beveridge. Starting with points of view which are not similar, they seem in the end to be happily complementary. Each suggests the importance of incidental figures in the Lincoln story, and these promptings take one back again to the *Journal* and the *Transactions.*

335

I wish to acknowledge indebtedness of many kinds and degrees to the people who have helped me shape my studies: to Theodore C. Blegen, formerly superintendent of the Minnesota Historical Society, now dean of the Graduate School of the University of Minnesota; to Arthur J. Larsen, present superintendent of the Historical Society; to Alburey Castell, of the Philosophy Department of the University of Minnesota; to S. N. Dicken, of the university's department of Geography; to Miss Helen K. Starr, Miss Helen Rugg, Miss Constance Humphrey, Miss Anna Heilmaier, of the James J. Hill Reference Library in St. Paul; to Miss Lois Fawcett and Mrs. Irene Warming, of the Minnesota Historical Library; to Earl Browning, of the Peoria Public Library; to Paul Angle, of the Illinois State Historical Library; to Frank Heinl, of Jacksonville; to Roy Swanson, of St. Paul; and to many others who have been generous in giving me of their time and of their knowledge.

Bibliography

ALVORD, CLARENCE WALWORTH (Editor), *Cahokia Records* —Vol. II, Illinois Historical Collections. Springfield: Illinois State Historical Library, 1907.
—————— *The Illinois Country, 1673-1818*, Centennial History of Illinois. Chicago: A. C. McClurg & Co., 1922.
—————— and CARTER, CLARENCE EDWIN (Editors), Vol. X, Illinois Historical Collections. Springfield: Illinois State Historical Library, 1915.
ANGLE, PAUL, *Here I Have Lived*. Springfield: Abraham Lincoln Association, 1935.
ASBURY, HERBERT, *Carry Nation*. New York: Alfred A. Knopf, Inc., 1929.
BALL, FLORENCE GRATIOT, *Galena's Memories of General Grant*, Journal of Illinois Historical Society, Vol. 21.
BALLANCE, C., *History of Peoria*. Peoria, Ill.: N. C. Nason, 1870.
BARTON, W. E., *The Life of Abraham Lincoln*. Indianapolis, Ind.: Bobbs-Merrill Co., 1925.
BECKWITH, H. W. (Editor), Vol. I, Illinois Historical collections. Springfield: Illinois Historical Society, 1903.
BEVERIDGE, A. J., *Abraham Lincoln, 1809-1858* (2 vols.). Boston: Houghton Mifflin Co., 1928.
BIRKBECK, MORRIS, *Letters from Illinois*. Philadelphia: M. Carey and Son, 1818.
BOGART, E. L., *The Industrial State*, Centennial History of Illinois. Chicago: A. C. McClurg & Co., 1922.

BREESE, SIDNEY, *Early History of Illinois*. E. B. Myers & Company, 1844.

BROWN, HENRY, *History of Illinois*. New York: J. Winchester, 1844.

BROWN, WILLIAM H., *Memory of Daniel P. Cook*. Chicago: Chicago Historical Society, 1857.

BUCK, SOLON JUSTUS, *Illinois in 1818*. Springfield: Illinois Centennial Commission, 1917.

BURNS, JOSEPH E., *Daniel P. Cook*—Vol. 6, Journal of Illinois Historical Society, 1913-1914.

CARR, CLARKE E., *The Illini*. Chicago: A. C. McClurg & Co. 1904.

CARTWRIGHT, PETER, *Autobiography*, W. P. Strickland, Methodist Book Concern, 1856.

CHARNWOOD, GEOFFREY RATHBONE BENSON, First Baron, *Abraham Lincoln*. New York: Henry Holt & Co., 1917.

CHESNEL, PAUL, *The History of Cavelier de La Salle*. Translated by Andree Chesnel Meany. New York: G. P. Putnam's Sons, 1932.

COLE, A. C., *The Era of the Civil War*, Centennial History of Illinois. Chicago: A. C. McClurg & Co., 1922.

COLLOT, VICTOR, *A Journey in North America* (2 vols.). Paris: Arthur Bertrand, 1826.

CONGER, JOHN LEONARD, *History of the Illinois River Valley*. Chicago: S. J. Clarke Publishing Company, 1932.

DAVIDSON, ALEXANDER, and STUVÉ, BERNARD, *A Complete History of Illinois, 1673-1873*. Springfield: Illinois State Journal Company, 1874.

DOUGLAS, STEPHEN ARNOLD, *Autobiography*. Edited by Frank E. Stevens. Springfield: Illinois State Journal Company, 1913.

EDWARDS, NINIAN W., *History of Illinois, 1778-1833, and Life and Times of Ninian Edwards*. Springfield: Illinois State Journal Company, 1870.

FALCONER, THOMAS, *On the Discovery of the Mississippi*,

with a translation from the original manuscript of memoirs by Robert Cavelier de La Salle and the Chevalier Henry de Tonty. New York: Samuel Clark, 1844.

FORD, THOMAS, *History of Illinois*. Chicago: S. C. Griggs & Co., 1854.

GERHARD, FRED, *Illinois as It Is*. Chicago: Keen and Lee, 1857.

GILLESPIE, JOSEPH, *Recollections of Early Illinois and Her Noted Men*. Chicago: Fergus Historical Series, Nos. 13-22, 1880.

GRANT, HELEN HARDIE, *Peter Cartwright: Pioneer*. New York: The Abingdon Press, 1931.

GRANT, U. S., *Personal Memoirs*. New York: C. L. Webster & Co., 1885.

GREENE, EVARTS BOUTELL, and ALVORD, CLARENCE WALWORTH, *The Governors' Letter Books*—Vol. IV, Illinois Historical Collections. Springfield: Illinois State Historical Library, 1909.

GREENE, EVARTS BOUTELL, and THOMPSON, CHARLES MANFRED, *The Governors' Letter Books*, 2d series—Vol. VII, Illinois Historical Collections. Springfield: State Historical Library, 1911.

HARRIS, N. DWIGHT, *The History of Negro Servitude in Illinois*. Chicago: A. C. McClurg & Co., 1904.

HART, ALBERT BUSHNELL, *A Source Book of American History*. New York: The Macmillan Co., 1899.

HEINEL, FRANK J., *Jacksonville and Morgan County*, Journal of Illinois Historical Society, Vol. 18, Part I.

HENNEPIN, LOUIS, *Discovery of Louisiana*. Minneapolis: University of Minnesota Press, 1938.

HERNDON, WILLIAM H., and WEIK, JESSE W., *Abraham Lincoln*. New York: Albert and Charles Boni, 1930.

HERTZ, EMANUEL (Editor), *The Hidden Lincoln*. New York: Viking Press, Inc., 1938.

HOBART, CHAUNCEY, *Peter Cartwright: A Sketch* (pamphlet). Red Wing, Minn.

340   BIBLIOGRAPHY

Hobbs, Clarissa Emely Gear, *Autobiography,* Journal of Illinois Historical Society, Vol. 17.

Hoffman, C. F., *A Winter In the Far West.* London: Richard Bentley, 1835.

Hutchins, Thomas, *A Topographical Description of Virginia, Pennsylvania, Maryland, and North Carolina.* Edited by Frederick Charles Hicks. Cleveland: Burrows Brothers Co., 1904.

Jones, A. D., *Illinois and the West.* Boston: Weeks, Jordan & Co., 1838.

Kenton, Edna (Editor), *The Jesuit Relations and Allied Documents.* New York: Albert and Charles Boni, 1925.

Lamon, Ward Hill, *The Life of Abraham Lincoln.* Boston: J. R. Osgood & Co., 1872.

Legler, Henry E., *Tonti.* Parkman Club Papers, 1896.

Lincoln, Abraham, *Complete Works of . . .* (12 vols.). Edited by John G. Nicolay and John Hay. New York: Tandy-Thomas, 1905.

Linder, Usher F., *Reminiscences of the Bench and Bar.* Chicago: Chicago Legal News Co., 1879.

Lovejoy, Joseph C., and Owen, *Memoir of the Reverend Elijah P. Lovejoy.* New York: John S. Taylor, 1838.

Mason, Edward G., *Chapters From Illinois History.* Chicago: Herbert S. Stone, 1901.

Masters, Edgar Lee, *Days In the Lincoln Country,* Journal of the Illinois Historical Society, Vol. 18.

—— *Lincoln, the Man.* New York: Dodd, Mead & Co., 1931.

Matson, Nehemiah, *Pioneers of Illinois.* Chicago: Knight and Leonard, 1882.

McCabe, James D., Jr., *Great Fortunes.* Cincinnati: E. Hannafird & Co., 1871.

McColloch, David, *History of Peoria County*—Vol. II, Historical Encyclopedia of Illinois.

McCormick, Henry, *The Women of Illinois.* Bloomington: Henry McCormick, 1913.

MOREHOUSE, FRANCES MILTON I., *The Life of Jesse Fell*. Urbana, Ill.: University of Illinois Press, 1916.

ONSTOT, T. G., *Lincoln and Salem*. Peoria, Ill.; Franks and Sons, 1902.

O'SHAUGHNESSY, FRANCIS, *General James Shields of Illinois*, Journal of the Illinois Historical Society, 1915.

PALMER, JOHN M., *Bench and Bar of Illinois*. Chicago: Lewis Publishing Co., 1899.

PARISH, JOHN CARL, *The Man With the Iron Hand*. Boston: Houghton Mifflin Co., 1913.

PARKMAN, FRANCIS, *La Salle and the Discovery of the Great West*. Boston: Little, Brown & Co., 1903.

PARRISH, RANDALL, *Historic Illinois*. Chicago: A. C. McClurg & Co., 1905.

PEASE, THEODORE CALVIN, *The Story of Illinois*. Chicago: A. C. McClurg & Co., 1925.

—— *The Frontier State*, Centennial History of Illinois. Springfield: Illinois Centennial Commission, 1922.

—— (Editor), *The French Foundations*—Vol. 23, Illinois Historical Collections. Springfield: Illinois State Historical Library, 1934.

PECK, J. M., *Gazetteer*. Philadelphia: Grigg and Elliott, 1837.

PRATT, HENRY EDWARD, *Judge David Davis*, Transactions of Illinois Historical Society, 1930.

PRICKETT, JOSEPHINE GILLESPIE, *Joseph Gillespie*, Transactions of Illinois Historical Society, 1912.

REED, CHARLES BERT, *Masters of the Wilderness*. Chicago: University of Chicago Press, 1914.

REPPLIER, AGNES, *Pere Marquette*. New York: Doubleday, Doran & Co., 1929.

REYNOLDS, JOHN, *Sketches of the County*. Belleville Ill., 1854.

—— *My Own Times*. Chicago: Fergus Printing Company, 1879.

—— *The Pioneer History of Illinois*. Belleville, Ill.: N. A. Randall, 1852.

RIDLEY, DOUGLAS, *The Geography of Illinois.* Chicago: University of Chicago Press, 1914.

ROGERS, CAMERON, *Robert Green Ingersoll.* Garden City, N. Y.: Doubleday, Page & Co., 1927.

SANDBURG, CARL, *Abraham Lincoln: The Prairie Years.* New York: Harcourt, Brace & Co., 1926.

SANDBURG, CARL, and ANGLE, PAUL, *Mary Lincoln, Wife and Widow.* New York: Harcourt, Brace & Co., 1932.

SAUER, C. O., *Geography of the Upper Mississippi, and Historical Development,* Illinois State Geological Survey, Bulletin No. 27.

SCHOOLCRAFT, HENRY R., *Travels In the Central Portion of the Mississippi Valley.* New York: Collus and Hannay, 1825.

SCOTT, FRANKLIN WILLIAM, *Newspapers and Periodicals of Illinois, 1814-1879,* Illinois Historical Collections. Springfield: Illinois State Historical Library, 1910.

SEITZ, DON, *Uncommon Americans.* Indianapolis: Bobbs-Merrill Co., 1925.

SEYMOUR, FLORA WARREN, *La Salle, Explorer of Our Midland Empire.* New York: D. Appleton-Century Co., 1939.

SHAW, ALBERT, *Abraham Lincoln: A Cartoon History.* New York: Review of Reviews Corp., 1929.

SHEAHAM, J. W., *Stephen A. Douglas.* Chicago: Fergus Historical Series, Vol. 15, 1881.

SPARKS, EDWIN ERLE, *The Lincoln-Douglas Debates*—Illinois Historical Collections. Springfield: Illinois State Historical Library, 1908.

STEPHENSON, GEORGE M., *The Religious Aspects of Swedish Immigration.* Minneapolis: University of Minnesota Press, 1932.

STEVENS, FRANK, *The Life of Stephen A. Douglas,* Journal of the Illinois Historical Society, Vol. 16, Illinois Historical Society, 1923.

STEVENSON, ADLAI E., *Stephen Douglas,* Transactions of the Illinois Historical Society, 1908.

STILES, HENRY REED, *Joutel's Journal of La Salle's Last Voyage.* Albany, Ill.: Joseph McDonough, 1906.

STUART, JAMES, *Three Years In North America.* New York: J. and J. Harper, 1833.

SWEET, WILLIAM H., *Peter Cartwright,* Transactions of the Illinois Historical Society, 1921.

SWISSHELM, JANE GREY, *Letters of* . . . Edited by Arthur J. Larsen. St. Paul: Minnesota Historical Society, 1934.
——— *Half a Century.* Chicago: Jansen, McClurg & Co., 1880.

TANNER, HENRY, *The Martyrdom of Lovejoy.* Chicago: Fergus Printing Co., 1881.

TARBELL, IDA, *Life of Abraham Lincoln.* New York: Lincoln Memorial Association, 1900.

TILTON, CLINT CLAY, *Lincoln and Lamon: Partners and Friends,* Transactions of Illinois Historical Society, 1931.

WALLACE, JOSEPH, *The History of Illinois and Louisiana Under French Rule.* Cincinnati: Robert Clarke & Co., 1893.

WOODWARD, W. E., *Meet General Grant.* Garden City, N. Y.: Doubleday, Doran & Co., 1936.

Other References

Drown's Record and Historical View of Peoria. Peoria: E. O. Woodcock, 1831.

Illinois in 1837: A Sketch. Philadelphia: S. Augustus Mitchell, 1837.

Traveller's Directory for Illinois. New York: J. H. Colton, 1840.

Illinois State Gazetteer and Business Directory, 1858-1859. Chicago: George W. Hawes.

J. C. W. Bailey's *Illinois State Gazetteer*, 1864-1865.

Illinois State Gazetteer and Business Directory, 1880.

The History of Peoria County. Chicago: Johnson & Co., 1880.

_____

Illinois Monthly, Vol. I. Vandalia: Robert Blackwell, 1831.

Illinois Monthly, Vol. II. Cincinnati: Corey and Fairbank, 1832.

_____

The files of the Alton *Telegraph;* the Peoria *Register and Northwestern Gazetteer;* the Peoria *Journal-Transcript;* the *Illinois State Journal;* the *Illinois State Register.*

Index

345